FOUR
VIEWS
ON **HEAVEN**

Books in the Counterpoints Series

Church Life

Evaluating the Church Growth Movement
Exploring the Worship Spectrum
Remarriage after Divorce in Today's Church
Understanding Four Views on Baptism
Understanding Four Views on the Lord's Supper
Who Runs the Church?

Bible and Theology

Are Miraculous Gifts for Today?
Do Christians, Muslims, and Jews Worship the Same God? Four Views
Five Views on Apologetics
Five Views on Biblical Inerrancy
Five Views on Law and Gospel
Five Views on Sanctification
Five Views on the Church and Politics
Five Views on the Exodus
Five Views on the Extent of the Atonement
Four Views on Christian Spirituality
Four Views on Christianity and Philosophy
Four Views on Creation, Evolution, and Intelligent Design
Four Views on Divine Providence
Four Views on Eternal Security
Four Views on Hell
Four Views on Moving beyond the Bible to Theology
Four Views on Salvation in a Pluralistic World
Four Views on the Apostle Paul
Four Views on the Book of Revelation
Four Views on the Church's Mission
Four Views on the Historical Adam
Four Views on the Role of Works at the Final Judgment
Four Views on the Spectrum of Evangelicalism
Genesis: History, Fiction, or Neither?
How Jewish Is Christianity?
Show Them No Mercy
Three Views on Christianity and Science
Three Views on Creation and Evolution
Three Views on Eastern Orthodoxy and Evangelicalism
Three Views on the Millennium and Beyond
Three Views on the New Testament Use of the Old Testament
Three Views on the Rapture
Two Views on Homosexuality, the Bible, and the Church
Two Views on the Doctrine of the Trinity
Two Views on Women in Ministry

FOUR VIEWS ON **HEAVEN**

John S. Feinberg

J. Richard Middleton

Michael Allen

Peter Kreeft

Michael Wittmer, general editor
Stanley N. Gundry, series editor

COUNTERPOINTS
BIBLE & THEOLOGY

ZONDERVAN
ACADEMIC

ZONDERVAN ACADEMIC

Four Views on Heaven
Copyright © 2022 by Michael E. Wittmer, John S. Feinberg, Peter J. Kreeft, Michael Allen, J. Richard Middleton

Requests for information should be addressed to:
Zondervan, 3900 Sparks Dr. SE, Grand Rapids, Michigan 49546

Zondervan titles may be purchased in bulk for educational, business, fundraising, or sales promotional use. For information, please email SpecialMarkets@Zondervan.com.

ISBN 978-0-310-09388-6 (softcover)

ISBN 978-0-310-09389-3 (ebook)

ISBN 978-0-310-12038-4 (audio)

Cover design: Tammy Johnson
Cover photo: © Nathan Nugent / Unsplash
Interior design: Sara Colley

Printed in the United States of America

22 23 24 25 26 27 28 29 30 31 /TRM/ 12 11 10 9 8 7 6 5 4 3 2 1

CONTENTS

CONTRIBUTORS

Michael Allen (PhD, Wheaton College) is the John Dyer Trimble Professor of Systematic Theology at Reformed Theological Seminary in Orlando, Florida. He is the author of *Grounded in Heaven: Recentering Christian Hope and Life in God*, *Ephesians*, and *Sanctification*.

John S. Feinberg (PhD, University of Chicago) is professor of biblical and systematic theology at Trinity Evangelical Divinity School. He is the author of *No One Like Him: The Doctrine of God*, *Light in a Dark Place: The Doctrine of Scripture*, and *The Many Faces of Evil: Theological Systems and the Problem of Evil*.

Peter Kreeft (PhD, Fordham University) is professor of philosophy at Boston College. He is the author of *Catholics and Protestants: What They Can Learn from Each Other*, *Heaven: The Heart's Deepest Longing*, and *Everything You Ever Wanted to Know about Heaven*.

J. Richard Middleton (PhD, Free University, Amsterdam) is professor of biblical worldview and exegesis at Northeastern Seminary at Roberts Wesleyan College in Rochester, New York. He is the author of *A New Heaven and a New Earth: Reclaiming Biblical Eschatology*, *Abraham's Silence: The Binding of Isaac, the Suffering of Job, and How to Talk Back to God*, and *The Liberating Image: The Imago Dei in Genesis 1*.

Michael Wittmer (PhD, Calvin Theological Seminary) is professor of systematic theology at Grand Rapids Theological Seminary. He is the author of *Heaven Is a Place on Earth*, *Don't Stop Believing*, and *Becoming Worldly Saints*.

INTRODUCTION

MICHAEL WITTMER

Most people have not thought too hard about heaven. They tend to think of it like the final line of a children's story, "And they all lived happily ever after." They assume that those who have died are now in heaven doing whatever they did on earth, only better. If someone enjoyed golf, he is smashing long drives down the middle of celestial fairways. If someone loved to paint, she is setting up her easel in front of a glorious vista. And if their friend played the banjo, he is now jamming in heaven's band. Which is unbelievable. *There are banjoes in heaven?!*

Seriously, even Christians have not thought too deeply about what happens when we die. We tend to run all of God's promised future together, assuming that we get everything he has promised all at once. Funeral sermons often say that our loved one is right now playing baseball, baking pies, or writing poetry that is out of this world. We seldom stop and ask, *Really? How is she doing these things?* We can see her body in the casket, awaiting its resurrection. Someday she may do all this, but now?

This is a good time to note that when it comes to eschatology, the Christian Scriptures teach the three Rs: the Return of Christ, the Resurrection of the body, and the Restoration of all things. Praise God that our loved ones who died in Christ are now "with the Lord" (2 Cor 5:8), but they apparently have not yet received all that God has promised them.[1] They are still waiting for their resurrection bodies that they will receive when Jesus returns to this earth (1 Thess 4:16). Like a wise parent who only allows her children to open their stockings on

---

1. I say "apparently" because some theologians posit that when believers die they join the eternity of God, while others say believers may be fast-forwarded to the new earth. In either case, believers would receive their resurrection bodies at the moment that they die.

Christmas Eve, so our Father does not give us every gift we have coming the moment we die. He gives us the best gift we have ever received, for we pass immediately from this life into the arms of our Savior. But God saves even more presents for the Christmas morning of Christ's return and our resurrection. Only then will our redemption be complete; only then will we be restored in every possible way.

Here is the point: many Christians make an eschatological mess by blurring together the various stages of the afterlife. Theologians typically avoid such confusion by distinguishing God's promised future for individual believers into the "intermediate state" and "the final state." The Bible says little about the intermediate state except that we are with the Lord (Luke 23:43; 2 Cor 5:6–8; Phil 1:21–23; 1 Thess 4:14). And this is enough. Unlike "heavenly tourism" books that celebrate the journeys of people who went to heaven and returned without laying eyes on Jesus, the Bible indicates that what makes heaven "heavenly" is the presence of Jesus. Yet the intermediate state is not the focus of Scripture. Its eye is on the end, when Jesus returns to resurrect and judge all people and restore all things (Acts 3:21; Col 1:20; Rev 20–22).

This will be our focus too. This book is not about the intermediate state, *what happens when Christians die.* It is about our final state, *what happens after that.* At the end of the day, when all is said and done, where will Christians live forever? What will that place be like, and what will we do there?

Given our focus on the final state, some readers may wonder whether *Four Views on Heaven* is the right title for this book. The term *heaven* is commonly associated with our disembodied, ethereal, otherworldly existence that begins the moment we die. It may not be the best word to use for our final state, which the Bible describes as "the new heavens and the new earth" (see Isa 65:17–25; 2 Pet 3:10–13; Rev 21:1–3). I agree. But most people still use *heaven* also to mean the final existence of the saved. In order to communicate with them, and to avoid privileging the "new earth" view, we have chosen to retain the term *heaven*, defining what we mean by it. The title also pairs well with another Counterpoint book. Think of our book as a cheerier counterpart to Zondervan's *Four Views on Hell.*[2]

---

2. Preston Sprinkle, ed., *Four Views on Hell*, 2nd ed. (Grand Rapids: Zondervan, 2016).

A Very Short History of Heaven

To help readers understand why there are four major views on heaven, here is a thumbnail sketch of the church's beliefs about our final state. I will keep this summary as neutral as possible in order to avoid influencing readers in one direction or another.

Like the Old Testament, which said the righteous will live on a new earth (Isa 65:17–25) yet dropped hints of them going to heaven (besides the translations of Enoch and of Elijah, see Pss 16:11; 49:15; 73:24–25; Eccl 3:21), the New Testament contains passages that could be used to support a final destiny both on earth (2 Pet 3:13; Rev 21:1–5) and in heaven (1 Cor 15:42–49; 2 Cor 5:1–8; Heb 11:13–16). The early church tried to say both, with an emphasis on heaven. Some scholars say the early church's heavenly focus was influenced by its surrounding Greek culture, which, following Plato, emphasized that the goal of every soul was to return to heaven where it might contemplate forever the eternal, unchanging, rational ideals (what Plato called the Forms). Others say the church was merely following Scripture's lead, which promised they would leave this corrupted world behind. Either way, the Christian's highest goal was to enter heaven and worship God forever.[3]

Consider Irenaeus (ca. 120/140–ca. 202), the church's first theologian and gnostic hunter. Against Gnosticism, which held a heretically low view of earth and the physical world, Irenaeus taught that our final destiny is a new heaven and earth that are substantially the same as our present creation. God will not destroy this earth. He will save it. But only for lesser Christians. Borrowing from Jesus's parable of the sower (Matt 13:3–9), Irenaeus said that disciples who bear a hundredfold fruit will be privileged to live forever in heaven, while those who produce sixtyfold will enjoy a middling paradise, and those who yield only thirtyfold will be stuck on earth. Each gets the reward he deserves.[4]

---

3. Summaries are found in Brian E. Daley, *The Hope of the Early Church: A Handbook of Patristic Eschatology* (New York: Cambridge University Press, 1991); Jeffrey Burton Russell, *A History of Heaven: The Singing Silence* (Princeton: Princeton University Press, 1997); and Colleen McDannell and Bernhard Lang, *Heaven: A History*, 2nd ed. (New Haven: Yale University Press, 2001). For the ancient Near Eastern and European backdrop of the biblical account, see J. Edward Wright, *The Early History of Heaven* (New York: Oxford University Press, 2000).

4. *Against Heresies* 36.1–2.

Irenaeus's preference for heaven was supported by the most influential theologians of both the Eastern and Western church. In the East, Origen's (185–254) writings were posthumously scrubbed of their controversial parts by an admiring Rufinus, so there is some dispute about his beliefs. Nevertheless, Origen apparently taught that the earth was created to supply an opportunity for souls whose love for God had cooled in a previous life to make their way back to him. God will create a succession of worlds—as many as necessary—until every soul returns to his loving, heavenly communion. He will upgrade their physical bodies so that they are fit to live in the "purer, ethereal, and heavenly regions." There believers will forever enjoy the beatific vision, gaining ever more knowledge of God as they gaze into his glory.[5]

In the West, Augustine (354–430) longed for our corruptible existence in time to be taken up into union with God and his eternity. Augustine's mature work *The City of God* affirms the earth and our physical bodies while longing for their transformation into a higher, heavenly key. When Jesus returns, our present earthly bodies will be "exalted to abodes which are material, albeit heavenly," and our present earth will be stripped to its foundations and rebuilt into an incorruptible environment that can accommodate them. No one escapes death. Those who are alive when Jesus returns must swiftly pass through death as they rise to meet him in the air (1 Thess 4:17). They will instantly be brought back to life, now with glorified, immortal bodies. God will hide his incorruptible saints in his unscathed, highest heavens while the world burns, then return us to the new creation where we will forever enjoy our beatific vision of God.[6] Given the incomprehensible privilege of seeing God "without interruption" and "in utter clarity and distinctness," Augustine could not imagine doing anything else. He wrote, "How great will be that felicity, where there will be no evil, where no good will be withheld, where there will be leisure for the praises of God, who will be all in all! What other occupation could there be, in a state where there will be no inactivity of idleness, and yet no toil constrained by want? I can think of none."[7]

---

5. Origen, *First Principles* 2.1–3 and 3.5–6. See Joseph Willson Trigg, *Origen* (Atlanta: John Knox, 1983), 108–15, and Daley, *Hope of the Early Church*, 50–54.

6. Augustine, *City of God*, trans. Henry Bettenson (New York: Penguin, 2003), 22.4 (pp. 1026–27). See also 22.16, 18, 20, and 24, and Daley, *Hope of the Early Church*, 131–50.

7. Augustine, *City of God*, 22.29–30 (pp. 1085–87).

The medieval church intensified the early church's focus on the beatific vision. Bernard of Clairvaux (1090–1153) wrote eighty-six sermons over eighteen years on the Song of Songs, using its erotic poetry to convey the Christian's ultimate, passionate union with Christ. This will happen after the resurrection, when, freed from the distractions of our currently "fragile, sickly bodies," we will finally not love God for our sake but love ourselves for his.[8]

Thomas Aquinas (ca. 1224–1274) argued that God's eschatological fire will not entirely consume our world; rather, it will cleanse the earth of its sin and corruption. However, it will burn the bodies of both the righteous and the sinners to ashes, though the former will feel no pain. God will then renew this world and the bodies of his saints, graciously elevating our finite natures so that we might know what is naturally unknowable and see what finitude cannot see. We will enjoy forever the end for which we were made, finding eternal happiness in our "immediate vision of God," becoming more like God as we participate in his blessedness and are increasingly able to "see God as he sees himself."[9]

The medieval view of heaven culminated in the *Divine Comedy* of Dante Alighieri (1265–1321). This masterpiece contains three books, *Inferno*, *Purgatorio*, and *Paradiso*, which describe Dante's mystical journey from an earthly paradise through the ascending levels of a celestial one. He is led upward by guides, his beloved Beatrice, and finally Bernard of Clairvaux, the greatest of all saints, through the various heavenly spheres. He passes through the moon, sun, and the planets, noting the various saints at each level, until he arrives at the first mover, the highest sphere that moves all the others. Dante has now reached the outer edge of the universe, beyond which no thing exists. Whatever lies outside is infinitely too real for that. Dante looks down from where he has come. Down, down, through dizzying spheres of light, he sees the earth lying at the bottom. He steadies himself and looks up and out and shields his eyes from a blazing point of light. This light does not exist

---

8. Bernard of Clairvaux, *On Loving God*, 10–12, Christian Classics Ethereal Library, https://ccel.org/ccel/bernard/loving_god/loving_god.xii.html.

9. Thomas Aquinas, *Summa Theologica*, trans. Fathers of the English Dominican Province (Westminster, MD: Christian Classics, 1948), 1a.12 (vol. 1:48–59); Supplement, Questions 74, 91–92 (vol. 5:2853–62, 2937–56); and *Summa contra Gentiles*, trans. Vernon J. Bourke (Garden City, NY: Image, 1956), book 3, part 1, chs. 47–54 and 61 (pp. 158–86, 200–201).

in time and space, yet it is the moral center of the universe, surrounded by angelic spheres descending down the other side. Dante looks toward this light, which simultaneously blinds and fills him with fresh, spiritual vision. He is overcome by love and light. The beauty of God is too much. With Bernard's coaching, and the Virgin Mary's help, Dante finally fixes his spiritual eyes on God. He cannot describe what he saw, except that he had "joined Infinite Being and Good itself." He now understood all that a creature can know and felt all the love and beauty a creature could stand, forever.[10]

Dante's otherworldly, luminescent heaven of love became the standard vision for the next three hundred years and more. It was challenged by the Renaissance, a cultural rebirth that envisioned heaven as the fulfillment of our human aspirations. Heaven would be a happy reunion of family and friends, a realm of peace and social harmony, in which God was relegated to the background, a benign deity who made our joy possible.[11]

The Reformers represented a theological wing of the Renaissance, and they attempted to combine the best of its humanist impulse with the church's historical focus on God. This produced some tension in their view of heaven, particularly in the unsystematic thought of Martin Luther. Luther's spiritual side asserted that we leave time and enter God's eternity the moment we die. We immediately reach the end of the world, as "each of us has his own Last Day when he dies."[12] Because we are in eternity, with no before or after, even "the patriarchs will not reach the Last Day before we do."[13] In heaven we will not desire food and wine but we "shall be satisfied by merely looking at God and contemplating him."[14] Nevertheless, Luther expressed some humanist concerns. He confessed, "I often think about it, but I cannot understand what we shall do to pass away the time; for there will be no change there, no labor, food, drink, and transactions. But I hold that in God

10. Russell, *History of Heaven*, 151–85.
11. Gerald Bray, "The History of Heaven," in *Heaven*, ed. Christopher W. Morgan and Robert A. Peterson, Theology in Community (Wheaton, IL: Crossway, 2014), 199–200.
12. Paul Althaus, *The Theology of Martin Luther*, trans. Robert C. Schultz (Philadelphia: Fortress, 1966), 416.
13. Althaus, *Theology of Martin Luther*, 416.
14. Ewald M. Plass, *What Luther Says*, 3 vols. (St. Louis: Concordia, 1959), 2:623.

we shall have enough to keep us occupied."[15] Unlike Johann Gerhard and Johann Quenstedt—later Lutherans who thought our present world will be annihilated (they did emphasize that this should not become an article of faith)—Luther himself believed, on the basis of Romans 8:21, that this world will be cleansed of its corruption and transformed, replacing its "workday clothing" with its "festive garment."[16] He wrote, "In short, whatever belongs to the nature of these temporal goods, whatever constitutes this transitory life and activity, shall all cease."[17] Luther hypothesized that in this renewed creation, the beatific vision will empower our resurrection bodies to be "so light and quick, that we shall speed along as a spark, yea, as the sun runs across the heaven, so that we shall in a moment's time be here on earth or up in the heavens."[18] We will "go out into heaven and earth and play with the sun and the moon and all other creatures."[19] Yet Luther conceded this is mostly conjecture. "We know no more about eternal life than children in the womb of their mother know about the world they are about to enter."[20]

John Calvin also illustrates the tension between earth and heaven, the physical and the spiritual. In book 3 of his *Institutes of the Christian Religion*, Calvin began his chapter on the resurrection by agreeing with Plato that our "highest good" is "union with God."[21] Yet he opposed Plato and the "monstrous . . . error" of the Manichaeans who scoffed at the notion of resurrection.[22] Calvin insisted that our present bodies will rise again. Nevertheless, despite his emphasis on the physicality of our end, Calvin consistently privileged its spiritual components. He said the Old Testament prophets described our destiny "in physical terms" only "because they could not find words to express that spiritual blessedness."[23] When Isaiah "speaks of 'new heavens' and a 'new

---

15. Plass, *What Luther Says*, 2:621.
16. Plass, *What Luther Says*, 3:1529. Surveys of Lutheran disagreement concerning the fate of this earth appear in Francis Pieper, *Christian Dogmatics*, vol. 3 (St. Louis: Concordia, 1953), 542–43, and John Theodore Mueller, *Christian Dogmatics* (St. Louis: Concordia, 1934), 631–33.
17. Pieper, *Christian Dogmatics*, 3:542–43.
18. Plass, *What Luther Says*, 2:623–24.
19. Plass, *What Luther Says*, 2:624.
20. Althaus, *Theology of Martin Luther*, 425.
21. John Calvin, *Institutes of the Christian Religion*, ed. John T. McNeill, trans. Ford Lewis Battles, 2 vols. (Philadelphia: Westminster, 1960), 2:988 (3.25.2).
22. Calvin, *Institutes*, 2:998 (3.25.7).
23. Calvin, *Institutes*, 2:1005 (3.25.10).

earth,'" he is referring to "the reign of Christ, by whom all things have been renewed."[24] He is not speaking about "trees, or beasts, or the order of the stars" but "the inward renewal of man."[25] The spiritual is most important, for "God contains the fullness of all good things in himself like an inexhaustible fountain," so "nothing beyond him is to be sought."[26]

Calvin's ambivalence toward this world is reflected in his description of its end. In his commentary on 2 Peter 3:10, he said the coming fire will both consume and cleanse the world of its corruption. The elements of this world "will be consumed only in order to receive a new quality while their substance remains the same."[27] Despite this continuity of substance, Calvin seemed to believe the new earth will not be this one. In his exegesis of Psalm 102:25–26, Calvin noted that the prophet said the heavens and earth would perish because their "renovation will be so complete that they shall not be the same but other heavens."[28] Calvin's application in both commentaries is similar: we must not "be engrossed with the things of earth" but "seek stability nowhere else but in God."[29] In sum, the same Calvin who lived decades in gorgeous Geneva wanted nothing to distract from his everlasting focus on God. When asked why God would bother to restore this world, given that his glorified saints will be like the angels, Calvin was not sure. But he assumed "the very sight" of the new earth, even if we do not use it, will fill us with "such pleasantness, such sweetness" and "happiness" that "will far surpass all the amenities that we now enjoy."[30] Calvin was not concerned about the eschatological tensions in his view, and he did not want to speculate to iron out the details. He dismissed questions about the specifics of heaven. "I not only refrain personally from superfluous investigation of useless matters, but I

---

24. John Calvin, *Commentary on the Book of the Prophet Isaiah*, trans. William Pringle, 4 vols. (Grand Rapids: Eerdmans, 1948), 4:437.

25. Calvin, *Commentary on Isaiah*, 4:437.

26. Calvin, *Institutes*, 2:1005 (3.25.10).

27. John Calvin, *Calvin's Commentaries: The Epistle of Paul the Apostle to the Hebrews and The First and Second Epistles of St. Peter*, trans. William B. Johnston, Calvin's New Testament Commentaries 12 (Grand Rapids: Eerdmans, 1989), 365.

28. John Calvin, *Commentary on the Book of Psalms*, trans. James Anderson, 5 vols. (Grand Rapids: Eerdmans, 1949), 4:123.

29. Calvin, *Hebrews and The First and Second Epistles of St. Peter*, 365, and idem, *Commentary on the Book of Psalms*, 4:123.

30. Calvin, *Institutes*, 2:1007 (3.25.11).

also think that I ought to guard against contributing to the levity of others by answering them."[31] He might have hated this book.

The seventeenth century seemed as puzzled as Calvin regarding the new heaven and earth. My colleague, John Duff, wrote his dissertation on what this biblical phrase meant in seventeenth-century England.[32] He discovered that some theologians understood it metaphorically, as representing either the new age of gospel proclamation that began in the first century or a future millennium in which the papacy would fall and true Christianity would flourish around the world. The majority took the new earth literally. They believed that our present world would be renovated rather than annihilated, but not for us. The saints are destined to live forever with God in the third, or highest, heaven, and we will look down upon the restored earth and delight in it as a monument to God's glory, wisdom, and power. The new earth might contain plants, fish, birds, and beasts, or it might not, but it will definitely not have people. It will be essentially a national park with a "no trespassing" sign: beautiful to look at but not for use. A few theologians believed the saints will live with Jesus forever on this restored earth, but only after Jesus resigns his position as head over his Father's heavenly kingdom. Jesus will ultimately receive an earthly kingdom, fulfilling God's promises to Abraham and David. Despite this minority report, most seventeenth-century English theologians anticipated a heavenly end for the people of God.

What was true of English Christians in general was true of most Puritans in particular. These fervent Protestants spoke often about the happiness of heaven and how its promise of rewards and "soul-ravishing" vision of God should motivate us to serve Jesus now. Sometimes they got a bit carried away. Arguably the greatest Puritan theologian, Jonathan Edwards (1703–58), believed that Jesus would return to earth to defeat his enemies at the day of judgment, then return to heaven with his resurrected followers. They will live forever up there, praising and serving God, as they lose themselves in his beauty and glory, perhaps a little too much. Edwards wandered into panentheistic territory when he carelessly exulted that the holiest saints "shall penetrate further into the vast and infinite distance that is between them and God, and *their delight in*

31. Calvin, *Institutes*, 2:1006 (3.25.11).
32. John Duff, "'A Knot Worth Unloosing': The Interpretation of the New Heavens and Earth in Seventeenth-Century England" (PhD diss., Calvin Theological Seminary, 2014).

annihilating themselves, that God may be all in all, shall be the greater."[33] The sublimation of the individual into God may seem spiritual, but it is more Buddhist than Christian.

Edwards's eighteenth century also signaled the arrival of the modern world, whose rising secularism challenged the very idea of heaven. The French Revolution dismissed heaven as a religious trick to pacify the oppressed, who would put up with a lot if they were promised heaven when they die. The Revolution punctured their naivete and encouraged them to overthrow their pious oppressors and seek to improve their living conditions in the here and now. Enlightened moderns did not worry much about the details of heaven; rather, they felt liberated in their belief that heaven does not exist. This emphasis on the here and now continues today. Consider the popular song "Imagine" by John Lennon, which counterintuitively inspires people during times of crisis to "imagine there's no heaven, it's easy if you try."[34] Religion is bunk, so rather than strive to get into heaven, people should use their energy to bring the ideals of heaven to earth. Love, peace, and socialism will promote "the brotherhood of man."

A religious version of this secular dream appeared in theological liberalism. Protestant progressives promoted the social gospel, which aspired to improve economic and educational conditions and bring the kingdom of God to earth. Most thought a future heaven was a distraction from the work that needed to be done here and now. Some stopped believing in heaven entirely. Reinhold Niebuhr admitted, "I do not believe in individual immortality," and Paul Tillich redefined eternal life as a present, existential relationship with the ground of Being.[35] The public theologians of the twentieth century tended to be panentheists. At death our individual selves dissipate into Being itself, a drop of humanity lost forever in the ocean of deity.

Not everyone accepted the conclusions of theological liberalism. Evangelical revivals regularly turned convicted hearts toward heaven, and black Christians, thanks to their biblical convictions and continued

---

33. Jonathan Edwards, "Miscellany #5," cited in John Piper, *God's Passion for His Glory* (Wheaton, IL: Crossway, 1998), 161 (emphasis mine). See also Gary Scott Smith, *Heaven in the American Imagination* (New York: Oxford University Press, 2011), 12–18 and 31–40.

34. John Lennon, "Imagine," *Imagine* (London: Apple Records, 1971).

35. Smith, *Heaven in the American Imagination*, 134–39, 162–66.

suffering and injustice, never gave it up. They longed for "Canaan's Happy Shore," where their endurance would be rewarded in God's righteous and everlasting reign. Another significant response arose from dispensationalism. This new hermeneutic began in nineteenth-century Britain and hit its stride in twentieth-century America. It promised to give lay Christians the key to resist liberalism and read Scripture for themselves. The secret to understanding many passages was to ask if they were speaking about Israel or the church. God has two distinct peoples that we must tell apart. Since Israel was God's earthly people and the church was his heavenly people, dispensationalism led Christians to focus on heaven. This was their true home. For a recent example, see *The Purpose Driven Life*, which tells Christians that earth "is not your permanent home or final destination. You're just passing through, just visiting earth." In fact, "many Christians have betrayed their King and his kingdom. They have foolishly concluded that because they live on earth, it's their home. It is not."[36]

Such heavenly pietism was challenged by Dutch Neo-Calvinism. This turn-of-the-twentieth-century movement was led by Abraham Kuyper and Herman Bavinck. They appreciated dispensational evangelicalism's conservative instincts, yet they desired to integrate its emphasis on personal salvation into a broader Christian worldview. So, they wrote about the goodness of creation, common grace, and the cultural mandate. They stressed that grace restores nature, so that following Jesus should lead Christians into the world rather than merely to rise above it. They noted that our final home was a new heaven and a new earth, and they emphasized the earth part. This vision of our earthly end can be found today in the Dutch theologians Al Wolters, Richard Mouw, and Cornelius Plantinga Jr. Its influence has also spread beyond the Dutch community and is apparent in such evangelicals as Randy Alcorn, N. T. Wright, Richard Middleton, G. K. Beale, and myself.[37]

36. Rick Warren, *The Purpose Driven Life* (Grand Rapids: Zondervan, 2002), 48–51. For an explanation of dispensationalism's heavenly focus, see Michael Williams, *This World Is Not My Home: The Origins and Development of Dispensationalism* (Fearn, Scotland: Mentor, 2003), 175–211.

37. Albert M. Wolters, *Creation Regained: Biblical Basics for a Reformational Worldview*, 2nd ed. (Grand Rapids: Eerdmans, 2005); Richard J. Mouw, *When the Kings Come Marching In: Isaiah and the New Jerusalem*, rev. ed. (Grand Rapids: Eerdmans, 2002); Cornelius Plantinga Jr., *Engaging God's World: A Reformed Vision of Faith, Learning, and Living* (Grand Rapids:

The pendulum is always swinging, and it is easy to overcorrect against one extreme and fall into the ditch on the other side. Recently some evangelical theologians, such as Todd Billings, Scott Swain, and Michael Allen, believe this has happened with some Neo-Calvinist writings. These writings focus so much on the earthiness of our end that they forget that the main business of heaven is Jesus.[38] In response, Dutch Neo-Calvinists might say that some correction was needed. Consider Moody Bible Institute, a dispensational, evangelical flagship that ends its doctrinal statement in article five with the church being "caught up to meet the Lord in the air ere He appears to set up His kingdom." A previous endnote to article three says this kingdom is Jesus's "millennial reign."[39] But that only lasts one thousand years. What happens after that? The statement does not say. Such common lacunae are what this book seeks to fill.

There is much more that could be said about the history of heaven, but this is enough to get the gist of how the church's views developed. Now that you are up to speed, you can better appreciate the differing views in this book and where their proponents are coming from.

Questions about Heaven

Our first contributor is John Feinberg, professor of biblical and systematic theology at Trinity Evangelical Divinity School and author of a forthcoming book on eschatology. Feinberg is a leading theologian who advocates the traditional evangelical Protestant view that our final destiny is largely discontinuous with our present earthly life. Like many evangelicals, Feinberg also comments at length on events that immediately precede our final state, such as the great tribulation and millennium.

Eerdmans, 2002); Randy Alcorn, *Heaven: A Comprehensive Guide to Everything the Bible Says about Our Eternal Home* (Carol Stream, IL: Tyndale, 2004); N. T. Wright, *Surprised by Hope* (New York: HarperOne, 2008); J. Richard Middleton, *A New Heaven and a New Earth* (Grand Rapids: Baker Academic, 2014); G. K. Beale, *The Temple and the Church's Mission: A Biblical Theology of the Dwelling Place of God*, New Studies in Biblical Theology 17 (Downers Grove, IL: InterVarsity Press, 2014); and Michael Wittmer, *Becoming Worldly Saints* (Grand Rapids: Zondervan, 2015) and *Heaven Is a Place on Earth* (Grand Rapids: Zondervan, 2004).

38. Michael Allen, *Grounded in Heaven* (Grand Rapids: Eerdmans, 2018); Michael S. Horton, Scott Swain, and Michael Wittmer, "The Need for Heaven," *Modern Reformation* (September–October 2016): 38–49; and J. Todd Billings, "The New View of Heaven Is Too Small," *Christianity Today*, February 15, 2018, www.christianitytoday.com/ct/2018/february -web-only/new-view-of-heaven-too-small-resurrection-hope.html.

39. "Moody Bible Institute Doctrinal Statement," www.moodybible.org/beliefs/.

Our second contributor is J. Richard Middleton, professor of biblical worldview and exegesis at Northeastern Seminary and author of *A New Heaven and a New Earth: Reclaiming Biblical Eschatology* (Baker Academic, 2014). Middleton refers to himself as a Kuyperian Wesleyan, since he is a Wesleyan biblical scholar who blends the Neo-Calvinist position with Wesley's mature view of the new creation. His position may be viewed as a response in part to the traditional view, as he emphasizes the earthly continuity between this world and the next.

Our third contributor is Michael Allen, professor of systematic theology and academic dean at Reformed Theological Seminary in Orlando and author of *Grounded in Heaven: Recentering Christian Hope and Life in God* (Eerdmans, 2018). Allen's chapter may be viewed as a response in part to the Neo-Calvinist position, which he suspects has so emphasized the earthiness of our final state that it has forgotten the most important part, our beatific vision of God.

Our fourth contributor is Peter Kreeft, professor of philosophy at Boston College and author of *Everything You Ever Wanted to Know about Heaven* (Ignatius, 1990) and *Heaven: The Heart's Deepest Longing* (Ignatius, 1989). Kreeft presents a contemporary, post-Vatican II Roman Catholic perspective on heaven. He is a graduate of Calvin College, the North American home of Dutch Neo-Calvinism, so Kreeft is particularly situated to nuance clearly how the Roman Catholic position is similar to and different from this popular Protestant view.

As you read my short history of heaven, you may have noticed a recurring tension that expressed itself in various ways. Sometimes felt as the tension between the earth and heaven, creation and redemption, time and eternity, the physical and the spiritual, or our cultural enjoyments and Christ, this tension goes a long way toward distinguishing this book's various views on heaven. To highlight these differences, I asked each contributor to answer the following ten questions in their chapter. The first six were mandatory, and the final four were optional (yet common questions that Christians ask). The contributors were free to say if they did not think the questions had clear answers, and they could address any other issues they deemed relevant. I also asked that they avoid idiosyncrasies that are not shared by others who hold their view, or at least inform readers when their particular slant is not essential to the position.

Here are the ten questions:

1. **Where is the final destiny of the saved?** How do you understand "the new heaven and the new earth"? Will we live forever in heaven or on earth?

2. **What will we *be* there?** Presently we are an integrated combination of body and soul, two distinct parts intertwined in a mysterious whole. What will we be in our final, glorified state? How will we be changed, and how will we remain the same? How do you understand Paul's phrase, "spiritual bodies" (1 Cor 15:42–50)?

3. **What will we *do* there?** Can you describe our worship of God in our final condition? Will we do anything else? If so, what? Can you describe these activities?

4. **How, what, and who will we see of God?** Will we only see Jesus, or will we also see the Spirit and the Father? If we see the Spirit and the Father, will our vision require mediation of some sort, or will we see them directly?

5. **How does your view of our end relate to the intermediate state?** How is it similar and how is it different?

6. **How does your view of our end relate to our present life?** How is it similar and how is it different? How should our end influence how we live now?

7. **Will we possess special powers?** What may our "spiritual bodies" be able to do that our present bodies cannot? For example, will we be inherently indestructible?

8. **Will we remember traumatic events of this life or loved ones who are not with us?** If so, how will that not steal our joy? If not, then have we lost a vital part of our identity?

9. **How will we relate to our spouses and other family members?** Will there be marriage, sex, or family units in our final state? Will we remain gendered, and if so, will we wear clothes?

10. **Will we be able to sin in our final condition?** If not, in what sense do we possess free will?

Now that you have met the contributors and viewed their questions, it is time to dig into their answers. I'll see you on the other side.

A TRADITIONAL EVANGELICAL
PROTESTANT PERSPECTIVE

JOHN S. FEINBERG

Everybody wants to go to heaven, but nobody wants to die.[1] Still, unless you know Christ as personal Savior and are alive at the time of the rapture, chances are extremely good that you will have to die in order to get to heaven. And then what? For Christians there has always been the hope that, upon death, they will enter heaven. Some nonbelievers are very good at imagining that there is neither a heaven nor a hell, but sooner than later they will learn the sad truth that physical death is not the end. There actually is a hell, and no matter how good one's imagination, those outside of Christ cannot and will not escape it.

But what happens after death to those who have placed their faith and trust in Christ as Savior? After the funeral (and even before), we know what happens to the bodies of dead believers. But what about their immaterial part, their soul? Is it immediately upon physical death ushered into God's presence, or is there a waiting period before that happens? Scripture teaches the ultimate resurrection of the body, but if your soul is already in God's presence, why do you need the body? And, once the resurrection occurs, will we still know one another? If a baby died in infancy, will it be resurrected as an adult? And once believers are

---

1. Unless otherwise noted, the following essay employs the NASB translation for biblical citations.

resurrected and glorified, then what? Will we find the nearest cloud and float around on it all day, joyously playing our harps? Or will there be something more meaningful to do? These are all intriguing questions, and no matter how much we trust Christ for today, it is natural to have questions about what happens once we die. Sadly, there is not a lot of Scripture that addresses such questions, though Scripture does reveal things that help us find answers.

According to Scripture, those who know Christ will experience a series of events before they reach their final estate for eternity. In order to understand this point, it would help first to sketch briefly my understanding of end-time events. Though a case could be made for the general timing of each event in the sequence, that is for another place. My purpose now is to help readers see what I mean when I say that the path to the believers' final destiny involves various stages and events. Once I clarify those events, I can then more clearly present my views about what happens to believers at death and after.

Before proceeding, however, I must affirm my total and unapologetic commitment to the complete inspiration, inerrancy, and authority of Scripture. Hence, if views about life after death contradict or could not even be a logical implication of clear biblical teaching, I reject them, regardless of how "attractive" they may seem. I should also add that I believe there is enough biblical revelation for us to formulate a picture of the afterlife, and views about eternity that contradict that portrait cannot be correct.

Overview of Eschatological Events

So, prophetically speaking, what does God have in store for believers and this world in which we live? As we move to the end of the current age, there will be times of trouble (e.g., Matt 24:4–14; 2 Tim 3:1–9). That era will culminate in a seven-year tribulation on earth known as Daniel's seventieth week (Dan 9:27). Jesus promised to return for his church (John 14:1–3; 1 Cor 15:51–57; 1 Thess 4:13–18), and Bible scholars who expect such a rapture believe it will occur in relation to the tribulation. They debate whether Christ will come before, during, or at the end of the tribulation, but all agree that he will return at one of those times. Those who expect the rapture before or in the middle of the tribulation believe that dead saints and living members of the church will be taken to heaven. Those who believe the rapture will occur at the end of the tribulation do not see believers going immediately to heaven. Instead, believers will rise to meet Christ in the air and then turn around to accompany him as he comes to earth to destroy his enemies at the battle of Armageddon. Those who believe in the rapture expect that believers will receive a glorified body when raptured (1 Cor 15:51–57; 1 John 3:1–2).

At the end of the tribulation, a worldwide confederacy of nations will surround and attack Israel (Zech 12:1–3). Jesus will ride out of heaven with his army (Old Testament and New Testament saints and angelic hosts) to destroy those who have come against him and his people (the battle of Armageddon, Rev 19:11–21). After their defeat, Jesus will gather from all ends of the earth believers alive at his second coming who did not lose their lives in this climactic battle (Matt 24:31). There will then be a judgment of all people still alive in natural bodies (judgment of the nations, mentioned in Matt 25:31–46). Those who know Christ as Savior will enter the long-awaited kingdom (v. 34). Nonbelievers will go away into eternal punishment (v. 46).

At the outset of the kingdom, according to Revelation 20:1–3, Satan will be bound and cast into a pit, so that he will not be free to deceive people as he has at other times in history. When the kingdom begins, it will be populated by Old Testament saints, the church, and tribulation saints who lost their lives (Rev 20:4 specifically mentions saints killed during the tribulation, and other dead believers from other times in history will also be resurrected and enter the kingdom in glorified bodies—the kingdom was promised to them as well, and when it finally comes, they will not miss out on it). All these saints will be in their resurrected and glorified bodies. Other believers who lived through the tribulation without dying will enter the kingdom in natural bodies. This kingdom, otherwise known as the millennial kingdom or the millennium, will last one thousand years. Many who enter the millennial kingdom in natural bodies will give birth to others (Isa 65:20). Those born during the millennium will need to accept Christ as Savior; many will, but not all. At the end of the millennium, Satan will be loosed and will lead one last rebellion against God; many of his followers will be people born during the millennium who never turned to Christ. Satan and his followers will be defeated and cast into the lake of fire (Rev

20:7–10). This understanding of Christ's millennial kingdom after he returns at the end of the tribulation identifies me as a premillennialist.

Revelation 20:11–15 introduces us to the great white-throne judgment. Verse 11 says that God will sit on a great white throne and that before his face heaven and earth have fled. There is no evidence that the millennial kingdom was not lived out on the current earth, so sometime between the end of the millennial kingdom and the great white-throne judgment, God will destroy the current heavens and earth. Second Peter 3 portrays this event not as an annihilation of matter but as a gigantic "meltdown" of all existing structures. Second Peter 3 does not say exactly when this will occur, but given the scene in Revelation 20:11 it is reasonable to believe that it will happen between the end of the millennial kingdom and the great white-throne judgment.

According to Revelation 20:11–15, "losers" at the great white-throne judgment will be cast into the lake of fire as their final abode. My understanding of this judgment is that there are no "winners." Whether or not one agrees, Revelation 20:11–15 does not say what happens to "winners," so if there are some, it is not clear where they go. After the great white-throne judgment, the old heavens and earth are still gone, but nothing else exists to take their place. However, Scripture predicts that God will then create a new heaven and new earth (Isa 65:17; 2 Pet 3:11–13). We get the fullest description in Revelation 21–22 of what this new age will be like, as John writes about life in the eternal state, in this new heaven and earth. The new heaven and new earth will also include a new Jerusalem. Revelation 21–22 says this new era will last forever. During the eternal state, Scripture is very clear that there will be no sin or sinners. It will be a time of perfect peace and righteousness that will continue uninterrupted forever. God (Father, Son, and Holy Spirit) will rule and reign forever in the eternal state.

The Intermediate State

The period between physical death and bodily resurrection is known as the *intermediate state*. Given the previous sketch of end-time events, what happens to believers in Christ who die before the rapture? Assuming that their body was not lost (and if not, assuming it was not cremated), after death the body will be buried in a tomb or grave of some sort. Common experience shows that this happens to most people when they die. But what about *believers'* immaterial part (soul/spirit)? The best biblical evidence teaches that their immaterial part goes immediately into the Lord's presence in heaven.

Here is some evidence in support of this view. In Philippians 1 Paul wrestles with a dilemma. He does not know whether he should depart and go to be with Christ (better for him), or stay alive so that he can continue to minister to the Philippians' needs. Though both options are appealing, Paul is certain that he will remain alive. It should be clear that what will remain if he dies is his body. There is no evidence that he thought anything but the body could remain if he died. Hence, he believed that when he died his soul would depart and go to be with the Lord.

In addition, in 2 Corinthians 5:8, Paul writes about being absent from the body but present with the Lord. What can this possibly mean other than his soul leaving his body when he dies? Paul does not describe this state as though it will be unique to him. The clear impression is that this is the lot of all believers who die.

There is also the story of the rich man and Lazarus (Luke 16:19–31). It is not clear whether this is a parable or a true story, but even if it is just a story to make a theological point, what is that point, and what does it teach about the afterlife? The rich man with no relation to God is portrayed as being in the torments of hell. The flames scorch him, and there is no escape from this torture. He asks if "Father Abraham" would send Lazarus with some cold water to put on his tongue so that he might have a moment of relief. The rich man is told that this cannot happen because there is a great gulf between him and Lazarus, and neither has access to the other.

If this is a true story, then the rich man has died and already been resurrected; he has likely faced his final judgment and has been consigned to the lake of fire, that is, he is one of the "losers" at the great white-throne judgment. If it is not a true story but only one to illustrate in general the final state of the saved and lost, then the story of the rich man does not necessarily make a *precise* point about the final abode of the wicked. It can merely signify that there is unrelenting judgment for the nonbelieving.

Similarly, what is said about Lazarus may be a fictional story or parable meant to teach that the godly will, in the next life, be greatly blessed. Or this story may intend to teach something specific about what happens to the godly after they die. If it is the latter, then we do not learn a lot from it. Is Lazarus embodied or disembodied? One is tempted to opt for the former, because that would fit with his ability to pour water on the rich man's tongue. But if it is only a story meant to show the different final states of the godly and the wicked, then we would be wise not to demand that the details of Lazarus's and the rich man's conditions make precise metaphysical points about a phase (or even all) of afterlife existence.

Finally, there is Jesus's comment to the repentant thief crucified next to him. In response to his faith, Jesus says, "Today you shall be with me in paradise" (Luke 23:43). While Jesus might have been predicting a miraculous removal from the cross and a transference of a living and glorified thief into God's very presence in heaven, that is not the most likely understanding of what he meant. Rather, Jesus knew that the thief would soon die, and he knew that his body would be buried. Jesus's comment affirms that there is a separable part of human nature, the immaterial soul, and that upon death the thief's soul would go to be with Jesus in God's presence in heaven ("paradise").

So, when believers die, their soul goes immediately into God's presence, while their body goes to the grave. Some bodies will be lost at sea, and others changed into a different form by cremation. No matter, for the God who created human bodies in the first place can later reconstitute them, even if they have changed form by means of cremation or some catastrophe.

The Rapture

What happens next to believers who have died? Scripture has more to say about this than we might expect (John 14:1–6; 1 Cor 15:50–57; 1 Thess 4:13–18; 1 John 3:2). Jesus told his disciples that he would soon leave them (John 14:1–6). However, he also promised that someday he would return for them and take them to be with him. Specifically, in John 14:2–3 Jesus revealed that he would go to his Father's house to prepare a place for his disciples. Later he would return to take them to be with him (v. 4). Many theologians and Bible scholars refer to this event as the rapture of the church. They debate whether it will happen before the seven-year tribulation at the end time, midway through it, or at the end of the tribulation. Regardless of the exact timing, Scripture teaches that when Christ returns, some believers will be alive while many others will have died. Jesus promised that neither of these groups will miss the rapture.

So, what will happen at this event? First Thessalonians 4:16 says that the Lord will return from heaven with a shout, the voice of an archangel, and the trumpet of God. Those who have died believing in Christ will be resurrected and caught up in the air to be with Christ. This means, among other things, that the immaterial part of their being will be reunited to their resurrected body. Then, believers alive at the time of the rapture will be caught up next. Paul adds "and so we shall always be with the Lord." It is not entirely clear whether this means that everywhere he goes we will be with him or simply that from then onward we will be in our resurrected bodies (even as Christ is in his) and hence prepared to be with the Lord and do whatever he asks us to do as we serve him in his kingdom. Both are possible, and each amounts to no more separation from the Lord, spiritually or otherwise.

But how, one may wonder, can believers in natural bodies do these things? Even astronauts who travel long distances in space must wear special equipment so that they can adapt to their new surroundings. I believe we have the answer in two key passages, one more general and the other more specific in what they reveal. First John 3:2 says that "we are children of God," but it does not now appear what we shall be. Yet we know that someday he (Christ) will appear. Given the rest of the verse, it is clear that the day when Christ will appear is the rapture. John says that when Christ appears, "we will be like him" (1 John 3:2).

This is an incredible promise, but we must clarify what it means. It does not mean that we will become deities of some sort. That is totally contrary to the teaching of the whole Bible, let alone 1 John 3. Nor does it mean that only believers who have died will be resurrected from the dead. If it meant that, there would be no change to believers *alive* at Christ's coming, but 1 John 3:2 is clearly about *all* believers, *all* who are the children of God through faith in Christ, not just about dead believers. And it says that all will be changed!

What will this change be? We can do no better than repeat Paul's explanation in 1 Corinthians 15:51–55. Paul says that not all believers will "sleep" (Paul's term for undergoing physical, natural death), but all believers will be changed (v. 51). When? At the last trump (v. 52; Bible scholars who see this as the trump of the rapture of 1 Thess 4 are, I believe, correct). Paul next explains what the change will involve. "The dead will be raised imperishable, and we will be changed. For this perishable must put on the imperishable, and this mortal must put on immortality" (v. 53). The ultimate result, Paul says, is that "death is swallowed up in victory" (v. 54).

This means that our bodies will no longer be capable of becoming ill, feeling any negative effects of aging, or dying. I take it that this means also that we will be able to go any place in the universe (as Christ can) without any negative effect to our being. In short, we will be in our glorified state. That is the sense in which we can say with John, "We will be like him."

While this is helpful, I believe we can be even more specific. After we are changed, we will still be an integrated combination of body and soul, but each part of human nature (material and immaterial) will be glorified. Our bodies will be glorified, so they will not be able to show negative signs of aging. They will not be able to get sick, deteriorate, or die. Our souls will be glorified, so they will be able to do everything our immaterial part did in its natural, unglorified state (e.g., think, reason, have and express emotions, deliberate and choose), but without the possibility of sin. Presumably, we will be able to do physical and mental work—generally whatever unglorified humans can do—but in ways that entirely please and honor God and in no way disobey any of his commands.

As to Paul's use of "spiritual bodies" in 1 Corinthians 15:42–50, he does not mean that our physical bodies will be spirit-like (what that would even mean is not clear). Rather, Paul uses the term in the sense of a glorified body. A glorified body (and mind) is totally separated from sin and its effects. Thus, it cannot sin in emotions, desires, deeds, willing, acting, or in any other way.

If this is what happens to living believers at the rapture, what happens to those who die before the rapture? The answer is the same as what happens to any believer at physical death. His or her body (if available) goes into the grave, and his or her immaterial part goes into Christ's presence. At the rapture, the bodies of dead believers resurrect from the dead and are each rejoined to their immaterial part. At this point, their whole person—body and soul—will be glorified in precisely the ways that John and Paul explain.

As referenced above, the time period between physical death and bodily resurrection is known as the intermediate state. The physical body is dead, buried (or cremated), and deteriorating in a grave, while the believer's immaterial part, upon physical death, goes immediately into God's presence. It cannot experience any of the mental maladies common to immaterial minds/souls while they are embodied. Does that mean that, in biblical terminology, the immaterial part of humans is "glorified" at that point? Scripture does not use such language of disembodied spirits, even when those spirits are in the presence of God in heaven (see 2 Cor 12:2–4 for what Paul says about a possible disembodied experience). Presumably, disembodied spirits can perform the same functions as they did while embodied, but with greater accuracy and knowledge. As to the eternal state, physical bodies are resurrected, rejoined to their respective immaterial parts, and the whole person (body and soul) is glorified. Christ died to save persons (body and soul), and until the body is resurrected and changed to its glorified state, it still bears the consequences of sin (death). Once resurrected and conjoined to their immaterial soul, the whole person is completely saved.

The Millennium

What happens next to these glorified saints, and what about saints saved after the rapture? As shared above, after the tribulation the Lord will set up his one-thousand-year millennial reign on earth. Scripture seems clear that at its inception the kingdom will only consist of believers. This involves three groups of people. The first is Old Testament saints. They will be resurrected and enter the kingdom in glorified bodies. If this seems odd, remember that the kingdom was promised to them too. When Christ's kingdom finally comes to earth, it is unthinkable that Old Testament saints would miss out on it! The second group of entrants into the kingdom will be those New Testament believers taken at the rapture. This includes all New Testament believers who have died and those who are alive at Christ's return. All will be glorified and will enter the kingdom.

After the rapture but before the start of the kingdom, many people in natural bodies will be saved (no doubt, many will be saved as a result of the evangelism efforts of the 144,000 witnesses; see Rev 7 and 14). This does not include everyone alive at that time; otherwise, there would be no "goats" at the judgment just prior to the start of the kingdom (Matt 25:31–46). Those included in this third group are people who, despite the persecution of God's people during the tribulation, somehow survived and did not die. When the kingdom arrives, they enter it in their natural bodies. It is from these people that others in natural bodies are born and live in unglorified bodies, as we do now. Isaiah 65:20 shows that during this reign of Christ on earth, people will be born and die (birth and death are true of people in natural bodies but not of glorified saints). Inhabitants of the kingdom will also do manual work (Isa 65:21–22). As for believers in natural bodies, they will live a long time (v. 20)—perhaps through the whole millennial kingdom, though perhaps some will die before the end of the kingdom. Scripture does not say whether such people who die will be immediately resurrected and glorified to live from then onward through eternity or whether they will be resurrected after the kingdom ends. Regardless, at some time during or just after the kingdom, all kingdom believers, dead or alive, will receive a glorified body. All of God's blessings promised to believers earlier in history also belong to kingdom saints.

Presumably, during the kingdom those in glorified bodies will have access to the current earth, and they will also be able to come and go from the current heaven, God's abode. What happens to believers after the kingdom ends? Scripture focuses more on what happens to nonbelievers at that time. As mentioned earlier, after the millennial kingdom God will destroy the current heavens and earth (2 Pet 3:10–12) and create a new heavens and earth. If there are believers who live in natural bodies to the end of the kingdom, undoubtedly God will give them a glorified body before he destroys the current heavens and earth. How else could they continue to survive?

Before God creates the new heavens and earth, one other solemn event will take place, the great white-throne judgment. John says that when this occurs, the current heavens and earth will no longer exist (Rev 20:11). All the godly dead would have been already raised and/or glorified to live through some or all of the kingdom. It is only the ungodly dead who are raised to stand at the great white-throne judgment.

After the great white-throne judgment, God will create a new heaven and new earth, where the saved of all ages, in glorified bodies, will live. As I understand Revelation 21 and 22, these saints will have equal access to the new heavens and the new earth. Revelation 21 also speaks of a new Jerusalem on this new earth. There will never come into it anything that is sinful in any way (Rev 21:27). Only those whose names are written in the Lamb's book of life will come into it. But the Lamb's book of life contains the names of everyone who is a believer, not just one or another group of believers. I take it that this means all believers from all places and eras will have access to the new heavens and earth and the new Jerusalem. I see nothing in Revelation 21 or 22 that limits any group of believers from the blessings of any part of the new heaven, new earth, and new Jerusalem. Believers from all ages will live there forever.

New Heaven and Earth

So what can we say about the very final state of believers from every age? Their final destiny will be the new heaven and the new earth. The godly dead of all ages before the kingdom will be raised to enter and live through the millennial kingdom (Rev 20:1–10). After the millennium, God will destroy the current heavens and the current earth (2 Pet 3). Then, there will be the great white-throne judgment where there is no heaven or earth (Rev 20:11–15). After this judgment, God will construct a new heaven and new earth (Rev 21–22). On the basis of 2 Peter 3:10–12, the destruction of the current heaven and current earth won't involve the annihilation of matter. Rather, 2 Peter 3:10–12 speaks of a gigantic meltdown of all existing structures. Matter from this will then be reformed into a new heaven and new earth as described in Revelation 21–22. As I understand biblical revelation about the new heaven and new earth (there is not a lot of it), we will have equal access to both. I do not see that one group will be sequestered in one place and another group elsewhere. By the time we come to the new heaven and new earth, all distinctions based on ethnicity, race, gender, etc., won't matter to those with whom you'll live. At least I see nothing in Scripture that suggests these distinctions will matter.

Those who contemplate life in the new heavens and new earth wonder what people will do in this final state. Of course, the immediate and most obvious answer is that we will worship God in song and message and with any deeds that bring praise to God. Though God will be the teacher or preacher most of the time, nothing suggests that a glorified human might not be able to give a testimony or even preach a sermon. Preparing such sermons and lessons will likely take much less time than they do now, but that is not to say they will not take any time. And might not there be libraries in the eternal state? Surely glorified persons will not be omniscient, and there is no indication (biblically or otherwise) that they will cease to be intellectually curious. Perhaps we will all be "speed readers," but even so we will need books to read.

Some may think this misunderstands worship in particular and life in general in a glorified body. They may think there is no need for cognitive content to be given when glorified people worship, and they may see no reason for glorified people to read and learn more about God. But I think this misunderstands glorification and human nature. Humans are not omniscient, and the glorified state will not make us so. Moreover, the glorified existence will not quench all intellectual curiosity. Glorified humans will still be finite, and as such there will be more we can learn about God. Our abilities to study and remember what we learn will be increased (e.g., fatigue, daydreaming, and racing thoughts that distract us in our nonglorified state from paying attention to sermons or even to Bible reading and devotions will not hamper us). I suspect that learning more about God will continue into eternity, and it will enhance our personal devotion to God as well as our corporate worship of him.

Is worship and study all we will do? I do not think so, though Scripture does not say much about what other things we might do. Still, I think there are things we can expect. For one thing, there will be much fellowship between ourselves and other believers. I suspect that we will have many questions for biblical figures like Jesus, Moses, Abraham, David, Peter, and Paul, let alone interesting conversations with people like Luther, Calvin, and Spurgeon. It is surely possible that there will be religious instruction for those with less biblical and theological knowledge, though Scripture does not mention this.

Will the new earth have gardens to tend, lawns to mow, houses to build? Will any of its structures (houses or buildings) need renovation? Scripture does not answer these questions. Suffice it to say that if there is need to "fix" any of these things, we can do so. Most likely there will be times simply to view and reflect on the beauty of the new heaven and the new earth in their glorified state. And there is no reason to think that we will not be able to travel to other parts of the earth (and perhaps even to the heavens) to enjoy these other places made and preserved by God's mighty hand.

There will probably also be a lot of eating and banquets. The marriage supper of the Lamb (Rev 20:7–9) happens in heaven, so everyone at this meal will be glorified. Some may wonder why glorified people will have any appetite for food at all. Though we are at a loss to explain the biological details of a hungry and thirsty glorified body, nonetheless Scripture is clear that there will be eating and drinking in the kingdom (e.g., see Luke 22:18, where Jesus speaks of eating and drinking in the kingdom), and nothing taught in Scripture about the eternal state precludes eating and drinking. People in glorified bodies can and will eat.

It is dubious that there will be animal sacrifices, even of a memorial nature. We also know that the Lord's Supper will not be celebrated, because Jesus told his disciples to remember him this way "until he comes" (1 Cor 11:26). But surely there will be much worship focused on Christ's death, burial, and resurrection for the forgiveness of sins. Also, it is not entirely clear whether glorified believers (before the eternal state) will know what the people on earth are doing. But if they do, there is no way to interact with them, because there is a significant gulf between them and us (see the parable of the rich man and Lazarus in Luke 16).

One of the most exciting truths for believers about the afterlife is that Scripture says we will see God (Matt 5:8 says that the pure in heart are blessed, for they shall see God). But what does this mean, especially when we consider that God is a pure spirit, and spirits are invisible? After physical death but before our resurrection, our disembodied souls will be in heaven with the Lord. Disembodied souls are pure spirit with no matter as part of them. Hence, at this point in our existence we will not have the "equipment" to see anything visually (as we do now in our embodied state). If it is possible to see something visual in that state, neither Scripture nor science nor any other academic discipline explains how. However, after our bodies are resurrected and reunited with our souls, then we will again have eyes (as well as the rest of our bodies), and presumably glorified eyes can see physical things. So, we will definitely then visually see Jesus in his glorified human nature. His divine nature, however, is pure spirit and is invisible, so it is hard to know how we could see that nature.

As to the Father and the Spirit, as pure spirit there is nothing to see visually. But many instances in both Testaments show that both can make their presence known by means of some physical manifestation (e.g., a cloud of smoke and pillar of fire or a voice from heaven). We do not know how we may visually perceive an immaterial substance, but that does not mean that something invisible can't make its presence known by acting and making the results of that action knowable in some sensory way. Hence, when Scripture says that the pure in heart are blessed, for they shall see God, it most likely means that we will be able to experience his presence in a more intimate way than before. How that relates to our visual experience or any other sensory experience of God is not revealed in Scripture, nor can science explain how that happens. It may mean only that God will manifest his presence to us in some physical form, and we will "see" him that way. Finally, if humans in a glorified state can see things visually that are invisible, then we will be able to see all three members of the Godhead visually. However, nothing Scripture teaches about our glorification suggests that glorified humans can see invisible things.

What about our other characteristics and abilities? Will we possess special powers in our spiritual, glorified bodies? Scripture is mostly silent on such matters, but we can say some things. For one, glorified people will be inherently indestructible. But does this mean that as glorified persons each of us will have identical intellectual and physical abilities? Probably not. Though we will likely be able to learn more easily and remember more, I do not think this means we will all be Einsteins. Likewise, I do not think being glorified will so increase my athletic abilities that I could play professional sports, or even be a better athlete than Michael Jordan in his prime. Perhaps this will be true, but Scripture does not say. One thing seems relatively sure: any enhanced abilities will not make it impossible to identify us as the person we were on earth, nor will it mean that all glorified people will simply be complete stereotypes of one another in regard to all abilities. Note, for example, that Peter, James, and John were able at the Mount of Transfiguration to identify Moses and Elijah, whom they had never met. Perhaps they introduced themselves to the three disciples, but the tenor of the passage suggests that the disciples just knew who they were (see Matt 17:1–8). Similarly, I will not lose my identity as John Feinberg; I will just be that same person in a glorified state.

As to our spiritual condition, neither sin nor any of its consequences will have any impact on us. I believe this means that we cannot be tempted, but even if we are, it will not be possible to fall into sin. Being immune to sin's consequences means that we will not get sick, experience the debilitating aspects of aging, or die. It is not even clear that we will be able to feel pain (if we can, it will not have any long-term, negative effects on us). We will not possess divine attributes, but our natural attributes will allow us to function maximally to whatever human attributes allow. Thus, we will not be omniscient, but we will probably learn things and remember them more easily and securely. Presumably, we will be able to travel more rapidly (e.g., see the saints of heaven riding out of heaven with Christ at his return in Rev 19:11–14), but exactly how this happens is unclear. It is unlikely that we will be able to starve, but whether we will eat simply to celebrate or because we need to eat in order to sustain existence is not clear. Perhaps some of both is involved. Finally, we will not fear physical death, because it will be impossible to die. Moreover, it is unclear that there will be anything else to fear. We will be saved forever, and we will experience much more of what that means than we do now. Scripture does not speak to this issue, but there seems to be no reason that we cannot grow in knowledge of the Lord or anything else (i.e., both our propositional as well as our experiential knowledge can still grow). Though we will not be able to sin, does that mean our spiritual condition will remain static? I doubt it. Growing to love the Lord more and growing closer relationally to him and to other believers will likely still be possible.

As a result of these blessings, we will likely also be happy much of the time and praising the Lord for our great salvation. Any doubts about God's existence and the gospel message will be answered as we receive the inheritance of salvation so clearly promised in Scripture. It seems also that believers will no longer be engaged in spiritual warfare, as all the opponents of our soul will have been consigned to the lake of fire. We will understand fully that Christ is victorious over every area of life, and that we are members of his winning team.

In the eternal state, how will we relate to those who were our spouse, children, and parents on earth when we lived and functioned in natural bodies? In answer to the Sadducees' attempt to trap Jesus by asking whose wife in heaven the woman would be who had had seven husbands on earth, he noted that the question erroneously presupposed that in heaven there will be marriage and perhaps even childbearing (Matt 22:23–30). Perhaps their question also assumed that there would be families and family life as we know it.

While Jesus's answer to the Sadducees suggests that these are wrong assumptions, neither he nor anything elsewhere in Scripture says that we will have nothing to do with others from our earthly families. While Scripture does not say that saved family members will live together in the eternal state, it does not forbid the idea either. But even if earthly familial relationships do not apply in the eternal state, that cannot nullify the fact that we had parents, spouses, and children when living on the current earth. Evidently, from what Jesus said, family life as we know it will not be present in heaven and, by implication, probably not in the eternal state. That does not mean we will not spend a lot of time with our former spouse, children, and parents; it just means we will not have family life with them as we did on earth in natural bodies.

Lest one worry that we will have to pick and choose our closest relationships, because there will not be time to establish ties with everyone, that simply will not be the case. An eternity will be plenty of time to establish a deep relationship with everyone there, regardless of whether we choose to do so or not.

Will we still be recognizable as the persons we were in our natural bodies, or will glorification make that impossible? This is actually a question about personal identity. There seems to be no reason that we will lose marks of personal identity. At the Mount of Transfiguration, Peter, James, and John knew they were in the presence of Moses and Elijah, and they could distinguish Moses from Elijah and vice versa. Moreover, the risen Christ still had marks of personal identity. There is no reason to think that will not be true of us as well. A key marker of personal identity is one's gender. Hence, in eternity men will still be men, and women will still be women.

Will we wear clothes or even need them? In Revelation 19, after the marriage supper of the Lamb, we see the church ride out of heaven with Christ to do battle at the end of the tribulation. Christ's bride is clothed in linen, white and clean (Rev 19:8; this represents the righteous deeds of the church). Will we lose those clothes once the kingdom starts and on into the eternal state? We simply are not told. As to the eternal state, since everyone will be glorified and incapable of sin, whether we are clothed or not will not actually matter to our spiritual condition. Moreover, questions about what the climate will be like in eternity and whether there will be seasons that require different kinds of clothes are impossible now to answer. And, even if there will be different seasons, it is not clear whether a glorified body can or cannot be affected by temperature and climate.

One of the most difficult questions to consider is whether hard and even tragic events in our lives now will still be remembered in eternity and tarnish our joy. Likewise, will the realization that some friends and relatives will spend a Christless eternity and suffer hell's torments steal or, at the very least, diminish the joy of being forever with the Lord? These are challenging questions to consider, let alone answer. Presumably, we will remember all the good things and blessings that happened. And if our memories are that strong, it is hard to believe that we will not also remember the traumatic events of our lives. But then we will know how everything turned out (Rom 8:28 won't be just a slogan but an experienced reality), and the fear and anguish that come with such events will be gone. Moreover, we will see how God used those events ultimately for our benefit, and we will praise him.

More difficult, though, is the matter of loved ones who are not there and the knowledge that they are suffering eternal torment that will never end. Especially troubling is the thought that had we witnessed to them (at all or more), they might have turned to Christ and spent eternity with him and with us. Because of the "great gulf" between the final states of the lost and the redeemed, it is unlikely that we will know by firsthand observation or even by secondhand reports from God exactly what they are feeling and experiencing at any one time or another. Even so, it is natural for us to think that such things will cause us much sorrow and even embarrassment (because we did not do more to point them to Christ). Scripture says, however, that God will wipe away all tears, and so it is reasonable to say that these facts will not spoil our joy and cause us to live with regret for eternity. How God will do this is not clear. But remember, God is omniscient, and so he is aware of every detail of every life that ends in the lake of fire. Christ died for them, and they could have had eternal life, but they chose not to establish a relationship with God. This realization could result in God being endlessly sorrowful and sad, but it does not. That does not mean God does not care about the lost but only that their fate does not ruin his joy. So whatever God does to maintain *his* joy despite his desire for all to be saved suggests that he can do whatever it takes to ensure that *we* do not lose our joy over these things. That, however, does not mean we will not care about the lost but only that their lost state will not put us in a perennially sad and grieving mood. But exactly how God will bring that to pass is not clear.

Some speculate that, once in heaven, we will perfectly understand the justice and righteousness of God, and hence we will agree that what has happened to the lost is totally deserved, causing us to praise God for his just ways. Others even speculate that the lost will come to see this and hence will not be angry at God for their lost estate. Of course, their admission of this will not save them or even reduce their time in the lake of fire. However, as noted, this is speculation; Scripture does not go into such details.

How should biblical teaching about the future for the saved impact our lives now? For one thing, in our current state of existence even believers can sin. However, in our glorified state that will be impossible. It is not even clear biblically whether someone in a glorified state can be tempted to sin. Does this mean we will not be free? A lot depends on how one defines freedom. If one defines it as *libertarian freedom*—the ability to do otherwise than what one does—then there will not be freedom in eternity. Yet this is the definition of freedom an indeterminist would hold, and it is not the only possible concept. For compatibilists like myself, free human action is defined as compatible with causal conditions that decisively incline the will without constraining it. In other words, one's acts are causally determined but not constrained (one does what one wants to do), and so one acts freely. For a compatibilist, being unable to sin will not make one unfree. This is especially so since the individual freely chose to be saved (the decision that made him or her incapable of sinning). Similarly, incompatibilists can say that though glorified humans cannot sin, their decision to accept Christ that resulted in their inability to sin was made using libertarian free will. Thus, in essence both sides say that a saved human freely (either with libertarian free will or with compatibilism) chose to accept Christ, so that the saved person's inability to sin resulted by an act of free choice. And thereby the person's freedom remains intact.

In 2 Peter 3, Peter discusses changes that are coming with a new heaven and new earth, and he asks the crucial question for those living before the eschaton: In light of what God will someday do, "what sort of people ought you to be" (v. 11)? Immediately he answers that we should live holy, godly lives. Thus, in view of where history is going and what will be our final goal, it would not be bad even now to adjust our life to what will be the norm and standard for behavior for eternity. Likewise, Paul, speaking about the rapture and the changes that it will bring for all believers, says, "Therefore comfort one another with these words" (1 Thess 4:18). Jesus, speaking of his need to go away and his intent to prepare a place for us and then return for us, says, "Do not let your heart be troubled" (John 14:1; i.e., do not worry about the ultimate outcome; trust me to take care of everything).

Thus, as we await the rapture, the kingdom, and eternity, we should pursue godliness. And as Peter suggests, we should eagerly await the return of our Lord Jesus Christ (2 Pet 3:12–14).

Some day we will behold him in all his glory! Along with saints throughout church history, we say, "Even so, come, Lord Jesus" (KJV).

RESPONSE TO JOHN S. FEINBERG

J. RICHARD MIDDLETON

My thanks to John Feinberg for the clear articulation of his eschatological perspective. There is much to applaud in Feinberg's chapter, including his commitment to the authority of Scripture and his desire to conform his beliefs and actions to what he understands biblical teaching to be on eschatology.

I am also struck by the many times he used terms like "perhaps" or "it is possible" and pointed out that the Bible does not give a clear answer on the particular topic he was exploring. This is laudable humility, since there is much about the eschaton that we would like to know but simply do not have enough scriptural information from which to form a firm opinion.

Dispensationalism

Feinberg's basic approach to eschatology is what I learned as a teenager growing up in the church. However, as I began to study the Bible in depth—not just eschatological texts, but the whole range of Scripture in both Testaments—I found this eschatological approach (typically known as *dispensationalism*) could not survive biblical scrutiny.

As historians know, the basic tenets of dispensational eschatology were not developed as a hermeneutical package until the mid-nineteenth century. Although there have been precursors of this or that detail of dispensationalism (and not every aspect of Feinberg's eschatology is unique to dispensationalism), this framework for reading the Bible is of relatively recent lineage, which means that the editor's decision to call it a "traditional" perspective is a bit of a misnomer. Even designating his chapter "Heaven" does not quite match his exposition of the new heaven and new earth as the final state of salvation.[1]

---

1. Editor's note: the contributor John Feinberg did not choose his title. The term

The Nature of Our Disagreement

Before I get to the details of our disagreement, I want to make clear that whatever differences we may have in our theology or interpretation of the Bible, I view John Feinberg as a faithful brother in Christ and respect him as a theologian and teacher of the church. Also, simply because I have a different opinion on these matters does not mean that I am necessarily right and he is wrong. Pointing out areas of disagreement is not itself an argument as to which approach is preferable. So allow me to explain the basis of my disagreement—first the general basis, then some of the details.

The core of my disagreement is that I perceive Feinberg brings to Scripture an external, preformed view rather than developing a perspective by taking all of Scripture into account. This may partially be an issue of how scholars in the disciplines of theology and biblical studies work. As a theologian, Feinberg seems to soar at a high level over the biblical landscape, using his framework as binoculars to scan the terrain for elements that fit the dispensationalist scheme. As a biblical scholar, I prefer to fly closer to the ground, often getting lost in the terrain, and building up my understanding of the landscape bit by bit until a coherent picture begins to form.

However, both Feinberg and I utilize a framework. No one just sees things as they are, "objectively." We are subjective beings who frame the data in a particular way to develop an interpretation. We both address the data of Scripture, though what we take to be relevant data is often dependent on the framework we are using.

A question I am constantly asking myself is whether I understand the patterns I notice in the Bible in a way that would make sense to the biblical authors, with their assumptions and cognitive environment. I suspect that much of Feinberg's eschatological framework would not be recognizable by biblical authors.

Now, let us get down to some specifics. Since Feinberg's chapter is (laudably) filled with interpretation of particular biblical passages, my focus will be on alternative exegesis of some of these passages. Since

---

"traditional" was assigned to his essay because his view seems to represent the most popular evangelical position today. It is what most evangelical Christians are most familiar with.

I have limited space, I will concentrate on those passages he cites in support of two prominent themes—the rapture and the intermediate state.[2]

The Rapture
1 Thessalonians 4

As support for the rapture, Feinberg cites the classic text in 1 Thessalonians 4:13–18, which says that after the dead in Christ are raised at his coming, those who are alive "will be caught up together with them in the clouds to meet the Lord in the air. And so we will be with the Lord forever" (1 Thess 4:17). In this passage Paul uses the ideas of the "coming" (*parousia*) of our Lord and our "meeting" (*apantēsis*) him in the air. As many recent studies have shown, the terms *parousia* and *apantēsis* are semitechnical terms in Greco-Roman culture for the coming of a dignitary to a city. The citizens go out to meet him as he arrives and then escort him back into the city.

Acts 28:15 uses *apantēsis* to describe the believers coming out of Rome to meet Paul and escort him into the city, while *hypantēsis* (a variant of *apantēsis*) is used for the crowds meeting Jesus at his triumphal entry into Jerusalem (John 12:13). Both *hypantēsis* and *apantēsis* are used in Jesus's parable of the wise and foolish virgins (Matt 25:1–13), where the wise virgins go out to meet the bridegroom and escort him to the wedding banquet.

The point is that the picture Paul paints in 1 Thessalonians 4:13–18 is not of being taken up to heaven but of the coming of Christ in victory to claim the earth as his rightful kingdom.

John 14

Neither are Jesus's words of comfort to his disciples at the start of John 14 a reference to the rapture. Speaking to the disciples before the crucifixion, Jesus gives this assurance: "My Father's house has many rooms;

---

2. I have addressed both 1 Thess 4 (the classic rapture text cited by dispensationalists), as well as Matt 24 (a popular rapture text in the church, which is *not* typically cited by dispensationalists), in J. Richard Middleton, *A New Heaven and a New Earth: Reclaiming Biblical Eschatology* (Grand Rapids: Baker Academic, 2014), 221–27. For more detailed analysis of texts typically thought to refer to the intermediate state, see *New Heaven and a New Earth*, 227–37.

if that were not so, would I have told you that I am going there to prepare a place for you? And if I go and prepare a place for you, I will come back and take you to be with me that you also may be where I am" (John 14:2–3).

Although Feinberg takes these words to refer to the rapture, they are more commonly thought to be about going to be with Christ in heaven, either eternally or for an interim time (the intermediate state). So I can see how Feinberg, who understands the rapture as the taking of the faithful from earth to heaven, could think that John 14 supports this idea.

However, it is not at all clear that "heaven" is where Jesus promises to take his disciples. The location is not explicitly stated (though they are assured that they will be with him). The rest of the New Testament suggests that after Christ's return we will be with him *on earth*, in the new creation.

Indeed, the reference to Christ going to "prepare" a place for the disciples fits a larger pattern of New Testament texts that link preparation in heaven (where the Christian hope is presently secure) to a future unveiling or revelation of that hope in the eschaton (on earth).

This pattern is illustrated in 1 Peter 1:4–5, which affirms that those who trust in Christ have received new birth "into an inheritance that can never perish, spoil or fade. This inheritance is *kept in heaven* for you, who through faith are shielded by God's power until the coming of the salvation that is ready to be revealed in the last time."

If we ask where this future revelation will take place, the answer is abundantly clear from the rest of Scripture. One place where this is explicit is Revelation 21, which describes a vision not only of "a new heaven and a new earth" (v. 1), but of "the Holy City, the new Jerusalem, *coming down out of heaven* from God, *prepared* as a bride beautifully dressed for her husband" (v. 2). Having been first prepared in heaven, the holy city does not remain there but is revealed in all its glory on earth, where God will dwell with the redeemed forever (v. 3).

I have traced this pattern of (present) preparation in heaven for (future) revelation on earth through various New Testament texts in *A New Heaven and a New Earth*. In these texts we are told of the promise of an inheritance, a salvation, a kingdom, a hope, a homeland, a city, a citizenship—all kept, reserved, or prepared in heaven for unveiling on earth at the last day.[3]

This pattern makes sense of John 14, where Jesus goes to prepare a place for his disciples. Indeed, for a first-century reader deeply immersed in the conceptuality of the Old Testament, "my Father's house" would not be taken as a reference to heaven but to the cosmos (heaven *and earth*), understood as God's temple or "house" where he wants to dwell with us (see especially Isa 66:1–2).

The Intermediate State
2 Corinthians 5

On the topic of the intermediate state, Feinberg cites 2 Corinthians 5:8, where Paul says that he "would prefer to be away from the body and at home with the Lord." Feinberg asks: "What can this possibly mean other than his soul leaving his body when he dies?" Apart from the fact that Paul has no doctrine of the "soul" as an immaterial part of the person, there are several exegetical considerations here.

First, the main thrust of 2 Corinthians 5:1–10 is Paul's expectation of the resurrection body, which is being prepared for him in heaven (this is part of the New Testament pattern of preparation in heaven for revelation on earth). In verse 1 Paul uses the metaphor of "the earthly tent" (his present mortal body) in contrast to "a building from God, an eternal house in heaven, not built by human hands" (the resurrection body), also called "our heavenly dwelling" (vv. 1, 2, 4). Paul says that he wants to be clothed (with the new body) so he is not "naked" or "unclothed" (vv. 3–4). Yet the intermediate state would be precisely a case of being naked or unclothed.

Paul says in verse 8 that he prefers to be with Christ ("at home with the Lord") rather than remain in his present mortal body (v. 4, in which "we groan"). But this preference does not refer to a disembodied, intermediate state; it refers to the resurrection. To understand this, we need to read 2 Corinthians 5:8 in the context of the previous chapter (chapter divisions are not part of the original text and are often artificial). In chapter 4 Paul speaks of his confidence and persistence in times of trial

---

3. For analysis of this "apocalyptic" pattern (from the Greek word for unveiling or revealing) through various New Testament texts, see Middleton, *New Heaven and a New Earth*, 212–21.

and suffering (vv. 8–12), explaining the *basis* for his confidence in verse 14: "We know that the one who raised the Lord Jesus from the dead will also *raise us with Jesus and present us with you to himself.*"

Note that Paul explicitly connects the resurrection with being in the presence of God and Christ. Given this statement in 2 Corinthians 4:14, which contextually precedes 5:8, there is no reason to distinguish Paul's statement about being "at home with the Lord" from the resurrection. Of course, if we first *assume* an intermediate state, we could take verse 8 as referring to it. But this passage does not clearly teach it.

Luke 23

Neither is the intermediate state to be found in Jesus's words to the criminal on the cross (Luke 23). When the criminal pleads, "Jesus, remember me when you come into your kingdom," Jesus replies, "Truly I tell you, today you will be with me in paradise" (vv. 42–43). First, the kingdom the criminal is referring to is God's rule, which will be consummated over all the earth when Jesus returns; it is not equivalent to "heaven." I realize that Feinberg did not make this claim, but it is worth clarifying here.

However, Feinberg does identify "paradise" with "heaven." But "paradise" (Greek *paradeisos*) is how the Septuagint translates the Hebrew term for "garden," as in the garden of Eden (Gen 2–3). Paradise refers to the location of the tree of life, which is currently inaccessible to human beings. Besides being guarded by cherubim (Gen 3:24), Jewish Second Temple theology understood the garden or paradise to have been taken up into heaven (the sky), sometimes pictured as on a high mountain between heaven and earth. Apart from Enoch and Elijah, who were taken up in bodily form before their death, paradise is inaccessible to human beings. But in the book of Revelation the risen Christ says: "To the one who is victorious, I will give the right to eat from the tree of life, which is in the paradise of God" (Rev 2:7). And since various aspects of the garden or paradise are incorporated into the description of the new Jerusalem in Revelation 21–22, it is no surprise that the tree of life is also there (Rev 22:2, 14, 19). The main point here is that paradise is not a reference to an immaterial heaven but to the final eschatological state, the new creation that is waiting for us—and it is incontrovertibly physical.

Luke 16

I will not say much about the parable of the rich man and Lazarus in Luke 16:19–31, since Feinberg admits that it might be "a fictional story or parable" making a theological point (I would say that it makes an *ethical* point about wealth, poverty, compassion, and repentance). Nevertheless, Feinberg goes on to distinguish between the rich man being in "the torments of hell," separated by a great gulf from Lazarus, who is with Abraham. Here I just want to point out that Lazarus and the rich man are both in Hades (the underworld), though in separate compartments (for the righteous and the wicked). This picture is found elsewhere in some Second Temple literature. Not only is the rich man not in "hell" (Gehenna or the lake of fire), but Lazarus is not in "heaven." We must be careful not to read the idea of heaven and hell as two ultimate destinations into the Bible (this framework developed only after the New Testament).

Beyond the exegetical points, I simply do not see how the idea of an intermediate state is relevant for Christian hope. The intermediate state is believed to be an unearthly, disembodied existence, and so it is worse in some ways than our present life. How would this motivate us to live toward the vision of the coming of the kingdom ("on earth as it is in heaven")?

A Concluding Appreciation

Although I disagree with John Feinberg on various aspects of his eschatology, I celebrate his moving beyond the traditional idea of an immaterial heaven as the final destiny of the believer to the biblical idea of a new heavens and new earth. I also think he is right to suggest that in the eschaton we will do many of the ordinary things we do in this life (with appropriate differences, not all of which we currently understand) and that there will be the possibility of learning and growth even after the return of Christ.

I am particularly glad that Feinberg ended his chapter by considering the implications of eschatology for our living today, citing 2 Peter 3:11 and 1 Thessalonians 4:18. To this we could add Paul's exhortation at the end of his long passage on the resurrection: "Therefore, my dear brothers and sisters, stand firm. Let nothing move you. Always give yourselves fully to the work of the Lord, because you know that your labor in the Lord is not in vain" (1 Cor 15:58). In my opinion, this is the primary purpose of eschatology in the Bible. Instead of crystal-ball gazing that tries to predict the future, we should ask ourselves: What does God require of us in the here and now so that his kingdom may come on earth as it is in heaven? Then we must live toward that vision.

MICHAEL ALLEN

I want to express my gratitude to Professor Feinberg for his reflections on the nature of heaven.

The title of his essay promises "a traditional perspective," and I wish to reflect on it under that banner and theme. In many ways, of course, he does commend a traditional perspective that involves the return of Christ, the resurrection of the body, divine judgment, and eternal life in heaven and hell. His willingness—signaled right up front—to stand where Scripture summons is commendable, not least in the face of the historicist and materialist tendencies of our wider world. In that respect, he does speak up for a theocentric and supernatural (though not supernaturalist or gnostic) Christianity and a consistently exegetical mode of reasoning. It might go unnoticed, so I do want to draw out this methodological point, namely, that his theocentrism and supernatural commitments lead to that exegetical commitment. Because there is this God revealed in the gospel and offering such hope, we are wise to tend to his speech as revealed in the writings of his prophets and apostles. Just so, I say. If I wore a hat, I would gladly doff it to these fundamental marks of his argument.

I do think that several strands of his thought might be furthered or enhanced by wrestling overtly with some witnesses from the Christian tradition. I hope to focus my response not on particular areas of disagreement—perhaps most notably his repeated reference to the rapture—but instead to consider a wider methodological issue. His exegetically infused approach does not really dip into the witness of the communion of the saints through the ages, or, at the very least, his essay does not explicitly attest that wrestling. Because his title suggests a "traditional perspective," and given that absence of historical engagement, I thought that I would suggest a few areas where I could imagine fleshing out, tweaking, or furthering the argument by means of retrieval of classic texts. In so doing, some of the powerful voices of the "great cloud of witnesses" can speak here, too, and help us as we seek to run "the race that is set before us" theologically (Heb 12:1 ESV).

First, Professor Feinberg affirms that in the heavenly state "humans are not omniscient," and he goes on to say that "glorified existence will not quench all intellectual curiosity." I greatly appreciate this reminder that we will remain finite, even if transfigured in God's glory. And I do think he is right to consider what intellectual goods might continue to be received anew throughout eternity. Thomas Aquinas would argue that in possessing the beatific vision, we would come to see not only God but other things in God as well. But we are not Christ, and everything does not hold together in us, and therefore our knowledge of other things in God would not be so wide as to be omniscient (as Thomas believed Christ's beatific vision was).

The significant voice who could help enhance this argument is Gregory of Nyssa, whose *Life of Moses* so powerfully explores the nature of perfection: "The perfection of human nature consists perhaps in its very growth in goodness."[1] Because this goodness is defined as God, not merely some discrete appendage or item passed on by him and separable from him, it is endless (as he is). Again, Nyssa: "Those who know what is good by nature desire participation in it, and since this good has no limit, the participant's desire necessarily has no stopping place but stretches out with the limitless."[2] Therefore, Moses's ascent—paradigm for us all and prefiguration of that of the incarnate and risen Christ—represents a real but unending journey into God. Perfection will never cease to grow and develop, because that is what finite creatures do when they seek to enjoy communion with the creator, who is infinite and ceaseless in his glory. Professor Feinberg could take up that notion of the glorious good of heaven, which, because it is a divine and infinite good, brings unending experiences of dependent reception of God's communicated blessings, and he could tease out its implications for thinking about intellectual goods in that eternally perfect but still developing

---

1. Gregory of Nyssa, *The Life of Moses*, trans. Abraham J. Malherbe and Everett Ferguson, Classics of Western Spirituality (New York: Paulist, 1978), 31.
2. Gregory of Nyssa, *Life of Moses*, 31.

state. In certain respects, there will not be change intellectually: no false hypotheses or fitful mistakes. But that is not to say that stasis is the right word for the heavenly life of the mind, and a Christian doctrine of God's transcendence and of creaturely finitude (even in transfigured glory) prompts further reflection here. I think Nyssa's whole text can serve to shape and provoke that pondering.[3]

Second, Professor Feinberg also commends a future with "a lot of eating and banquets." In so doing, he takes language of the "marriage supper of the Lamb" in more than metaphorical register. That figure speaks of intimacy and celebration that exceeds the best wedding reception, no doubt, but that also includes no less than real feasts. Food is not a blank sign, in other words, but a constitutive element of the heavenly good. God provides it. Even immortal humans are composed so as to run on it. And it provides an occasion for such social and relational fellowship, such revelry and festivity that it marks out the happiness of our creaturely experience. The feast will go on.

I do think we could and should wrestle with the fact that eating is not uncomplicated. Perhaps because I have Crohn's disease, I am more attuned to this reality than others, but all humans bear the marks of indigestion, even if they do not suffer more serious maladies. There will be no more sickness. This will not be merely the absence of autoimmune diseases but also, presumably, of lesser ailments like occasional bloating. It is not beneath us to speak of such realities. We can go a step further, though, in thinking about the fact that even a healthily functioning digestive system connects to an excretory system. The fact that food in means excrement out has always struck thinkers as something less than glorious. I've yet to encounter an account of the heavenly mansion, whether in medieval or modern reflection, that pauses over the toilet when recounting its many rooms. But a feast will be followed by a flush, providing an opportunity for us to consider the physiological nature of this new resurrection life.

Here I am struck by a passage that appears in Thomas Aquinas's

---

3. The argument of Jonathan Edwards's sermon, "Heaven Is a World of Love," also presents an ongoing developmental notion of perfection that could be teased out in its intellectual aspect as well; see "Charity and Its Fruits (Sermon 15: Heaven Is a World of Love)," in *Ethical Writings*, vol. 8 of *The Works of Jonathan Edwards*, ed. Paul Ramsey (New Haven: Yale University Press, 1989), 366–97.

account of humanity's original state, in particular humanity's physical condition in the state of innocence prior to the fall (*Summa theologiae* 1a.97.3). In the fourth objection to his argument that food was needed in innocence, he observed that some find a "certain filthiness" to mark any excretion, which "would not have befitted the dignity of the original state." His reply is to say that God is quite capable of making human excrement, apart from the fall, such that there is not "any offensiveness."[4] Somehow God sanctifies the excrement, so that it is the physiologically appropriate waste product of human eating and yet in no way leads to a detrimental experience of that paradise.

Thomas goes on to say that the resurrected body will not need food at all. He does not deny that there is eating in the resurrected body, however, for he plainly knows that Jesus ate fish at the lakeside (John 21:9–14). The question of whether food is needed is a distinct query, but the presence of eating ensures that digestion and excretion will be part of that heavenly, transfigured experience. I think it goes without saying, then, that something like that earlier miracle of innocent paradise must also mark this later, eternal feasting. The feast is great, and there is no morning-after effect of bloating or anything else. Even what may seem the most animal of our bodily instincts is not thwarted, though it is transformed. We may not assume a medieval text helps take us further into exploring the physiological constitution of this paradise to come, but Aquinas does help prompt us to consider these deeper issues.

Third, Professor Feinberg affirms that the beatific vision involves physiological sight of Jesus—who is incarnate and can thus be seen in his human nature only—and some other mode of perceiving the Godhead. He does importantly signal that Scripture regularly uses sensory language to speak of God being revealed and experienced (even in non-incarnational settings). I think he is on to something very significant here, namely, that we do need to continue to affirm the invisibility of God, but also to note that God makes himself known in sensory manner (albeit not as a physical object or being, apart from the incarnate presence of the Son). It is here that the doctrine of the spiritual senses might prove helpful in charting ways that a range of theologians have

---

4. Thomas Aquinas, *Man Made to God's Image (1a.90–102)*, vol. 13 of *Summa theologiae*, trans. Edmund Hill (New York: McGraw-Hill, 1963), 143–45.

taken those scriptural occurrences (of fire, cloud, voice, or fragrance; of lover touched or caressed) as being metaphorical at times as well as analogical. All our perception is shaped in some way, more or less, by our embodied character in this life (though not in the intermediate state), but God (apart from the incarnate Son) is not a physical component of the universe. Depicting ways in which Scripture like Exodus 3 or 34 may prompt us to speak of distinctly spiritual senses that are analogously attested by means of sensory terms (sight and touch, for instance) seems important, and theologians from Origen to Wesley could prove helpful here (though I might personally attest a preference for the textured approach of Augustine of Hippo, wherein the reunification of all the senses will be involved in the experience of conversion[s] now and the eventual perception of God's glory in the hereafter).[5]

In conclusion, I want to return to my appreciation for this essay, its exegetical tenor, and its concern to commend traditional—especially creedal—elements of our living hope. I hope I may have signaled ways that these classic commitments could be explored in a more overtly "traditional" register. In so doing, I do not mean to call anyone away from Holy Scripture, only to suggest that it calls for reading it within the communion of saints and thus mindful of the history of biblical exegesis within the one, holy, catholic, and apostolic church.[6]

---

5. This tradition of discussion can be encountered in the many historical studies found in Paul Gavrilyuk and Sarah Coakley, eds., *The Spiritual Senses: Perceiving God in Western Christianity* (Cambridge: Cambridge University Press, 2012).

6. For more on this methodological argument, see Michael Allen and Scott R. Swain, *Reformed Catholicity: The Promise of Retrieval for Theology and Biblical Interpretation* (Grand Rapids: Baker Academic, 2015).

PETER KREEFT

General Reactions

I was gratified to find the four of us in agreement on a deep level, even when we were in disagreement on many surface levels. Let me give two examples of this, one general and the other specific.

In general, we seem very different. One obvious difference is that we come from different theological traditions, which have tragically diverged since 1517—tragically because we are separated brethren who have a lot to learn from each other as long lost brothers in Christ. This little ecumenical enterprise on one specific but important dimension of our faith (eschatology) is one of the small stones in the avalanche of honest ecumenical dialogue that has sought to address that tragedy in the last few generations. By a happy paradox, the more clearly we disagree, the more resolved we are to discuss our differences and learn from each other.

Another, perhaps even deeper, general agreement was that all four of us not only said but clearly saw the importance of eschatology and how it was of a piece with the rest of the whole seamless garment of our Christian faith.

Still another, and perhaps even more determinative, agreement was more subjective than objective, more personal than theological: all four of us, on many issues, manifested a prudent and humble holy agnosticism. The things "God has prepared for those who love him," the things "no eye has seen" (yet, in experience), and no "ear heard" (clearly, in Scripture), these things that "the heart of man" has not "conceived" (1 Cor 2:9 RSV)—on these things we were all unready to pontificate and instead ready to discover rather than to impose, to open rather than close possibilities. I think this personal attitude, a combination of firm unity in essentials, open discussion of disagreements on nonessentials, and charity in both, is the key to ecumenical hopes.

As far as specific issues are concerned, I was surprised and gratified to find that all four of us, explicitly or implicitly, gave the same answer to perhaps the most difficult eschatological question of all, how any of us who share God's love can possibly be happy in heaven if we know that any of the friends or family members we knew on earth are in hell. For all four of us, the first and most essential answer was that we will solve that problem in heaven in the same way God does, *whatever* that way is. (My own guess is that our love will become totally active, not passive or reactive. But that is only a guess. I think it is a good one because it comes from St. Thomas Aquinas, no second-rate theologian.)

A Response to Feinberg's Essay

My essential criticism of this essay is with a single word in its title. The essay does not seem to me to be at all "traditional."[1] It confines itself to questions that are central only for the fundamentalist and dispensationalist traditions, both of which are only a century or two old.

I have not the expertise to say much about Dr. Feinberg's essay, since I am not part of or very familiar with these recent traditions. But overall, my reaction to this very clear and impressive essay is not that it appears to me as necessarily wrong, or false, or heterodox, but as a very well-argued answer to a very overrated question. This question is essentially, What would be the newspaper headlines and stories of the last days if any newspaper was allowed to do what *The New York Times* once famously claimed, namely, to print "all the news that's fit to print." (I suspect that contemporary ideological constraints would censor all reports of the second coming, especially in the *Times*, which is why Christians read not the *Times* but the eternities.) What Dr. Feinberg's essay did show me, especially when compared with the other three, more clearly than I had realized before, was how much closer other evangelical Protestant theological traditions are to my own Catholic tradition, and I to them, than any of us are to the fundamentalist or dispensationalist tradition—not in doctrine but in focus; not in answers but in questions.

---

1. Editor's note: John Feinberg did not choose his title. The term "traditional" was assigned to his essay because his view seems to represent the most popular evangelical position today. It is what most evangelical Christians are most familiar with.

By the way, even though I am the only Roman Catholic among the four of us (would that an Eastern Orthodox voice had been added, for completeness!), and the only one who accepts not only Scripture but also the dogmas of the church as an authoritative dimension of divine revelation—the "deposit of faith" left to us by Christ and his apostles—I did not find that this difference factored necessarily into any of our four essays or the differences between them, except perhaps when it came to Purgatory.

But even that is, I think, much less of a deal-breaker than any other specifically Catholic dogma, since the three premises on which Purgatory is based are so clearly in Scripture: (1) that we are all sinners by nature (1 John 1:8), (2) that nothing sinful or defiled can enter heaven (Matt 5:48; Rev 21:27), and (3) that the gap between the perfect personal holiness we must have in heaven and the deep habits of selfishness and sinfulness that we have on earth is a Grand Canyon that must be bridged. How can any Christian ignore or mitigate any of these three premises? And do they not evidently prove the essence of purgatory, which is simply God completing our sanctification, not the "spiritual technology" by which he does it?

The details of what will happen collectively at the end of this present age, frankly, do not concern me very much. And I think this is not just a personal proclivity. Dr. Feinberg's focus seems rather like a contemporary, patriotic American citizen spending much of his time and energy focusing on the future state of America a thousand years from now, then arguing about crystal-ball predictions concerning the newspaper headlines of this remote future.

Granted, the American citizen has no scriptural data for the future of that little blip on the historical screen that is America, while we have quite a lot of scriptural data for the future of the whole "world" (that is, the age, or *aeōn*, rather than the planet, or *gaia*). But the scriptural data are not clear and unambiguous but highly suggestive, symbolic, or allegorical. And there has always been more disagreement about that part of our scriptural data than about any other part of it. That is probably a large part of the reason why the book of Revelation was a book of the New Testament about which there was in the early church considerable dissent concerning its canonicity and divine inspiration.

I agree with the three other essayists about the importance of eschatology for our present spiritual life and regret that this is far from universally perceived and admitted; but (in line with Dr. Middleton's point that "the purpose of eschatology is primarily ethical," p. 66) I am more concerned about the ethical dimensions of my personal eschatology than about those others (the chosen few) who will be alive at the end. Both Dr. Allen and Dr. Middleton made the telling point that perhaps it is our questions, rather than our answers, that first need correcting. This is something I think Dr. Feinberg and the whole church need to learn from John 21:19–23. Peter's "What about this man?" (v. 21 RSV) was the same kind of diversionary tactic that both Adam and Eve used after the fall (Gen 3:12–13). It is a diversion, not a version; a temptation, not an invitation. I do not claim that Dr. Feinberg is making the same mistake as Peter and Adam, but surely that is a clear and present danger. It is always more comfortable to look through a spyglass than to look in a mirror.

In Dr. Feinberg's essay I missed the deep symbolic, mystical, linguistic, and liturgical dimensions of eschatology that I found in the other two essays. I realize that no one can do everything, and I appreciate the diversity of perspectives that we bring to eschatology. I also admit that the focus on future history and events on earth is a legitimate dimension of eschatology. But is it primary? My two questions are (1) Why not spend more time on what we will be and do in eternity? and (2) Why not pay attention to our past church history in interpreting Scripture? The fathers of the church and most of the saints did not make either of these mistakes. They did not focus their eschatology on temporal end-time events on earth but rather on the nature of personal eternal life in heaven, and they did not ignore the traditional answers (and questions) of their historical predecessors in church history.

I would like to add what I think is one important specific theological correction in light of the fact that one of the twelve articles of the Apostles' Creed is "the communion of saints." Dr. Feinberg says, "It is not entirely clear whether glorified believers . . . will know what the people on earth are doing." But I think Hebrews 11 and 12:1 make it very clear. They are not all "witnesses" in the sense of martyrs, but they are all "a great cloud of witnesses" in the broader sense, like spectators in the stadium that has become earth.

To the objection that there is a great door that is shut between the worlds of nature and the supernatural or between earth and heaven, I reply that Christ opened that door, and *is* that door (John 10:9).

And the "great chasm" that is "fixed" (Luke 16:26 RSV) is not between heaven and earth, as Dr. Feinberg claims, but between heaven and hell. For God's love and presence and communion is stronger than death and as communal as the Trinity. God is not a Unitarian or a libertarian or an individualist. Christians, unlike Gnostics and Neoplatonists, do not go "alone into the Alone."

REJOINDER

I begin with several words of thanks. Thanks to our editor Michael Wittmer for working with the publisher and the authors and for making sure we addressed the ten key questions and each other. Thanks also to Zondervan for publishing this volume. And special thanks to my co-contributors. I think each addressed the issues clearly and fairly. Though we disagree on many items, in our broader theologies there is likely much agreement. It has been a pleasure to work with and to learn from them!

Space is limited, but I must address two issues my colleagues raise. The first concerns dispensationalism. First and foremost, I affirm that dispensationalism has *nothing* to do with my answers to questions 2–10. Nothing in dispensationalism logically entails those answers or even predisposes one to answer as I have. Nor do my answers entail dispensationalism. As to question 1, dispensationalism does matter for how I see end-time events leading up to the final state of the godly, but it is irrelevant to what I think believers' final state will be.

Second, many beliefs are associated with dispensationalism, in part because of views some of its earlier proponents espoused. I reject those beliefs, just as my co-contributors would. Furthermore, though I appreciate the work of progressive dispensationalists, I do not see myself as a progressive dispensationalist either. Instead, I see the issues dividing non-dispensationalists and dispensationalists as ultimately about whether there is more continuity or more discontinuity between the testaments. I see both continuity and discontinuity, but I am in the discontinuity camp because I see more discontinuity. I believe my

60

co-contributors are in the continuity camp. For my specific views on dispensationalism, see my "Systems of Discontinuity" in *Continuity and Discontinuity*.[1]

Third, many dispensationalists are accused of adopting their views as a result of being taught a whole eschatological system that they accept even though they aren't taught an exegetical basis for it (assuming there is one). Having adopted the system, they then impose it on Scripture wherever they deem it necessary to uphold the system.

Undoubtedly some dispensationalists do this, even as others in a similar way adopt and use Roman Catholic thinking and various "Reformed" eschatologies. But that was definitely *not* my path to dispensationalism. In seminary I was an Old Testament major, and I had a special interest in Old Testament prophecies. Many of those prophecies are about the first advent, but many fit better with the second advent. By doing the exegesis and studying those passages in detail, I came to a certain understanding of end-time events. Similarly, I studied in the same way New Testament prophecies about the end time. I came to see that there is significant discontinuity between the testaments, but also some very important continuity. In particular I was especially interested to learn whether Old Testament prophecies made to Israel are still going to be fulfilled, despite Israel's national rejection of her messiah. From careful study of passages like Christ's Olivet Discourse and Romans 9–11, I concluded that promises made to Israel are yet to be fulfilled at the end times to a believing remnant in Israel.

As I studied those passages, I did not impose any eschatological system on the texts. At that time I did not have one. I just did the exegetical work and then put together what those texts teach to come to my understanding of eschatology. It was only later that I learned about dispensationalism. My exegetical work supports some dispensational tenets, but not all. Because many of my major eschatological conclusions coincide with tenets of some form of dispensationalism, I am seen as a member of that camp. But I think it is more accurate to see me as a member of the discontinuity camp. My key point, though, is that I did not acquire my eschatological views by having them forced on me

---

1. John S. Feinberg, "Systems of Discontinuity," in *Continuity and Discontinuity: Perspectives on the Relationship between the Old and New Testaments*, ed. John S. Feinberg (Wheaton, IL: Crossway, 1988).

"from above." My understanding arose from careful exegesis of many Old Testament prophecies and then putting those teachings together with New Testament teaching.

One final point about dispensationalism. In their responses to me, Drs. Middleton and Kreeft claim that dispensationalism is of recent vintage, stemming from thinkers who lived not more than 150 or so years ago. I have several responses. First, at the heart of my position (and of dispensationalism) is a commitment to premillennialism. Surely Middleton and Kreeft know that premillennialism has been around since the early days of Christianity. Even more, if my understanding of *biblical* teaching about the kingdom is correct, such views go back to biblical revelation. In addition, dispensationalism affirms the eternal state and says many things my co-contributors say about it, because those things also go back to Scripture. So, it is just false that *all* of dispensationalism's understanding of end-time events is of recent invention.

But why does it matter, if true, that some dispensational tenets are of recent vintage? Middleton answers in a passing remark, whereas Kreeft says a bit more about it. As a philosopher Kreeft knows (and Middleton likely does too) that their comments about the "newness" of dispensationalism border on committing the genetic fallacy.[2] Thankfully, neither Middleton nor Kreeft say that because dispensationalism is of recent origin that is proof (or even an argument) that its views are wrong. Saying that would blatantly commit the genetic fallacy. Yet then why mention at all the supposed "recent arrival" of this understanding? If they do not intend to argue something in the neighborhood of the genetic fallacy, what do their comments accomplish?

My colleagues raise a second issue, and it is extremely important. They correctly note that my essay and responses include very little, if any, references to the views of historical figures in church history. Though they do not quite say so, I believe they think my views would have greater credibility if I had cited various theologians throughout church history who have held views like mine. So, why didn't I?

It is not because I think views of other Christian theologians are unimportant. Instead, I took the approach I did for several reasons. First,

---

2. The genetic fallacy is damning a view because of its origin. That can refer either to its newness or to its founders' having a dubious character, holding suspect views, or engaging in questionable actions.

I thought it most important to answer the ten questions the book focuses on and to support my answers, as possible, with scriptural teaching. None of the contributors to this volume had unlimited space to state and defend their views. All of us had to make decisions on what to include and what to omit. Had I answered the ten questions as thoroughly as I did, provided biblical and other support for my answers, and still had space to include the views of historical figures, I would have done so. But readers have my essay before them. Where is there room to include views of historical figures? My readers may think I should have left some things out and covered views of theologians of the past, but I disagree. I deemed it important to explain as clearly and thoroughly as I could my views and their support. This seemed all the more necessary because I believed as I wrote (and I was right) that my views would be the most different and distinct of all the positions in this volume.

Second, I took the approach I did because of my views about authority. As argued in my initial essay, Scripture is the touchstone of my theology. Thus, I had to articulate biblical teaching on these topics. Historical views, though important, are not as authoritative as Scripture.

Finally, even if historical figures agreed with everything I hold, that would not prove my views are correct. You do not win a debate by having the most thinkers on your side. Only Scripture, God's word, is the final, authoritative arbiter of truth.

As I close, I must add that even more important than our *views* about heaven is whether each person is going there. Scripture teaches, as I showed, that trusting Christ is the only way. I certainly hope and desire to see all of our readers there.

A NEW EARTH PERSPECTIVE

J. RICHARD MIDDLETON

Eschatology is not superfluous to the gospel. Rather, eschatology is integrally connected to the entire biblical story as its logical climax and fulfillment. If we pay attention to the overarching story the Bible tells, we find that it culminates in God's redemption of creation, with his presence permeating heaven and earth. Indeed, these two themes—cosmic redemption and divine presence—are integrally connected.

This chapter argues that our human vocation as the image of God (*imago Dei*) involves mediating God's presence from heaven into earthly life by righteous living in the temple of creation. But this vocation has been blocked by our rebellion against our creator, which has corrupted and distorted human life in numerous ways and prevented the fullness of God's presence from permeating earthly life. When Jesus returns and removes sin and its curse from the earth, then the glory and presence of the creator will fill not only heaven but also the earth. We will finally exercise our human calling unimpeded by sin, to the honor and glory of God.

Although there are discontinuities between our present life and the world to come, I believe that the eschatological future for redeemed humans consists in the ordinary cultural pursuits that God intended from the beginning, now freed from the bonds of sin and death, in full communion with God, whose presence will fill creation.[1]

---

1. This chapter draws upon the fuller analysis of the topic in J. Richard Middleton, *A New Heaven and a New Earth: Reclaiming Biblical Eschatology* (Grand Rapids: Baker Academic, 2014) and various other articles I have written. I have tried, however, not to be too repetitive of what I have written elsewhere.

I do not claim to have a precise picture of what human life on the new earth will be like. The Bible typically uses figurative language to describe the eschaton. This is because the purpose of eschatology is primarily ethical. The Bible's vision of the future does not necessarily answer every question we might have, but it is sufficient to inspire us to live toward that future even now.

Nevertheless, glimpses of this promised future will emerge from our sketch of the biblical story as we attend to the two themes I have highlighted—earthly redemption and the presence of God. At the conclusion of the sketch, I will attempt to answer the specific questions posed to the authors in this volume.

Underlying the entire biblical story from creation to eschaton is God's profound love for his world. One of the most famous (and best loved) verses in the Bible is John 3:16. "For God so loved the world that he gave his one and only Son, that whoever believes in him shall not perish but have eternal life."[2]

God so loved the world—the *kosmos* in Greek. Could that mean what we mean today by the "cosmos"? Does God love this universe—the galaxies, the earth, all life forms?

Clearly, the Gospel of John could not be referring to our contemporary conception of the universe—that would be anachronistic. But could John 3:16 mean that God loves the entire cosmos as understood in ancient times?[3]

To answer this question, we need to reflect on how the Bible portrays the created world. Indeed, it is easy to go astray in our understanding of redemption and its eschatological climax if we do not ground this understanding in God's intentions for creation. So how does the Bible understand the created cosmos?

Creation as a Habitable Building

As is well known to biblical scholars, Scripture shares the ancient Near Eastern portrayal of the earth as a flat land mass situated above the subterranean waters, with mountains at the extremities of the known lands functioning as the pillars of heaven that go down into

---

2. My default Bible translation will be the NIV, unless otherwise noted.
3. The word *kosmos* has a variety of meanings in the Gospel of John, depending on the passage in question.

the underworld and hold up the firmament above. The firmament is conceived of as a solid transparent or semitransparent dome that holds back the waters above the heavens, thus providing an air space for earthly life to flourish.

In other words, the Bible and other cultures of the ancient Near East typically picture the cosmos as a building or house.[4] Proverbs describes God's creation of the world and the building of a house in nearly identical terms.

Proverbs 24:3–4 describes a house:

> By wisdom a house is built,
> and through understanding it is established;
> through knowledge its rooms are filled
> with rare and beautiful treasures.

Proverbs 3:19–20 describes creation:

> By wisdom the LORD laid the earth's foundations,
> by understanding he set the heavens in place;
> by his knowledge the watery depths were divided,
> and the clouds let drop the dew.

The Hebrew terms "wisdom" (*khokmah*), "understanding" (*tevunah*), and "knowledge" (*da'at*) are virtually synonymous, referring to God's careful construction of the world.[5]

At one level, then, Genesis 1 agrees with the ancient Near Eastern world picture of the cosmos as a building or a house. However, the Bible

---

4. For a fuller account of the biblical understanding of the cosmos as a building, see J. Richard Middleton, *The Liberating Image: The Imago Dei in Genesis 1* (Grand Rapids: Brazos, 2005), 77–81; also Raymond C. Van Leeuwen, "Cosmos, Temple, House: Building and Wisdom in Ancient Mesopotamia and Israel," in *From the Foundations to the Crenellations: Essays on Temple Building in the Ancient Near East and Hebrew Bible*, ed. Mark J. Boda and Jamie Novotny, Alter Orient und Altes Testament 366 (Münster: Ugarit-Verlag, 2010), 399–421.

5. As in Prov 24, so in Prov 3 the structure of the house is first described, then its provisions are mentioned. As Raymond Van Leeuwen puts it, "In the Bible, house building and filling is the fundamental metaphoric domain for divine creation" (Van Leeuwen, "Cosmos, Temple, House," 404). This is also how the creation account in Gen 1 is structured: the first three days describe the structure, while the next three days describe the filling. See J. Richard Middleton, "The Genesis Creation Accounts," in *T&T Clark Handbook of Christian Theology and the Modern Sciences*, ed. John P. Slattery (London: Bloomsbury T&T Clark, 2020), 15–31.

goes significantly beyond what is found in the rest of the ancient Near East in that it conceives of creation as a very specific sort of building. Our home is a temple.

Creation as God's Cosmic Temple

If we attend to Scripture's worldview, we will notice that many biblical texts describe heaven and earth as God's sanctuary or cosmic temple, of which the tabernacle and the Jerusalem temple are only microcosms. Since in the cosmic building of creation, the sky or heaven is normally inaccessible to humans (it is *transcendent*, in the sense of *beyond* us), heaven becomes a symbol for *God's* place, where the creator has his throne and from which he rules the earth.

An interesting testimony to this idea is the vivid picture of Moses, Aaron, and the elders of Israel who went up Mount Sinai and "saw the God of Israel. Under his feet was something like a pavement made of lapis lazuli, as bright blue as the sky" (Exod 24:10). Or as the NRSV reads, "Under his feet there was something like a pavement of sapphire stone, like the very heaven for clearness." This clear blue structure under God's throne is the sky, the dome of heaven (*shamayim*). Even when the image is not so vividly portrayed, it is a pervasive theme in the Bible (e.g., Ps 103:19: "The LORD has established his throne in heaven, / and his kingdom rules over all").

Yet heaven belongs to the created cosmos. After all, "In the beginning, God created the heavens and the earth" (Gen 1:1). So heaven as the seat of God's throne means that God has chosen to *indwell* the cosmos (initially in its transcendent sphere). Paradoxically, then, the statement that God's throne is in heaven is an image not only of God's transcendence but also of his immanence.

Isaiah spoke of seeing "the Lord, high and exalted, seated on a throne; and the train of his robe filled the temple" (Isa 6:1). This vision of God seated on his heavenly throne (far above the temple in Jerusalem) challenged the truncated view of the rulers of Judah, who believed that God was confined to the holy of holies (which they thought provided religious grounds for their monarchy). But rather than being enthroned between the cherubim on the ark of the covenant, the true God has established his throne in heaven, and the ark is merely where his feet touch down. Indeed, the entire Jerusalem temple is filled with just the lowest edge of his robe.

Matching the cosmic scale of this vision is the proclamation of the seraphim: "Holy, Holy, Holy is YHWH of Hosts. / The fullness of the entire earth is his glory" (Isa 6:3; my translation).[6] This proclamation makes two important points. First, the entire earth, and not just the Jerusalem temple, attests to God's glory. Second, and contrary to most translations, the text does not actually say that the earth is presently full of God's glory. The dominant theme of Scripture suggests that this fullness is still future, a point to which we will return.

A similar picture of God enthroned in heaven is found at the end of Isaiah, where God challenges those who would rebuild the Jerusalem temple after the Babylonian exile.

This is what the LORD says:

"Heaven is my throne
    and the earth is my footstool.
Where is the house that you will build for me?
    Where will my resting place be?
Has not my hand made all these things,
    and so they came into being?"
declares the LORD. (Isa 66:1–2a)

This text is not opposed, in principle, to the rebuilding of the Jerusalem temple. It only opposes the idea that this temple would replace God's cosmic dominion or in some way limit God's reign to Israel or Jerusalem. Rather, the entire cosmos of heaven and earth is God's intended habitation.

Because God's presence does not yet fill the earth, the temple in Jerusalem should allow the nations to have access to Israel's God. This is the basis of YHWH's proclamation just a few chapters earlier in Isaiah: "My house will be called a house of prayer for all nations" (Isa 56:7), a line quoted by Jesus in the New Testament (Mark 11:17).

---

6. The NASB has a footnote at this point: "Lit *the fullness of the whole earth is His glory*." Jon Levenson is among those biblical scholars who make a point of translating this correctly (Jon D. Levenson, "The Temple and the World," *Journal of Religion* 64.3 [1984]: 289 [entire article 275–98]).

Humanity as *Imago Dei* in the Cosmic Temple

One further indication that the cosmos is God's temple is the appointment of Bezalel to oversee construction of the tabernacle in the wilderness. To this end, God fills Bezalel with wisdom, understanding, and knowledge (Exod 31:1–5; 35:30–33)—the same triad of terms by which a house is built in Proverbs 24 and by which God created the cosmos in Proverbs 3.

Through these endowments Bezalel is enabled "to make artistic designs for work in gold, silver and bronze, to cut and set stones, to work in wood, and to engage in all kinds of crafts" (Exod 31:2–5). Bezalel's work in "all kinds of crafts" reflects God completing "all his work" of creation (Gen 2:2, 3). The Hebrew phrases are virtually identical. This suggests not only that the tabernacle is a microcosm of God's cosmic sanctuary, but that Bezalel, by his wise craftsmanship, is the image of God. Indeed, Bezalel is filled with "the Spirit of God" (Exod 31:3; 35:31), which echoes the presence of the same Spirit hovering over the initially formless and empty world (Gen 1:2). As the Spirit at the start of Genesis 1 suggests the presence of God's wisdom in guiding the construction of the cosmos, so the Spirit of God is present in Bezalel, directing construction of the sanctuary in the wilderness. We might say that good craftsmanship is the fruit of the Spirit and reflects God's work as creator.

However, there is a significant discontinuity between tabernacle construction in Exodus and the creation of the world in Genesis 1:1–2:3. When the building of the tabernacle was completed (Exod 40:34–35), it was filled with the glory-presence of God (what later Jewish writers would call the Shekinah).[7] God's glory cloud also filled the Jerusalem temple when it was complete (1 Kgs 8:10–11; 2 Chr 7:1–3). This might lead us to expect that the mention of the Spirit of God in Genesis 1:2 is a prelude to the creator breathing his presence into the cosmos that it might be filled with his glory. Yet when world construction in Genesis 1 is complete, there is no reference to God filling the cosmic sanctuary with his presence.

---

7. *Shekinah* is derived from the verb *shakan* ("to dwell"); the word for "tabernacle" (*mishkan*) is a noun derived from this verb.

Instead, in the following creation account, God breathes into a human being, formed from the dust of the ground, causing the human to become alive (Gen 2:7). This divine inbreathing in the garden reflects ceremonies known from the ancient Near East for the dedication of images or cult statues after they have been manufactured. These ceremonies imagine the spirit of the god entering the statue, with the result that it becomes the living image of that god, which is then placed in the god's temple and is understood as mediating divine presence from heaven to earth.[8] In contrast to this pagan idea, Genesis 2 claims that human beings are the true image of God.

Since every temple in the ancient world had an image or statue of the deity being worshiped, and without the image the temple was not thought to be complete, it is no wonder that God has placed his own authorized image—human beings—in the temple of creation. While the phrase "image of God" (Hebrew *tselem 'elohim*) in Genesis 1:26–27 has been the subject of much speculation, Old Testament scholars today are fundamentally united in understanding this phrase as designating the human vocation of representing God on earth and channeling God's presence and power from heaven (the cosmic holy of holies) to the earthly realm (the holy place). In different ways, then, Genesis 1 and 2 affirm that humanity is the authorized image of God in the cosmic temple of creation, charged with the royal-priestly vocation of representing, and thus mediating, the divine presence from heaven to earth.[9]

In the vision of Genesis 1, it is the human task to "fill the earth" (Gen 1:28) not just with descendants but—by implication—with God's presence, a task accomplished by faithful representation of the divine king who rules from heaven. The filling of the cosmic temple with God's presence is not automatic. It is missional. It is furthered or

8. For an excellent study of the so-called "mouth washing" or "mouth opening" ritual in Mesopotamia and Egypt, see Catherine L. McDowell, *The Image of God in the Garden of Eden: The Creation of Humankind in Genesis 2:5–3:24 in Light of the* mīs pî pīt pî *and* wpt-r *Rituals of Mesopotamia and Ancient Egypt*, Siphrut: Literature and Theology of the Hebrew Scriptures 15 (Winona Lake, IN: Eisenbrauns, 2015).

9. This was the function both of cult statues vis-à-vis their worshipers and of kings vis-à-vis the people they ruled in ancient Egypt and Mesopotamia, which is why both were called the image of a god. For a full analysis of this ancient Near Eastern background to the image of God, see Middleton, *Liberating Image*, esp. chs. 3–5. For specific references to kings (and sometimes priests) in ancient Egypt and Mesopotamia as the image or likeness of a particular deity, see Middleton, *Liberating Image*, 108–22.

hindered by how humans exercise power and agency on behalf of the king of the universe.[10]

The *Imago Dei* and the Cultural Mandate

Whereas God reigns from heaven, earth is the distinctively human realm. Psalm 115:16 explains, "The highest heavens belong to the LORD, / but the earth he has given to mankind." And what has God given us the earth *for*?

Genesis 1 unpacks the *imago Dei* in terms of our God-given dominion over the earthly realm: "Let us make mankind in our image, in our likeness, so that they might rule over the fish in the sea, and the birds in the sky, over the livestock and all the wild animals, and over all the creatures that move along the ground" (1:26). This human purpose to exercise power over the animals is repeated in Genesis 1:28, combined with the task of subduing the earth: "Be fruitful and increase in number; fill the earth and subdue it. Rule over the fish in the sea, the birds in the sky and over every living creature that moves on the ground." Humanity is commissioned to have dominion over animal life and to "subdue" the earth, twin tasks that referred in their original context to animal husbandry and agriculture—both of which are foundational to the development of complex human culture.

Psalm 8 picks up on the first of these tasks, namely, dominion over animals. This psalm views dominion as equivalent to being crowned with glory and honor (vv. 4–5).[11] Since God is the creator and ultimate ruler of the cosmos (v. 3), human dominion on earth is equivalent to being god-like (v. 5)—the phrase "little lower than God [*'elohim*]" is parallel to the *imago Dei* in Genesis 1.[12]

Genesis 2 picks up on the second of the tasks mentioned in Genesis 1, as it focuses on humans tilling and keeping (or working and

---

10. For my own exposition of this priestly or sacramental understanding of the *imago Dei*, see Middleton, *Liberating Image*, 74–90; *New Heaven and a New Earth*, 37–50 and 163–76; and "The Role of Human Beings in the Cosmic Temple: The Intersection of Worldviews in Psalms 8 and 104," *Canadian Theological Review* 2.1 (2013): 44–58.

11. The English verse numbering for Psalm 8 is given here. The Hebrew verse numbers in the Masoretic Text (MT) are one higher, since the MT treats the superscription as verse 1.

12. The NIV translates this phrase as "a little lower than the angels," following the Septuagint, which is quoted in the New Testament (Heb 2:7). While *'elohim* is used most often for God, it can sometimes be translated "gods" (referring to either angelic beings or the gods of the nations).

protecting) the garden (v. 15). This garden is an agricultural project that God himself began (v. 8; God planted the garden), and God expects humans to continue working it (an implicit image-of-God theme). Even after being expelled from the garden due to their rebellion, the human race is expected to work or till the ground outside the garden (Gen 3:23; see 2:5).

Psalm 104 likewise highlights human agricultural prowess in the way it contrasts humans with cattle. Although God gives grass to cattle and plants to humans (v. 14), cattle are content to eat the grass that God provides, whereas humans cultivate the plants that God gives them. Through our ingenuity we become farmers who turn grapes, olives, and wheat into wine, oil, and bread for our own sustenance and enjoyment (v. 15).

By this twofold emphasis on agriculture and animal husbandry, which are foundational to complex societal organization, biblical creation texts ground the development of all aspects of culture, technology, and civilization in God's commission to humanity. This is the pre-fall "cultural mandate" that God gives those made in his image and that precedes the degradation and difficulty of work that is the result of sin (Gen 3:17–19). It is the original human mission to exercise power in such a way that we transform our earthly environment into a complex sociocultural world that glorifies God, thus manifesting God's lordship over all the earth.

Creation was never meant to be static. When God made the world, it was good—indeed, very good (Gen 1:31), but its full potential was not yet unleashed. God expected change and development as humans worked to unfold the vast possibilities of earthly life.

This expectation makes sense of the human cultural accomplishments recounted in Genesis 4, such as the building of the first town or human settlement (v. 17), the origin of nomadic livestock herding (v. 20), musical instruments (v. 21), metal tools (v. 22), and the beginnings of worship—the offerings of Cain and Abel (vv. 2–4) and people calling on God's name (v. 26). The fact that cultural practices and products like these came into being is due to people exercising their agency as the image of God to develop the world beyond its primitive beginnings—in accordance with God's purposes for earthly flourishing.

The *Imago Dei* and the Meaning of Worship

Here it is important to notice that "worship," in the narrow sense of our focused attention given to God in praise and prayer, is only part of the human purpose—though a very important part—that ought to guide our entire lives. There is a broader sense of worship, corresponding to all that we do in obedience to God, which is what ultimately gives God glory and enhances his reputation. "Worship" in the narrow sense ought to strengthen our allegiance to God so that we glorify God in all we do.

We can see this wider sense of worship in Paul's admonition to the church in Rome: "Therefore, I urge you, brothers and sisters, in view of God's mercy, to offer your bodies as a living sacrifice, holy and pleasing to God—this is your true and proper worship" (Rom 12:1). Paul's point is consistent with Jesus's challenge to the Pharisees that actions typically regarded as expressing devotion (such as tithing) are of less importance than a life of justice, mercy, and faithfulness, which he calls "the more important matters of the law" (Matt 23:23–24). Jesus echoes those Old Testament prophets who critiqued Israel for their sacrifices, solemn assemblies, Sabbaths, new moon festivals, and fasts that were not backed by obedience to God, an obedience demonstrated especially in love for their neighbors and justice toward the needy. According to these prophets, "worship" in the narrow sense, without appropriate actions to back it up, is downright repugnant to God.[13]

As far back as Psalm 15, the question was asked about what was necessary to live in God's presence: "LORD, who may dwell in your sacred tent? / Who may live on your holy mountain?" (v. 1). The answer has to do with a person's way of life, including their integrity and righteousness, and especially how they treat their neighbors (vv. 2–5). Here we clearly see the link between character and actions, on the one hand, and the possibility, on the other, of remaining in God's holy presence.

The prophet Micah raised a similar question: "With what shall I come before the LORD / and bow down before the exalted God?" (Mic 6:6a). Micah wonders if God wants excessive worship (in the narrow sense), consisting in burnt offerings, thousands of rams, even giving up

---

13. See Isa 1:10–20 (esp. 1:12–17); 58:1–14; Jer 7:1–15; Amos 5:1–25 (esp. vv. 4–7, 11–12, 14–15, 21–24); Mic 6:1–8 (esp. 6:6–8).

his firstborn (vv. 6b–7). The answer, of course, is no. Micah concludes, "He has shown you, O mortal, what is good. / And what does the LORD require of you? / To act justly and to love mercy / and to walk humbly with your God" (v. 8). Intimate fellowship with God requires our moral transformation. We must reflect God's purposes for interpersonal righteousness in all our doings.

This view of life as worship, by which we glorify God, is fully consistent with the biblical understanding of the cosmos as God's temple and humans as God's authorized image, commissioned to represent the creator in the entirety of our doings as we develop the world, unfolding its possibilities to God's honor and glory.

The Entrance of Sin: An Impediment to God's Purposes and Presence

Our trouble is that sin has distorted human life, and with it our ability to manifest God's presence in the cosmic temple. The human violation of God's prohibition in Genesis 3 devastated our relationships. Specifically, the original harmony between men and women degenerates into men exercising power over women (Gen 3:16). Furthermore, the original harmony between humans and the ground from which we were taken is fractured, as the ground is cursed for human sin (vv. 17–19).[14]

In the next generation, Cain kills his brother Abel (Gen 4:8), which results in a curse on Cain himself and his further alienation from the ground, such that he can no longer farm it (vv. 10–12). Cain's descendant, Lamech, kills a young man for injuring him and boasts about this act of vengeance to his two wives (vv. 23–24). So along with positive cultural developments, Genesis 4 narrates the proliferation of acts of violence (the misuse of the same God-given agency that allows humans to develop the earth). Whereas God desired a world filled with his presence, by Genesis 6 the world is filled instead with violence. All flesh and the earth itself have become corrupted in God's sight (Gen 6:11–12).

The earthly part of the cosmic sanctuary is desecrated, polluted by sin, so God brings the flood to cleanse the earth. The flood anticipates

---

14. For a more detailed analysis on the relational breakdowns that resulted from the original disobedience in Genesis 3, see J. Richard Middleton, "From Primal Harmony to a Broken World: Distinguishing God's Intent for Life from the Encroachment of Death in Genesis 2–3," in *Earnest: Interdisciplinary Work Inspired by the Life and Teachings of B. T. Roberts,* ed. Andrew C. Koehl and David Basinger (Eugene, OR: Pickwick, 2017), 145–73.

God's preexilic warning to Israel that when their sins pollute the land it will vomit them out (Lev 18:25; 20:22). After the flood, the human race proliferates into many nations, peoples, and languages, thus filling the earth—but the transformation of the world into a fit place for God's habitation has not yet happened. God's plan has been blocked by human sin.

Israel as God's Priestly Kingdom

God responds by calling Abraham out of the nations, promising to bless him with many descendants and with a land of his own, as a microcosm or model of God's purposes for humanity on earth. The long-term purpose of this blessing on Abraham and his descendants is that through them blessing shall accrue to the other nations of the world (Gen 12:3; 18:18; 22:18; 26:4; 28:14).[15] But this long-term blessing is delayed as Abraham's descendants settle in Egypt because of a famine. Although they are not in their own land, they begin to multiply and fill the land of Egypt (Exod 1:7), thus echoing God's original purposes for humanity (Gen 1:26–28). Although the reigning Pharaoh enslaves and oppresses them and tries to kill their newborn baby boys, they continue to multiply in the land (Exod 1:8–20).

In response to the people's cry for help (2:23–25), God intervenes to deliver them by the hand of Moses from Egypt, through the miracle of the sea to Mount Sinai (Exod 3–19), where the Torah is given as part of the covenant God made with Israel (Exod 20–24). When the newly redeemed people arrive at Sinai, God speaks to them through Moses and clarifies their calling: "Now if you obey me fully and keep my covenant, then out of all nations you will be my treasured possession. Although the whole earth is mine, you will be for me a kingdom of priests and a holy nation" (Exod 19:5–6a).

God's elect people, chosen for a royal-priestly role, were intended to carry on the holy task—forfeited by humanity because of sin—of mediating God's blessing and presence into the world. In response to the disobedience of the human race, which was not fulfilling its created

---

15. This is an admittedly quick summary, which does not adequately address how blessing will accrue to the nations through Abraham. For a more detailed analysis, see J. Richard Middleton, "The Blessing of Abraham and the *Missio Dei*: Reframing the Purpose of Israel's Election in Genesis 12:1–3," in *Orthodoxy and Orthopraxis: Essays in Tribute to Paul Livermore*, ed. Douglas R. Cullum and J. Richard Middleton (Eugene, OR: Pickwick, 2020), 44–64.

purpose, Israel is called to be *imago Dei*. They are to do this by modeling the sort of righteous life that God intends for all people, in obedience to the covenant that God has made with them at Sinai.

God's concern for the flourishing of his people in the ordinary matters of everyday life is evident in the laws found in Exodus, Leviticus, and Deuteronomy, as well as in the range of matters addressed in Israel's wisdom literature. These Scriptures cover issues relating to family life, interpersonal justice, work, indebtedness, clothing, housing, food, disease, sexuality, war, speech, anger, worship, and leadership. There are instructions for the protection of the disabled, the poor, widows, orphans, and aliens or sojourners, and even laws that address the well-being of domestic and wild animals, birds, trees, and the land itself. As Old Testament scholar John Stek explains, "Yahweh's will for Israel ranged across the whole spectrum of Israel's life: personal, familial, and national. All aspects of Israel's life came under his regulation: social, political, economic, educational, and cultic. No corner of life, no private domain, no human relationship lay outside the sphere of his royal authority; his rule was absolute. In all things Israel was to be 'holy,' consecrated *in toto* to the service of Yahweh."[16]

Given that the God of the covenant is the God of all creation, there is no distinction between sacred and secular to be found here. The God of the Scriptures is concerned for the entire range of earthly life, and he desires the flourishing and well-being of both human beings and the nonhuman creation. Thus the guidance provided in the Torah and wisdom literature of Israel's Scriptures aims to nurture holistic, earthly flourishing, restoring the whole of life to what it was meant to be. We will shortly see how important this foundation is for the Bible's vision of eschatological renewal.

The Purpose of the Tabernacle and Temple

We must never sever God's intention for Israel's earthly flourishing from their priestly vocation of mediating God's presence among the nations. It is precisely by their faithfulness to the covenant that they will be a testimony to God's presence in the world. Yet God's covenant people

---

16. John H. Stek, "Salvation, Justice and Liberation in the Old Testament," *Calvin Theological Journal* 13 (1978): 150.

will only function as a kingdom of priests (Exod 19:6) as they experience God's presence in their midst. Thus we find a significant part of the book of Exodus taken up with preparations for God to dwell among his people (Exod 31–40).

Between Sinai and the promised land, God travels with Israel in a pillar of cloud by day and fire by night. Beyond that guiding presence, he dwells in the tabernacle and/or tent of meeting.[17] God explains, "I will put my dwelling place among you, and I will not abhor you. I will walk among you and be your God, and you will be my people" (Lev 26:11–12). The Hebrew for "dwelling place" here is *mishkan*, usually translated "tabernacle." This theme of the God of heaven coming down to dwell (*shakan*) with his people on earth testifies to God's desire for his presence to fill all creation (not just heaven but also earth). During the exile Ezekiel elaborated on God's presence with his people: "My dwelling place [*mishkan*] will be with them; I will be their God, and they will be my people. Then the nations will know that I the LORD make Israel holy, when my sanctuary is among them forever" (Ezek 37:27–28).

It is important to understand the relationship of the tabernacle and temple, on the one hand, and the cosmos as God's sanctuary, on the other. Just as Israel as a kingdom of priests was a partial fulfillment of God's call to all humanity to be his image in the world, and just as the Sabbath was a partial consecration of time (one day out of seven), with the eschaton as the fulfillment of the Sabbath (when all time is holy), so the tabernacle and temple represent the partial sanctification of space, until the day when all the earth will be filled with God's glorious presence. Whereas Numbers 14:21 records God's promise that his ultimate purpose of filling the earth with his glory would not be thwarted by Israel's disobedience, Psalm 72:19 declares the ardent desire that God's glory would fill the entire earth.[18] Isaiah and Habakkuk envision a day

---

17. It is unclear if these are two different ways of referring to the same structure or references to two different structures.

18. In Numbers 14 God swears an oath: "Nevertheless—as I live, and as all the earth shall be filled with the glory of the LORD . . ." (Num 14:21 NRSV). Although the NIV renders the imperfect verb as present tense ("is filled"), the NRSV's translation of the verb as future ("shall be filled") is the typical sense of the imperfect and makes much better sense of the context (and is supported by the Septuagint's use of the future tense), namely, that Israel's disobedience will not prevent God's ultimate purpose from being fulfilled.

when the earth will, indeed, be filled with the knowledge of God, or of his glory, "as the waters cover the sea" (Isa 11:9; Hab 2:14).

The Exile and the Prophetic Promise of God's Returning Presence

As the bondage in Egypt was an impediment to God's initial purposes for Israel to model God's righteousness to the nations as a kingdom of priests, so the Babylonian exile, and with it the destruction of the Jerusalem temple, seemed to put an end to Israel's hopes of God's presence filling the earth.

But this does not reckon with the amazing faithfulness of God. While in Babylonian exile, Ezekiel saw a vision of the glory of YHWH exiting the Jerusalem temple because of the abominations of his people. God's glory is transported from the holy of holies by cherubim and departs through the east gate of the temple toward the mountains east of the city, while judgment is proclaimed against the city (Ezek 9–11; see especially 9:3a; 10:1–5, 18–19; 11:22–23).

This vision functions as a flashback in the book of Ezekiel, meant to clarify the opening vision of the book (Ezek 1–3), where the prophet, newly exiled to Babylon, describes in vivid detail what seems to be a chariot throne transported by cherubim arriving in Babylon, with a figure in the midst of it wreathed in glory and mystery. The God of Israel has, indeed, departed the Jerusalem temple. But he has not abandoned his people. Rather, YHWH has accompanied his people into exile. He is truly Immanuel, God with us.

It is the departure of God's presence from Jerusalem and its temple (which was then destroyed by the Babylonian armies in 586 BC) that explains an important series of exilic and postexilic visions of various prophets who expect YHWH's return to Zion and the temple. Thus we have an oracle in Isaiah 40 addressed to exilic Israel, which speaks of God's return from Babylonia to Jerusalem: "In the wilderness prepare / the way for the LORD; / make straight in the desert / a highway for our God. /. . . . And the glory of the LORD will be revealed, / and all people will see it together" (Isa 40:3, 5). Then a herald is instructed to announce God's returning presence: "You who bring good news to Zion, / go up on a high mountain. . . . / say to the towns of Judah, / 'Here is your God!'" (v. 9).

Later in Isaiah we find an oracle addressed to the inhabitants of Jerusalem as they look toward the same eastern mountains where Ezekiel saw YHWH depart: "How beautiful on the mountains / are the feet of those who bring good news, / . . . who say to Zion, / 'Your God reigns!' / . . . When the LORD returns to Zion, / they will see it with their own eyes" (52:7–8). Indeed, "The LORD will lay bare his holy arm / in the sight of all the nations, / and all the ends of the earth will see / the salvation of our God" (v. 10).

The prophet Zechariah also recounts God's promised return to Zion. "This is what the LORD says: 'I will return to Zion and dwell in Jerusalem. Then Jerusalem will be called the Faithful City, and the mountain of the LORD Almighty [lit. LORD of hosts] will be called the Holy Mountain'" (Zech 8:3).[19]

Ezekiel himself has a vision of God returning to the temple from the east, the same direction toward which his glory had departed:

> Then the man brought me to the gate facing east, and I saw the glory of the God of Israel coming from the east. . . . The glory of the LORD entered the temple through the gate facing east. Then the Spirit lifted me up and brought me into the inner court, and the glory of the LORD filled the temple. (Ezek 43:1–2, 4–5)

Ezekiel hears YHWH speaking from the temple: "Son of man, this is the place of my throne and the place for the soles of my feet. This is where I will live among the Israelites forever" (v. 7).

However, even after the exile has ended and many Israelites had returned to the land, the return of YHWH is not complete. God has not yet returned to take up residence in the holy of holies. One fascinating testimony to this is the observation in the Talmud (both the Bavli or Babylonian Talmud and the Yerushalmi or Jerusalem Talmud) that there were five differences between the original temple built by Solomon and the Second Temple that was built after the Babylonian exile. We find in both versions of the Talmud (which compiled authoritative sayings of

---

19. The NIV consistently translates YHWH *tseva'oth* (LORD of hosts) as LORD Almighty, which obscures this distinctive title for God. This title is first used in 1 Sam 4:4 in conjunction with God's enthronement above the cherubim on the ark of the covenant, which was kept in the holy of holies.

various rabbis in the first centuries of the Christian era) a notation that among the items missing from the Second Temple was the Shekinah, the glorious presence of God.[20]

Yet we have Malachi's announcement, after the exile, of God's intention to return to the temple, a return that would require the purification and refining of the priesthood: "'I will send my messenger, who will prepare the way before me. Then suddenly the Lord you are seeking will come to his temple; the messenger of the covenant, whom you desire, will come,' says the LORD Almighty [lit. LORD of hosts]" (Mal 3:1).

The Coming of the Shekinah in the Word Made Flesh: Immanuel

By the time we get to the New Testament, the sense that God is noticeably absent from the temple—indeed, from Zion—can be discerned from the opening of the Gospel of Mark, which quotes both Malachi 3:1 and Isaiah 40:3.

> The beginning of the good news about Jesus the Messiah, the Son of God, as it is written in Isaiah the prophet:
>
> "I will send my messenger ahead of you,
>   who will prepare your way"—
> "a voice of one calling in the wilderness,
> 'Prepare the way for the Lord,
>   make straight paths for him.'" (Mark 1:1–3)

That messenger, in the interpretation of Mark and the other Synoptic Gospels, is John the Baptist, who comes to prepare the way for Jesus, who fulfills, in his person and mission, God's promise to return to his people.

After the glory of God filled the Jerusalem temple at its completion (1 Kgs 8:10–11), Solomon pondered God's condescension to dwell with Israel and asked in amazement, "But will God really dwell on earth? The heavens, even the highest heaven, cannot contain you. How much less this temple I have built!" (v. 27). Today we have a

---

20. In the Babylonian Talmud, it is found in b. Yoma 21b, taught in the name of R. Shmuel bar Inya. The same idea shows up in y. Ta'anit 2:1 (65a) and two other parallel texts in the Jerusalem Talmud, cited in the name of R. Aha (quoted by R. Shmuel bar Yana, who is the same as R. Shmuel bar Inya of the Bavli).

clearer understanding of just how immense "the heavens" are, so we can appreciate Solomon's words even more. Yet God has condescended not just to dwell in the heavens, and not just to dwell on earth in the tabernacle and temple. It is the audacious claim of the New Testament that the creator became incarnate in Jesus of Nazareth, the Word made flesh (John 1:14), the paradigmatic *imago Dei* (2 Cor 4:4–6; Col 1:15; Heb 1:3), the second Adam, who accomplished through his obedience (even unto death) what the first Adam failed to do through disobedience (Rom 5:12–19).

Given the biblical teaching of humanity as God's authorized image, who is intended to represent the creator and mediate the divine presence from heaven to earth, the New Testament's affirmation of Jesus as the definitive *imago Dei* is equivalent to the claim that Jesus succeeded—where the human race failed—in manifesting God's character and presence in the full range of his earthly life. Matthew understands the birth of Jesus as the fulfillment of Isaiah's prophecy of Immanuel or "God with us" (Matt 1:22–23), while Paul explains that "God was pleased to have all his fullness dwell in him" (Col 1:19), and Jesus himself tells his disciples, "Anyone who has seen me has seen the Father" (John 14:9).

John describes the incarnation in language that reflects God's presence in the tabernacle and temple: "The Word became flesh and made his dwelling among us. We have seen his glory, the glory of the one and only Son, who came from the Father, full of grace and truth" (John 1:14). Whereas YHWH's "glory" was said to dwell with Israel in the tabernacle and temple, the phrase "made his dwelling" renders the Greek verb *skēnoō*, which is often used in the Septuagint to translate the Hebrew verb *shakan* ("to dwell"), from which we get both the noun for tabernacle (*mishkan*) and the later Jewish term *Shekinah*, used by the rabbinic tradition to refer to God's glorious presence with Israel.

There is a rabbinic saying, quoted in the Mishnah, that "if two sit together and words of the Law [are spoken] between them, the Divine Presence [lit. Shekinah] rests between them."[21] This makes sense of

---

21. Mishnah tractate Avot 3:2. This translation is taken from Benedict Thomas Viviano, *Study as Worship in Aboth and the New Testament*, Studies in Judaism in Late Antiquity 26 (Leiden: Brill Academic, 1978), 67. The first word in square brackets is Viviano's insertion; the second is mine.

Jesus's words to the disciples that "where two or three gather in my name, there am I with them" (Matt 18:20). As N. T. Wright explains, Jesus spoke and acted "as if he were the Shekinah in person, the presence of YHWH tabernacling with his people."[22] It is now widely recognized in New Testament scholarship that against the backdrop of Second Temple Judaism, the Gospels portray Jesus as the genuine temple, the definitive site of divine presence and means of connection with God.

The Church as God's Temple

After Jesus was raised from the dead, he breathed on his disciples, saying, "Receive the Holy Spirit" (John 20:22). Acts 2 recounts that, after Jesus's ascension, the Spirit came on the disciples at Pentecost, leading to an increase in the company of Christ followers. Through the power of the Spirit, the risen and ascended Jesus is now the head of an international community of Jews and gentiles reconciled to each other and to God, described by Paul as the "body of Christ" (1 Cor 12:12–27) and as the "new humanity" (my translation), renewed in the image of God (Eph 4:24; Col 3:9–10; see also 2 Cor 3:18).[23]

Given the coming of the Holy Spirit (God's Shekinah presence) and the renewal of the church as God's image on earth, it is no surprise that the church is also described as God's temple (1 Cor 3:16–17; 6:19; 2 Cor 6:16). Indeed, Paul combines these ideas in Ephesians 2, first describing the church as the "one new humanity" of Jew and gentile (v. 15), then calling the church "a holy temple in the Lord" (v. 21), which is being built into "a dwelling in which God lives by his Spirit" (v. 22).

These images of the body of Christ, the new humanity, and the temple of God are all integrally connected, since they refer to the vocation of God's people to continue the Messiah's mission to bring God's saving presence fully into earthly life, resulting in the forgiveness of sins and the process of healing the brokenness that sin has caused. Not only does the empowerment of the Spirit lead to the healing of human life,

---

22. N. T. Wright, *The Challenge of Jesus: Recovering Who Jesus Was and Is* (Downers Grove, IL: InterVarsity Press, 1999), 114.

23. Although *kainon anthrōpon* in Eph 4:24 ("new man" in the KJV) is often translated as "new self" in many contemporary versions (such as the NIV), the rendering "new humanity" better gets at the communal meaning of Paul's language, signifying a renewed human race; the church is called to fulfill the original purpose of imaging God that sin had prevented humanity from achieving.

but the reality of this Spirit-filled community being healed and transformed into God's likeness testifies to God's presence in their midst.

A New Heaven and a New Earth: The Renewal of All Things

The Bible envisions a day when the presence of God will spread beyond the church and permeate all creation. This is the vision John recounts in Revelation 21–22, beginning with a new heaven and a new earth (Rev 21:1) and the new Jerusalem (signifying redeemed humanity) descending from heaven as a bride prepared for her husband (v. 2), shining with the glory of God (v. 11).

John's vision of the redemption of human beings (the new Jerusalem) in their creational context (the new heaven and new earth) is rooted in the biblical understanding of humans as earth-creatures, made not only *from* the earth (Gen 2:7) but also *for* the earth (Gen 2:5, 15). Humanity and the natural world are inextricably intertwined—what affects one invariably affects the other. This is why Genesis not only describes the normative pre-fall human calling as working the ground (2:5, 15) but also portrays human disobedience as causing the ground to be cursed, such that its fruitfulness worsens (3:17). This ecological vision is found in much of Israel's covenantal and prophetic literature, which describes the consequences of human action for the natural world. In many of these biblical texts, human action affects the land, its vegetation, and animal life; and these consequences rebound on people due to the inextricable bond between humans and the ground.[24]

The prophetic literature also promises a day in which God will restore humanity, the earth, and its panoply of creatures to harmony and flourishing. This promise continues into the New Testament, which speaks of the lifting of the curse from the earth (Rev 22:3) and the liberation of creation from its bondage to corruption (Rom 8:19–21), leading to a new heaven and new earth, in which righteousness dwells (2 Pet 3:13; Rev 21:1). In Ephesians 1, Paul affirms that it is God's plan to bring together or unite in Christ "all things" in heaven and on earth (Eph 1:10). And in Colossians 1, he explains that whereas "all things" in heaven and earth have been created through Christ (Col 1:16) and "all

---

24. For a fuller exploration of this ecological vision in the Torah and Prophets, see Middleton, *New Heaven and a New Earth*, ch. 5: "Earthly Flourishing in Law, Wisdom, and Prophecy."

things" presently hold together in Christ (v. 17), so God will one day reconcile to himself "all things" in heaven and earth through Christ, by the blood of the cross (v. 20).

This cosmic vision of the redemption of "all things" through Christ is grounded in the ecological vision of the early chapters of Genesis, where humans and their earthly environment are intrinsically intertwined—so that human salvation is unthinkable without the renewal of the world. Given the reality of the bodily resurrection, which is a central theme in the New Testament, it makes sense that humans will be redeemed along with the wider created world of which we are a part. The church father Methodius insightfully links the redemption of the body to the renewal of the cosmos, noting that "it is silly to discuss in what way of life our bodies will then exist, if there is no longer air, nor earth, nor anything else."[25]

The Consummation of Creation: God's Permeating Presence

This cosmic renewal is also grounded in the sacramental understanding of the world as God's temple. While the earth does not currently experience the fullness of God's presence (due to sin), the Bible promises that even this small portion of the cosmic temple will ultimately be filled with the glory of God, as the waters cover the sea.

Not only does God plan to redeem "all things," but according to Ephesians 4 the ascension of Christ from the earth is only a prelude to his return to "fill all things," or as the NIV puts it, "to fill the whole universe" (Eph 4:10). Given the cosmos as God's intended sanctuary, cosmic redemption and cosmic filling go hand in hand. Paul elsewhere explains that after Christ has conquered death on the last day (1 Cor 15:26) and handed the kingdom over to the Father, then God will be "all in all" (v. 28). In other words, God's presence will permeate the temple of creation.

The cosmic temple is described in vivid imagery in the final chapters of Revelation. John hears a voice from God's throne that declares, "Look! God's dwelling place is now among the people, and he will dwell

25. Methodius, *Discourse on the Resurrection* 1.9. English translation taken from William R. Clark, in *Ante-Nicene Fathers*, vol. 6, ed. Alexander Roberts, James Donaldson, and A. Cleveland Coxe (Buffalo, NY: Christian Literature, 1886), available online: www.newadvent.org/fathers/0625.htm.

with them. They will be his people, and God himself with be with them and be their God" (Rev 21:3). The Old Testament promise will finally come to fruition.

But where is God's throne, from which the voice comes? Throughout the Old Testament we have the consistent claim that God rules the earth from his throne in heaven (the cosmic holy of holies). But once the curse is lifted from the earth so that the holy place in God's cosmic temple is no longer desecrated by sin, the throne of God shifts decisively from heaven to earth—it is now found in the midst of the new Jerusalem, which has descended from heaven (Rev 22:3; also 21:3, 5; 22:1). The center of God's governance of the cosmos is now permanently established on a renewed earth. The destiny of the cosmic temple is complete. God's kingdom has come on earth as it is in heaven (Matt 6:10).

Given the presence of God in the new Jerusalem, it is no wonder that John states, "I did not see a temple in the city, because the Lord God Almighty and the Lamb are its temple" (Rev 21:22). And since the city is the central locus of God's presence on earth, John describes it as having "the glory of God" (Rev 21:11; see also v. 23).

But John goes further, describing the city as a cube (it is "as wide and high as it is long"; Rev 21:16). This is a clear allusion to the only other cube mentioned in the Bible, the holy of holies in the Jerusalem temple (1 Kgs 6:20). But while the holy of holies was a relatively small structure, the new Jerusalem is enormous—twelve thousand stadia, nearly one thousand five hundred miles (Rev 21:16). We are, of course, here dealing with eschatological imagery and so should not be overly literalistic. The point of the enormous size of the city is, first of all, that this will be the center of God's presence in the entire universe. But it also suggests that there is room for many people (there is a wideness to God's mercy). And, indeed, John reports that he saw "a great multitude that no one could count, from every nation, tribe, people and language" (Rev 7:9), ransomed for God to serve him on earth (5:9–10).

The Destiny of Redeemed Humanity: The Cultural Mandate Renewed

The new Jerusalem is a complex image. It is a place—a city—where people will live. It is also a people—the bride of the Lamb (Rev 21:2). This image of a people-as-city suggests that God does not redeem isolated individuals. He saves people in community, even in their socio-cultural, urban setting.

This means that there is an important role for human culture on the new earth. We are told that "the glory and honor of the nations" will be brought into the city (Rev 21:26), a reference to the best of human workmanship that has been developed throughout history. The human contribution to the new Jerusalem should not be downplayed.

The reference to nations in the new creation is a telling signal that cultural, even national, diversity is not abrogated by redemption. Salvation does not erase cultural differences; rather, the human race, still distinguished by nationality, now walks by the glory or light of the holy city, which is itself illuminated by the Lamb (Rev 21:24).

And what will redeemed people *do* in the renewed temple of creation? Since God made humans in his image to represent him by ruling the earth, working the ground, and developing culture (Gen 1:26–28; 2:15), it should come as no surprise that Revelation 5:9–10 states that those ransomed by Christ from all tribes and nations will become a kingdom and priests serving God and will "reign on the earth."

The Bible is amazingly consistent here. God planned to fill creation with his presence through the royal-priestly mediation of humans who would live to his honor and glory in the full range of their earthly lives. This mission was blocked by humanity's disobedience, but it has been reactivated in Christ, and in the eschaton we will fulfill our original purpose, unhindered by sin. Indeed, the redeemed will "reign forever and ever" (Rev 22:5). This is our glorious, final state.[26]

The fact that the new Jerusalem does not encompass the entirety of the new creation but represents the central locus of God's presence further suggests that the cultural development of the earth is a continuing human task, as the redeemed do their part in filling the earth with the healing presence of God, thereby extending the parameters of the city and participating in the eschatological destiny of the world.

---

26. Haley Goranson Jacob's important study of Paul's theology of glory in Romans focuses on what Paul means by framing the goal of salvation as our being "conformed to the image of his Son, that he might be the firstborn among many brothers and sisters" (Rom 8:29). Jacob decisively shows that Paul's theology of glory means that believers will share in Christ's eschatological rule of the earth. See Haley Goranson Jacob, *Conformed to the Image of His Son: Reconsidering Paul's Theology of Glory in Romans* (Downers Grove, IL: IVP Academic, 2018).

The Nature of Resurrection Life

It is, of course, very difficult to comprehend fully what exactly the new creation will be like. The Bible suggests there will be discontinuities between the present age and the age to come. The primary discontinuity will be the absence of sin. Since none of us have experienced life without sin, it is difficult to imagine what our world will be like without it. How will communal life be organized if there is no crime or war? What will interpersonal relationships be like if there is no human dysfunction? What will work be like without the distorting and burdensome effects of sin? The answers lie beyond our imagination (1 Cor 2:9).

There is another important discontinuity. We will be transformed from our present mortality into the immortality of resurrection. Paul contrasts Adam, described as a man of dust (alluding to his creation from the dust of the ground in Gen 2:7), with Christ, the second Adam, who was raised immortal, never to die again (1 Cor 15:47–49).

Throughout the Old Testament, "dust" is a consistent symbol of transience and mortality, evident not only in Genesis 3:19 ("you are dust, and to dust you shall return" [NRSV]) but also in Psalm 103:14, which affirms God's compassion on his children, "for he knows how we are formed, / he remembers that we are dust" (using the very words "formed" and "dust" from Gen 2:7). Likewise, Psalm 90 contrasts the everlasting God with the short human life span (v. 10: seventy or eighty years) and describes death as God turning people "back to dust" (v. 3). It is no surprise that to be raised from "the dust of the earth" is how the Old Testament speaks of resurrection (Dan 12:2).[27]

One of the ways that Paul signifies human mortality, beyond our creation from dust, is his statement that the first man became "a living being" (*psychēn zōsan*). This is a quotation from the Septuagint of Genesis 2:7, which translates the Hebrew *nephesh khayyah*. The KJV renders this expression (whether in Gen 2:7 or in 1 Cor 15:45) as "a living soul." Instead of *having a* "soul" (as postbiblical Christian theology came to affirm), a human in the Old Testament *is* a "soul," a

---

27. The dust metaphor is applied to all living things in Ps 104, which notes: "when you [God] take away their breath, / they die and return to their dust" (Ps 104:29). This makes sense of the expression "the dust of death" in Ps 22:15, as well as a reference to "all who go down to the dust" (Ps 22:29).

nephesh, indeed a living *nephesh*. A better translation for *nephesh khayyah* would be something like "living organism." The phrase is used also of nonhuman animals in Genesis 2:19. Thus, it describes ordinary, mortal life, whether human or animal.[28]

Having described the first man as a living *psychē*, Paul goes on to speak of our present body as "natural" (NIV) or "physical" (NRSV), in contrast to the "spiritual body" we will have in the resurrection (1 Cor 15:44; see also v. 46). Both the NIV's "natural" and the NRSV's "physical" obscure the fact that the word Paul uses is *psychikos*, the adjectival form of *psychē*. Whether it is the noun for "soul" (*psychē*) or the adjective "soulish" (*psychikos*), Paul's point is that our ordinary human life is mortal and transient.[29]

In contrast to this, Paul describes the resurrection body as a "spiritual" (*pneumatikos*) body. He does not mean by this a body composed of immaterial substance. Just as we need to rid ourselves of modern, unbiblical notions of what "soul" means, we need to do the same for "spirit."

Whereas the first Adam "became a living being," the last Adam became (through his resurrection) "a life-giving spirit" (1 Cor 15:45). Paul is not saying that the risen Jesus is disembodied; this would contradict the Gospels, where Jesus, after his resurrection, told the disciples: "Look at my hands and my feet. It is I myself! Touch me and see; a ghost does not have flesh and bones, as you see I have" (Luke 24:39). When the disciples still found it difficult to believe, Jesus asked for something to eat (vv. 40–41). "They gave him a piece of broiled fish, and he took it and ate it in their presence" (vv. 42–43).

So what does Paul mean when he says that Christ became a life-giving spirit? Note the parallel terms Paul uses in speaking of the transformation of the mortal human body through resurrection: "It is sown in dishonor, it is raised in *glory*; it is sown in weakness, it is raised in *power*; it is sown a natural body, it is raised a *spiritual* body" (1 Cor

---

28. To pair "living" (*khayyah*) with "being" or "organism" (*nephesh*) is not redundant, since a dead *nephesh* refers in the Bible to a *corpse*, an organism after its life has left (Num 5:2; 6:6; 9:6–7).

29. See J. Richard Middleton, "Paul on the Soul: Not What You Might Think," *Creation to Eschaton*, October 23, 2014, http://jrichardmiddleton.wordpress.com/2014/10/23/paul-on-the-soul-not-what-you-might-think/.

15:43–44). To be spiritual is to be aligned with glory and power. And, indeed, God's Spirit throughout the Bible is the energizing power of God to remake the world, to transform it into his glorious kingdom.

Paul elsewhere explains: "If the Spirit of him who raised Jesus from the dead is living in you, he who raised Christ from the dead will also give life to your mortal bodies because of his Spirit who lives in you" (Rom 8:11). So when Paul says that Jesus was raised as "a life-giving spirit," his point is that the risen Jesus has the power to impart resurrection life to us, his followers. Indeed, Paul says that Christ is the "firstfruits" of those who have died (1 Cor 15:20–23), implying there is a large harvest to come—the resurrection of the redeemed. Just as we have participated in the mortality of the first Adam, so we shall participate in the immortality of the resurrection that comes through the risen Christ, the second Adam. And that is an *embodied* immortality.[30]

Things will clearly be different in the new creation.[31] But none of this leads me to dismiss the idea that we will be engaged in ordinary cultural activities (suitably transformed for a world without sin). Not only does the logic of the biblical story suggest this, but John's vision of the honor and glory of the nations finding their way into the new Jerusalem assumes the existence of culture. We should also take seriously Paul's idea that while some of our works will burn in the fire, others will be purified as they pass through God's judgment into the age to come (1 Cor 3:12–15). Not only will the best of past human works endure, but there will also be a whole new world for us to explore with creativity that is finally unhampered by sin.

At the same time, pushing to know too many details about the new heaven and new earth presses eschatological language too far, since such language is largely metaphorical or symbolic and evokes that which currently lies beyond human experience. The primary point of such

---

30. For a brilliant contextual analysis of the nature of the resurrection body, see James Ware, "Paul's Understanding of the Resurrection in 1 Corinthians 15:36–54, *Journal of Biblical Literature* 133.4 (2014): 809–35.

31. One of the discontinuities that Jesus mentions between the present age and the age to come (in a conversation with the Sadducees) is that there will be no marriage in the resurrection (Matt 22:30). Most likely, the underlying logic is that there is no need for the birth of children in a world of immortals. Yet even if there will be no marriage in the new creation, it makes sense to believe that God will provide a way to meet the deepest human needs for companionship that marriage meets in the present age.

language is not to satisfy our curiosity about the world to come but to motivate us in the present to be faithful to God in all that we do.

Complex Answers to Simple Questions

It is now time to make explicit my answers to the questions assigned to the authors of this book, keeping in mind the limitations of our knowledge. Although ten questions were presented to the authors, I will focus on the first six, since my answers to the remaining four would simply be too speculative.

1. **Where is the final destiny of the saved?** I believe that the Bible is clear that we will live on a redeemed earth in the context of a new heaven and new earth, God's cosmic temple, which has been sanctified and filled with his holy presence.

2. **What will we *be* there?** I believe that Scripture teaches that we will be raised from the dead as embodied and immortal human beings.

3. **What will we *do* there?** My sketch of the biblical trajectory of humanity renewed in God's image, serving him in the cosmic temple of creation, suggests that we will live in our full sociocultural complexity, developing the new world to God's glory. And, of course, "worship" in the narrow sense of the word will be a part of that, as we respond in thanksgiving and praise to God for who he is and what he has done for us.

4. **How, what, and who will we see of God?** This is a difficult question to answer, since it depends on how we take the many biblical texts about people seeing God in the Bible. The visibility of God is a pervasive theme in much of the Old Testament, often connected to seeing his "glory" (*kavod*). We can think of Isaiah seeing the Lord, high and lifted up (Isa 6:1), or the elders of Israel seeing God seated on the heavens as they ascended Mount Sinai (Exod 24:9–10). There is also the account of Jacob wrestling by the river at night with "a man" who tells him that he has struggled with God; Jacob calls the place "Peniel" (lit., face of God), saying, "I saw God face to face" (Gen 32:24–30).[32]

---

32. These are the English verse numbers for Genesis 32, which are one lower than the verse numbers in the Hebrew text.

Yet according to John 1:18, "no one has ever seen God" until the decisive revelation of Jesus, the Word made flesh. Is this simply hyperbolic language, to contrast previous revelations with the radical nature of the incarnation? What about 1 Timothy 6:16, which says that "no one has seen or can see" God? Or Colossians 1:15, which refers to Christ as the image of "the invisible God"? When 1 John 3:2 notes that "when Christ appears, we shall be like him, for we shall see him as he is," is this referring specifically to seeing the risen and ascended Christ but not God the Father?

Jesus seems to be referring to the Father in the Beatitudes when he says, "Blessed are the pure in heart, / for they will see God" (Matt 5:8). It is possible that the point of seeing God is not visibility but rather the idea of coming into the presence of the King, being invited into the divine throne room (Heb 4:16, boldly approaching the throne of grace). Whether or not we emphasize visibility, this "beatific vision" will not be a matter of standing still in God's presence. Rather, given the context of Jesus's earlier affirmation in the Beatitudes, "Blessed are the meek, / for they shall inherit the earth" (Matt 5:5), the vision of God, however it is understood, will be intertwined with our ordinary, earthly activities.

5. **How does your view of our end relate to the intermediate state?** The intermediate state is not important for biblical eschatology. Whatever happens between death and resurrection, the New Testament hope is never focused on this. Rather, our Christian hope is in God's final overthrow of evil, setting us free from the bondage of death into resurrection life and bringing his kingdom on earth as it is in heaven. I have my own opinion about the intermediate state, based both on the holistic view of the human person taught in the Bible (which makes me think that there is no consciousness without the body) and on my exegesis of the few biblical texts that are typically cited as evidence for such a state (none of which clearly support it).[33] I think that in the

---

33. For my exegesis of these texts (there are typically only six that are cited), see Middleton, *New Heaven and a New Earth*, 228–37.

consciousness of the believer, the next thing we will know after death is the resurrection. But that is just an opinion, since the Bible does not focus on this. In the end, my hope for the future is not dependent on having a theory of what happens between death and resurrection but on God, who is able to raise the dead and bring about a new creation.

6. **How does your view of the end relate to our present life?** I believe passionately in the truth underlying the petition in the Lord's prayer, "Your kingdom come, your will be done, on earth as it is in heaven" (Matt 6:10). This suggests that our expectations of the eschatological coming of God's righteousness and justice at the last day ought to motivate us to live in accordance with that vision even now. As I have been saying of late, ethics is lived eschatology.[34] If we really believe that God wants to redeem earthly life and fill the earth with his presence, we will live toward that vision.

Of course, we live in a broken world where we cannot always embody the perfection of the future kingdom. And in the depth of our brokenness, we often experience God as far off instead of present by his Spirit. We must be devoted to prayer as a means of drawing near to God in times of difficulty. We must hold ourselves to the highest standards of righteousness—without making excuses for our failures—while coming to God in penitence, seeking his forgiveness where we have fallen short. And we must extend grace to others, knowing that there are many roadblocks to the perfection of holiness in this complicated world, even as we seek to embody the kingdom in our lives here and now.

None of this can be done without Christian community; we are members of the body of Christ, and while we each have gifts by which we contribute to that body, we also need the body for our own growth in faith and life. Indeed, the vision of a multicultural people of God on the new earth (Rev 5:9–10; 7:9) should encourage us to seek out fellowship with Christians of different backgrounds, cultures, and ethnicities in order that the church might benefit from the contributions of the whole people of God.

---

34. Middleton, *New Heaven and a New Earth*, 24.

For God So Loved the World

While there is much that is still mysterious in the Bible's portrayal of the eschaton, its overarching thrust is summed up in these memorable words: "God so loved the world that he gave his one and only Son" (John 3:16).

The shed blood of Christ is the basis not only for individual salvation but also for God's redemption of the cosmos. The Bible is clear: the entire creation will participate in the same salvation—the same liberation from death—that redeemed people will experience in the resurrection. When John 3:16 says that "God so loved the world," there is nothing to stop us from taking this in the widest possible sense.

If we can believe John 3:16—read intertextually and canonically within the eschatological arc of the biblical narrative—it was love for this creation (human and nonhuman) that moved the creator to become incarnate in Christ Jesus, ultimately to suffer and die on behalf of this broken and groaning creation, in order to bring it to its true destiny—its true *telos* or goal—which even sin cannot finally impede.

Ultimately, the biblical promise of a new heaven and a new earth signifies the very heart of God. Praise be to the Lord, the creator—*and redeemer*—of heaven and earth!

JOHN S. FEINBERG

Professor Middleton's essay offers his understanding of Scripture's teaching about the final goal or end of God's program for the universe ("the cosmos," as Middleton calls it). Most of his essay is his presentation of Scripture's story line. Readers will find it relatively easy to understand and will likely agree with most of it. In fact, when Middleton merely relates the biblical story of God's redemption of people, it is hard to disagree with most of what he says.

Nonetheless, I think Middleton's piece is actually a rather sophisticated presentation of a particular eschatological view about the end times.[1] His eschatology includes his belief that the final state of the saved of all ages will be their living out eternity on a redeemed earth.

While I find many things in Middleton's piece with which I can agree, he and I have some significant differences. I cannot cover all of them here, but I want to focus on a crucial one, namely, his hermeneutics and how he applies them to yield his understanding of the eschaton.

First, I must clarify Middleton's hermeneutics in his essay. He helps us out by various comments he makes about them. On page 66, Middleton says that "the Bible typically uses figurative language to describe the eschaton." This sounds rather innocuous, as Scripture uses figurative language when discussing many different things. The crucial point is what Middleton thinks about the proper interpretation of biblical teaching on the eschaton, and which parts of that teaching he deems figurative and which he takes as literal.

Consider two other claims Middleton makes about hermeneutics.

---

1. If I had to attach a label to it, I suppose I would see it as somewhere between an amillennial and a premillennial, nondispensational understanding of the kingdom of God.

On pages 85–86 we find a section on God's permeating presence in the final eschatological order. Middleton explains details about that time as found in Revelation 21–22. He gives his understanding of the temple in that passage, but as he offers his interpretation, he makes a claim that not only applies to his interpretation of Revelation 21–22 but also seems to be an appropriate way to understand his interpretation of end-time prophecies. After giving his interpretation of the dimensions of the temple in the eternal state, Middleton adds:

> *We are, of course, here dealing with eschatological imagery and so should not be overly literalistic.* The point of the enormous size of the city is, first of all, that this will be the center of God's presence in the entire universe. But it also suggests that there is room for many people (there is a wideness to God's mercy). And, indeed, John reports that he saw "a great multitude that no one could count, from every nation, tribe, people and language" (Rev 7:9), ransomed for God to serve him on earth (Rev 5:9–10).[2]

Note as well Middleton's final paragraph in a section in which he describes "the nature of resurrection life":

> At the same time, pushing to know too many details about the new heaven and new earth presses *eschatological language too far, since such language is largely metaphorical or symbolic and evokes that which currently lies beyond human experience.* The primary point of such language is not to satisfy our curiosity about the world to come, but to motivate us in the present to be faithful to God in all that we do.[3]

Before turning to my complaints, I note that, using the hermeneutics outlined above, Middleton concludes that there will be an actual new earth on which redeemed humanity will dwell with the Lord. It is true that we cannot describe in detail all the features of that new earth, but Middleton has no doubt that the phrase "new earth" has a referent that

---

2. Page 86 (emphasis mine).
3. Pages 90–91 (emphasis mine).

denotes an actual thing that will exist in a real universe created by a real God. However, though texts like Revelation 21–22, 2 Peter 3:13, and Isaiah 65:17–25 speak of a new heaven that God will also create, Middleton does not see glorified human beings in a future day having access to this new heaven, and so their lives will be confined to the new earth. Why is this so? While Middleton does not say explicitly why he thinks this is so, from his passages quoted above one suspects that he thinks belief in a real new heaven (with even minimal descriptions of life therein) would be an "overly literalistic" understanding of biblical language about a new heaven. What other reason does he offer for not thinking "new heaven" refers to some actual thing that will not only exist but be a place where glorified believers can live?

Let me now turn to my concerns about Middleton's hermeneutics. First, what is the difference between literal and symbolic/metaphorical language and interpretation? Middleton never defines any of this, and that makes one suspicious about how he understands the difference(s). Do not mistake my comments here. There is a difference between the two types of language. But the crucial point is that even metaphorical language has a referent. For example, when Jesus called Herod "that fox" (Luke 13:31–32), what he said is a metaphor (Herod wasn't an actual fox; he was a human man). But that does not mean the phrase tells us nothing about Herod's nature. Metaphors work by noting a similarity between the metaphorical thing designated (what is thought to be true of a fox's "nature" as a fox) and the literal thing in the world on which the metaphor is predicated (Herod's personality, thought processes, and actions).

Now the problem with Middleton's understanding of the eschaton can be clarified. Though he claims that talk of "the new earth" and "the new heaven" are metaphorical or symbolic, oddly he believes we can designate the actual thing to which "new earth" refers, but we cannot do the same for "new heaven." And we can say many things we believe will be literally true of life on this future "new earth" but can say little, if anything, about life in the "new heaven." And, therefore, we must limit eschatological existence of the redeemed to the new earth alone. But the *exact nature* of the "new earth" is just as unclear as the *exact nature* of the "new heaven." Similarly, we know less about the exact nature of the current heaven than about the current earth. But Middleton doesn't seem to think we can say much of anything literally true of the new heaven. Doesn't "new heaven" have a referent? Of course it does; otherwise talk of it would be gibberish. Granted, we know less about the referent of "new heaven" than we do about the referent of "new earth." That does not mean we know nothing about the new heaven or that passages that speak of the redeemed in the new heaven make no sense at all to us now.

Second, in the first passage (above) quoted from Middleton, he supports his interpretation of humans in the eschaton by saying that we need to be careful not to be "overly literalistic." But he never explains what this means, nor does he define what proper literalism looks like. Nor does he tell us why belief in redeemed humanity dwelling on a "new earth" handles the biblical text with "appropriate literalism" (whatever that is), but belief in a "new heaven," in which redeemed people may also dwell and to which the redeemed may come and go, handles the text in an "overly literalistic" way. How does he know this? What hermeneutics text teaches us how to distinguish properly literalistic language and interpretation from overly literalistic language and interpretation? Because he tells us none of these things, his decision to see talk of a new earth as having a literal "enough" referent so that we can say that is where glorified saints will be, while talk of a new heaven is "overly literalistic," so we cannot say glorified humans will live there seems to be purely *stipulative* on his part. It is hard to discover what in biblical texts about these entities (new heaven and new earth) allows us to make such distinctions.

Let me make this point another way. Why is language about a *new earth* (as Middleton describes it) symbolic and metaphorical, and yet he sees it as being about some specific thing, and he can tell us many things about life on the new earth that will be literally true of it? And yet language about a *new heaven*, though also symbolic or metaphorical, is language about something whose referent is about things of which we can say little that is literal, and so we should assume that in the eschaton the redeemed will not live there but only on the new earth. This is not only problematic hermeneutics. It leads to an unwarranted logical leap, namely, because we know little about a new heaven that is literally true, that means that glorified humans will not live there. The point about language simply does not warrant the conclusion that the glorified saints will not be there. At best, it warrants a conclusion that we just do not know whether the redeemed will have access to and/or live in the new heaven or not. Middleton's position draws a conclusion about the new heaven that is unwarranted by what he says about eschatological language. Eschatological language, including language about a new heaven, does refer to something actual, even if we do not know a lot about the thing to which the language refers.

My concerns can be seen in another passage from Middleton. In the second passage quoted above from Middleton's essay, he says that trying to know too many details about the new heaven and earth pushes "eschatological language too far, since such language is largely metaphorical or symbolic and evokes that which currently lies beyond human experience." This is truly remarkable! Though we should not try to know too many details about the new heaven and earth because language about them as metaphorical or symbolic evokes things that "currently lie beyond human experience," nonetheless Middleton does not hesitate to affirm that glorified believers will definitely dwell on a new earth and do many different things he describes *in some detail* in his essay. Put differently, he claims (1) that things said about a new heaven evoke things currently beyond human experience and so don't tell us that glorified humans will have access to the new heaven. Yet he also affirms (2) that things said about the new earth, though also by his own admission about things beyond current human experience, definitely reveal many details about the future life of the redeemed on a new earth that *he can and does detail.* As a result, we can affirm that the saints of all ages will have access to and live on the new earth, but we cannot say whether those same saints will have much, if any, access to the new heaven. How does he know these things? The logic of this maneuver escapes me, and so do the hermeneutics that supposedly warrant it.[4]

---

4. I should also add that if we cannot say much about and must deny the existence of things that are beyond human experience (current or otherwise), what does that mean about belief in the Trinity and/or the hypostatic union of Christ? These doctrines, like eschatological language about places, persons, and events, have referents, and even though there is much about these doctrines we do not know, there surely is no ground for rejecting altogether the things of which they speak.

MICHAEL ALLEN

I salute Professor Middleton for this essay. He begins with this claim that "these two themes—cosmic redemption and divine presence—are integrally connected" and uses that to structure the bulk of his essay. I find this to be a significant step forward from his earlier book, *A New Heaven and a New Earth: Reclaiming Biblical Eschatology*. I read that book and found it to be overly focused upon the redemption of this world and either not enough about or even dismissive of the notion of heaven. Therefore, I wrote a short book in response, titled *Grounded in Heaven: Recentering Life and Hope in God*.[1] I found this essay to be far more balanced and serviceable, so I really do want to begin with a salute and statement of appreciation.

What strikes me as so serviceable here? Here that twinned theme plays such an elemental role, not merely of "creation as a habitable building" but also of "creation as God's cosmic temple." God plays an active role here, not merely as provider of eternal life, the resurrected body, and this new heavens and new earth, but his very presence becomes a defining element of its glory. Middleton develops that temple theme in a thoughtful way by drawing on Reformed covenant theology and a number of biblical theologians. As with his earlier book, a high point here is his discussion of the purpose of eschatology to form Christians ethically. For these and other reasons, I begin with gratitude.

Yet I still have my disagreements or hesitancies. I am a bit struck at the denial of the intermediate state. I am less surprised to find him denying it than by the rather stark way in which he states that there is

---

1. Michael Allen, *Grounded in Heaven: Recentering Life and Hope in God* (Grand Rapids: Eerdmans, 2018).

no biblical evidence for it. Yet he does not really engage those who have argued for two millennia that some texts do teach just such a doctrine. And I remain curious as to whether Professor Middleton is now affirming the presence of God as a definitive reality of this glorious kingdom or also (I hope, but don't assume) its most distinctive feature, the *sine qua non* of that place that has no temple and no sun, for the glory of the Lord is there (Rev 21:22–23). I gather from this essay that there is more commonality in our approaches than was earlier evident, but I am still not sure to what extent I'd call this eschatology a theocentric one. These are illustrations of a range of queries that might pop up in a longer conversation.

I want to turn to something else that Professor Middleton says, which may provide a tangential path into this ongoing discussion and hopefully prompt deeper reflection for all of us on matters of real consequence. He repeatedly speaks of worship occurring on the new earth and of human agency or activity more broadly. I want to think with him—trying to synthesize what he says and explore its cogency—in expectation of his response. I trust the dialectic allows each of us to explore matters in a deeper way.

In a section entitled "The *Imago Dei* and the Meaning of Worship," Middleton says, "It is important to notice that worship in the narrow sense of our focused attention given to God in praise and prayer is only part of the human purpose—though a very important part, which ought to guide our entire lives. There is a broader sense of worship, corresponding to all we do in obedience to God, which is what ultimately gives God glory and enhances his reputation. 'Worship' in the narrow sense ought to strengthen our allegiance to God so that we glorify God in all we do."[2]

Liturgy might be used as a term for what he calls "worship in the narrow sense." He itemizes its essential elements as "focused attention to God in praise and prayer." My reservation is that this description fixes our eyes

---

2. Page 74. Middleton returns to these claims briefly at the end of the essay in the subsection answering the question, "What will we *do* there?" His answer there matches his earlier claim: "My sketch of the biblical trajectory of humanity renewed in God's image, serving him in the cosmic temple of creation, suggests that we will live in our full sociocultural complexity, developing the new world to God's glory. And, of course, 'worship' in the narrow sense of the word will be a part of that, as we respond in thanksgiving and praise to God for who he is and what he has done for us" (91).

on the human agent in worship as actor: our praising God, our praying to the Lord. There is no language here of receptivity on our part and action on God's part: God granting his word and offering his sacraments as the Lord provides for his covenant family. I trust that Middleton affirms all this, but it is notably absent here. I will leave the matter of divine action in the liturgy here and return to what he says. He argues that liturgy or worship in that narrow sense equips and strengthens so that one may then glorify God in the broader arena. There is a centrifugal force to these liturgical rhythms of devotion, where praise and prayer fit and send us out to glorify God attentively in other areas.

Life in its fullness—every day, each activity, all aspects—marks the setting for glorifying God. Relationships and production and even culture-making supply the context for honoring the King of kings. This whole-life devotion is what he terms "worship in the broader sense." At times it seems as if Middleton is arguing that these secular activities, when rightly performed, are equal to liturgy in giving glory, laud, and honor to God. He will say in this vein that the narrow sort of worship "is only part of the human purpose," which seems to convey a call simply for coordination of liturgy and all of life. In other moments, though, it appears that liturgy is meant to form us for this more ultimate exercise of human agency, life in its full reach beyond the space of the liturgy. In this regard, it is notable that he uses the language of ultimacy only in talking of the broader sort of worship ("which is what *ultimately* gives God glory," p. 74). He speaks later even of the *visio Dei* as being "intertwined with our ordinary, earthly activities" (92). Because the verb "intertwined" remains unelaborated in context, I will resist saying more about what that might mean. It is suggestive and likely connected, however, to this question of how liturgy and life relate as what he calls narrow and broad forms of worship.

A few questions come to mind. Am I reading this right? Is the wider sphere where the "ultimate" or real action is? Is liturgy penultimate as a mere preparation for that wider mission? Or, perhaps, is there not rather more that we need to say? Could we not also speak of a centripetal motion where broader activities are meant to equip and sustain lives and communities that can then turn in prayer and praise to God in that liturgy to which the Psalms so regularly summon us? I do not question the way in which the liturgy fits us for life (by God's transforming presence), though I do wonder if the *ultimate* purpose of praising the name of the Lord has been dropped.

Perhaps his argument is really integrated with another feature of his argument, namely, a tendency to speak of a "sacramental" world. I do not question the way that he is challenging any idea that the secular world might be construed godlessly or as of no religious consequence; I would agree with his Neo-Calvinist sort of concern in that direction. But I do think we are wise to ask if transferring the liturgical language of sacrament to my lawncare does not merely alert me to the value of sustaining a good neighborhood and caring for the earth but also (unintentionally) undersells and downplays the singularity of what's offered when God provides the grace of real mysteries (*sacramenta*) in the liturgy. If everything is a sacrament, we do well to ask if anything is really a sacrament, that is, a mystery marking the apocalyptic and gracious presence of heaven above in particular places, times, and religious rites or ordinances on earth.[3]

This view of liturgy and life more broadly construed has significance not merely for the hereafter but also for today. I agree entirely with Professor Middleton about the ethical bent of eschatological teaching. That is another source of my wondering, namely, whether his argument sustains the kind of liturgical focus (or ritual focus) that is found in the Scriptures of both testaments. David Peterson has argued that New Testament teaching prioritizes all-of-life worship over against liturgical worship, and there is something significant to note in that observation.[4] Whether it is the prophets of the Old Testament or the apostolic writings of the New Testament, the summons to wholeness and integrity (to worship in all of life and not just in liturgy) is a crucial cry. In this regard the contrasts of Matthew 5:21–6:18 are perhaps the most helpful in describing the need to pursue "perfection," that is, com-

---

3. Most of the same objections apply to the "sacramental ontology" commended by Hans Boersma, *Heavenly Participation: Weaving a Sacramental Tapestry* (Grand Rapids: Eerdmans, 2011). I would suggest that the appropriate intuitions of Boersma (and possibly also of Middleton here) can be theologically attained through the language of providence and participation without turning to the language of sacrament or sacramental action. Doing so invariably leads to confusion (at best) about the distinction of general revelation and special revelation and mangles the fundamental connotation of the term "sacramental" (*mysterium* conveying singularity or distinctiveness, not simply enchantment).

4. David Peterson, *Engaging with God: A Biblical Theology of Worship* (Downers Grove, IL: InterVarsity Press, 1992).

pleteness or integrity: not treating friends well and enemies with hatred, not regulating one's body but allowing one's thought life to run haywire, not participating in liturgy that commends love of God without also leaning in to love our neighbors. That said, we cannot read the Sermon on the Mount or the New Testament more broadly in a noncanonical way. The Sermon, the book of Acts, or even the New Testament are not a sufficient guide to Christian worship. That instruction begins with the Old Testament (and, even more specifically, with the law found therein) and is applied to later, varied circumstances in prophetic and apostolic texts.

Professor Middleton offers a lengthy sketch of the history of redemption, so I want to specify what I mean here. We must read the prophetic summons and the later apostolic teaching as a fulfillment in a stream of ongoing revelation given to Israel, but we need to grasp that progress in its canonical and literary shape (where the law remains fundamental). Prophets call the people back to the law in its totality. Apostles summon the church toward the law as it is fulfilled or completed. As Professor Middleton notes, there is a long-standing prophetic tradition warning against those whose lips say one thing and whose lives manifest another. But the rebuke against half-hearted devotion must be read rhetorically, as a chiding denunciation of those who lack integrity. Of course, prophetic correctives emphasize what is missing. As we seek to step back and offer a fuller account of our hope and its ethical implications, we must appreciate that the law provides that wider sketch to which the prophets of Old and New Testaments recall us (in both its initial and its later fulfilled forms). While prophets help us not to forget the range of worship, I do wonder if perhaps the Pentateuch might serve a bit more fundamentally to define its priorities and emphases. Again, we need to appreciate how the canon works rhetorically and literarily, not just redemptive historically.

In one sense, I read Professor Middleton's earlier book and this contribution as a prophetic rebuke offered to many in the modern church. He is calling those influenced by a dispensationalist theology not only to remember that our future hope involves a new earth but also that it must engage all our active capacities. Still further, he is helping us see that this should help Christians imagine ways that each of their present areas of agency can and should have theological or religious significance.

I am grateful for this rebuke that he offers to us. In many spots, it is needed (not just in the days of Micah but also in our consumer age). Yet it is not the oldest concern (with dispensationalism being a modern error), and it may not be the most predominant concern today (at least in many places). I do not think it addresses the remarkably anti-religious character of aggressive secularism (even its "spiritual" guise) at all, nor does it confront the instrumental approach to religion that demands a renewed Reformed iconoclasm or Augustinian emphasis on ordering loves (à la Matt 6:33). Even if I am wrong that it is not the most dominant concern, I trust Professor Middleton would agree that it is not the only concern. We also need to call our contemporaries to a theocentric hope and a liturgical ethic. I find this essay to do more in the former instance, though I am not sure it delivers on the latter. And I look forward to hearing back from Professor Middleton.

RESPONSE TO J. RICHARD MIDDLETON

I thought Dr. Middleton's essay accomplished some of that redirection of focus that Dr. Allen called for in his essay, in that Dr. Middleton brought attention to God's presence, both now and then, in his earthly temple (the cosmos) and in his image (humanity). "Presence" is a concept that is as mysterious as it is important, and theologians and philosophers have largely neglected it. Like "time" and "being," we all understand "presence" and even recognize it when we experience it, yet we cannot clearly conceptualize it. It is more than mere presence in thought, memory, or desire and more than mere bodily presence; it is more than both together (e.g., accidentally knocking down a person while at the same time thinking about him is not yet personal presence).

I was very impressed by Dr. Middleton's synthesis of cosmic Christocentrism (reminiscent of the Eastern Orthodox), hermeneutical linguistics (reminiscent of Von Balthasar), the psychology of sacred space and time in mythology (reminiscent of Mircea Eliade), the Calvinist "cultural mandate" (reminiscent of Abraham Kuyper), and his intuitive perception of analogies and connections (reminiscent of Augustine). A multidimensional, commodious mind!

When Dr. Middleton shared with us his copious gifts of linguistic illumination by unpacking the riches contained in common words like "temple" and "holy," I felt like a little child opening wondrous Christmas presents left by Santa Claus, or my first discovery of Tolkien's love affair with names in reading *The Lord of the Rings* and *The Silmarillion*. I thought of Heidegger's insight that "words and language are not wrappings in which things are packed for the commerce of those who write and speak. It is in words and language that things first come into being and are."[1]

And, regarding temples and tabernacles and sacred buildings, I felt that the little child who answered the question "what is the church" so simply and concretely by saying, "It's that building there on the corner where we go to worship every Sunday" was not so shallow or stupid as we usually think.

I had few problems with any of Dr. Middleton's essay, and I appreciated his emphasis on two things: (1) the moral dimension of eschatology and (2) the continuity between this world and the next. But I think the first of these themes deserves a more detailed treatment, and the second a more dialectically nuanced one.

Regarding (1), if, as Dr. Middleton affirms, the primary difference between this world and the next is the moral one—that our relation to God will be sinless—then the consequences of this are fascinating and radical. One of them concerns one of the four features of the resurrection bodies of the blessed that St. Thomas Aquinas made famous, namely, "agility." (The other three are "impassibility" or freedom from vulnerability, "subtlety" or freedom from obstacles to communication, and "clarity" or beauty, glory, and brightness.) "Agility" means that the matter, time, and space of the new earth will be totally obedient to the resurrection body when it is perfectly subjected to the perfectly sanctified will and that will is perfectly subjected to God. In other words, we will have "magical" powers when we can be trusted with them. Our universe will obey us like an obedient pet when we become God's obedient children. How will this affect travel, art, science, technology (even Eden had technology), and our appreciation of nature? Will the new world be as unimaginably large as this one? Will we discover and commune with other rational/moral/spiritual species on other planets? One need not have or expect to have answers to such questions in order to ask and ponder them with profundity and profit.

Regarding (2), more generally Dr. Middleton's emphasis on the continuity or identity between this old earth (or, as we now say, "the universe") and the "new earth," between us now and us then, and between

---

1. Martin Heidegger, *An Introduction to Metaphysics* (New York: Doubleday, 1961), 11.

our natural cultural human activities in this world and the next, need to be balanced by an emphasis on the discontinuities, which he does clearly affirm. In general, will God destroy this universe and create a new one, or will he transform it? What will happen to entropy? How will our natural and cultural human activities be transformed? I would love to see how he might apply his Augustinian principle of embracing dialectical paradoxes (e.g., predestination and free will, divine grace and human freedom) to specific questions. He does this already with the paradox that we will "see" God even though God "dwells in inaccessible light." What about other questions? Will marriage, like all other essential dimensions of human life, be transformed rather than simply abolished, and if so, how? Will there be a spiritual or mystical marriage with all, so that a type of promiscuity becomes virtuous? How will we do justice to unique individuality and unique relationships? Obviously, we do not know and can only speculate, but the principles of such speculations are as important and relevant to us now as the detailed answers are not.

J. RICHARD MIDDLETON

I am delighted to be able to make some final comments (a "rejoinder") to the responses of Professors Feinberg, Allen, and Kreeft to my essay on the new earth.

Response to John Feinberg

John Feinberg raises the important issue of hermeneutics in relation to the question of how we distinguish figurative from literal readings of biblical texts. He suggests (correctly) that I do not provide any clear criteria for making this distinction. Part of the reason for this is that I am wary of appealing to hermeneutical theory in advance of actual interpretation to prescribe how we should proceed; biblical interpretation is more art than science, and good theory is reflection, after the fact, on practice. But perhaps I do, indeed, need to work on articulating some basic guidelines, derived from my study of Scripture.

Another reason why I avoided providing clear criteria for the distinction between "literal" and "figurative" is that I do not typically use the terms as contrasts. This is a modern distinction, where "literal" is usually taken to mean that there is a one-to-one correspondence between the text's language and features of the external world. I call this modern approach "literalistic" rather than "literal." I tend to follow the usage of "literal" (*ad litteram*) by the church fathers and Reformers to designate the intent of the text (equivalent to reading according to its genre and social conventions). So, paradoxically, a figurative reading might well be the literal (intended) meaning of the text.

In principle, I have no trouble thinking that we can understand the referent of figurative language; it is just that the details about what this would look like in the external world may be somewhat ambiguous. In this connection, there is a comment Feinberg makes in the final footnote of his response that puzzles me. He critiques my position by claiming that just because we cannot say much about a particular topic (because it lies beyond human experience) does not mean we should deny the reality of this topic. I agree fully with this point and do not see how this is a critique of anything I actually said.

It is possible that Feinberg is thinking here of my claim that the new earth (in opposition to "heaven") is the destiny of the redeemed. Indeed, he suggests that it is problematic that I deny that the redeemed will have access to "heaven" in the eschaton. But I did not actually deny this; I just did not address it, since the Bible never does. Indeed, the entire tenor of the biblical story (which I traced) is for God's presence to come from heaven to earth.

I am wondering if Feinberg is thinking of "heaven" in the same way that I do. As I outlined in my essay, "heaven" in the Bible refers to part of the created order, the non-earthly part of creation, which is "up there" (the sky, the realm of the heavenly bodies). My study of Scripture leads me to conclude that the term "heaven" does not refer to an immaterial realm (which Feinberg may be assuming). Even in the history of interpretation, "heaven" does not come to mean an immaterial realm until the late medieval or early modern period. The reason that Psalm 148 lists the angelic host as inhabitants of heaven, along with the sun, moon, and stars, is that these are all creatures that transcend ordinary earthly life (and there are biblical texts—in both testaments—that treat angels as equivalent to stars).

Although the Bible does not portray the redeemed living in heaven in the eschaton, let's speculate, shall we? If by "heaven" we mean the created universe beyond earth (including other habitable planets), then I am open to the possibility that we may be able journey beyond the earth and perhaps visit other sentient beings whom God has created (a point pondered also by Peter Kreeft in his response). But this clearly goes beyond what we can know for sure.

Response to Mike Allen

In Mike Allen I discern a kindred spirit, even if we have our differences. I am glad that he thinks my emphasis of God's presence is an important point that he can affirm. However, I do not understand how he thinks this is significantly different from my treatment of eschatology in *A New Heaven and a New Earth* (2014), since I haven't changed my position in any fundamental way. Indeed, I even emphasized in chapter 4 of the book that God's intent to dwell with Israel was essential to understanding the *exodus pattern*, which ought to guide our reading of salvation in later Scripture (pp. 89–90). And my exposition of the biblical story, from *creation* in chapter 2 (pp. 39–49), followed by the trajectory of *redemption* in chapter 8 (pp. 163–75), was written as a consistent story line of God's intent for his presence to permeate the world (even though it was then split up between two chapters). My essay in the current volume basically repeats this narrative, with (admittedly) more detail.

Let me attempt to respond to some of the questions Allen posed (which are asked in a very beautiful, gracious way). Allen wonders if I take the presence of God as "*a* definitive reality" of God's kingdom or as "its *most* definitive feature" (emphases added). Given that he calls the second option "theocentric," this suggests that my subordinating worship or liturgy in the narrow sense to the broader worship of an obedient life might be thought of as anthropocentric (though he does not use this term). I detect here an unnecessary worry, analogous to Richard Bernstein's point that many scholars after the demise of modernity are troubled by what he calls "Cartesian anxiety," the perhaps unconscious thought that the status of their knowledge is somehow inferior because it does not measure up to the (unattainable) standard of Descartes's claim to absolute certainty.[1] I am not quite sure what to call Allen's anxiety— perhaps "Calvinian anxiety," taking as a point of departure a somewhat stereotypical understanding of Calvin as emphasizing the sovereignty and glory of God to the detriment of human responsibility and agency (this is not actually Calvin's view, but it can be found in some of the Reformed scholasticism that came after Calvin).

Or maybe it is a form of "Platonic anxiety," thinking that if we do not explicitly emphasize that which transcends the mundane world there is a fundamental problem in our worldview and theology. That there is a Platonic accent to this anxiety is suggested by the way that Allen poses

---

1. Richard Bernstein, *Beyond Objectivism and Relativism: Science, Hermeneutics, and Praxis* (Philadelphia: University of Pennsylvania Press, 1983), 16–20.

questions about my emphasis on whole-life obedience as the "ultimate" purpose of liturgy or worship in the narrow sense. He asks (note the words I have italicized): "Is the wider sphere [whole-life obedience] where the 'ultimate' or *real* action is? Is liturgy penultimate as a *mere* preparation for that wider mission?" Since it was Plato who famously thought that the penultimate was a mere shadow of the ultimate and that the mundane world only tenuously participated in the reality of the ultimate, this phrasing betrays an implicit Platonism (though perhaps not intended by Allen). Yet this is very far from a biblically based view of reality, where God (the ultimate) declares the contingent world to be "very good" (Gen 1:31).

Response to Peter Kreeft

Peter Kreeft's response is mostly appreciative, and I am glad to see a philosopher of his stature reflecting on (and excited by) biblical theology (especially temple theology). There is a significant movement today of analytic philosophers and theologians grappling with how a careful reading of the Bible in its own context can inform their conceptual reflections. This is, of course, a two-way street, since such reflections can help to unpack and further clarify theological concepts that are intrinsic to Scripture.[2]

Kreeft raises an important issue, which he would like me to have explored in more depth, namely, the extent of continuity and discontinuity between the present creation and the eschatological world that we are awaiting. Along those lines, he asks all sorts of fascinating questions, including whether matter will any longer be subject to entropy, how marriage will be transformed, etc. I agree with Kreeft that "one need not have or expect to have answers to such questions in order to ask and ponder them with profundity and profit."[3]

---

2. An impressive example of the two-way street at work is James T. Turner Jr., "Temple Theology, Holistic Eschatology, and the *Imago Dei*: An Analytic Prolegomenon in Response to N. T. Wright," *Canadian-American Theological Review* 8.1 (2019): 16–34. This essay responds to Wright's inaugural lecture for the Logos Institute for Exegetical and Analytical Theology at the University of St. Andrews, published as "History, Eschatology, and New Creation in the Fourth Gospel: Early Christian Perspectives on God's Action in Jesus, with Special Reference to the Prologue of John," *Canadian-American Theological Review* 8.1 (2019): 1–15.

3. One major work that explores how matter might be transformed beyond entropy in the eschaton (without any final resolution of the question) is David Wilkinson, *Christian Eschatology and the Physical Universe* (London: Continuum T&T Clark, 2010). Wilkinson is

In conclusion, let me offer my thanks to Mike Wittmer for his generous invitation for me to contribute to this four-views Counterpoints volume. It has been an honor to dialogue with fellow Christian theologians about the nature of eschatological hope. Even if we do not agree on all points, I look forward to continuing the discussion—and getting to know my interlocutors better—in the eschaton.

---

a theologian and astrophysicist, and currently both principal of St John's College, Durham and a professor in the department of theology and religion at Durham University. His PhD in astrophysics was on star formation; the book cited here was his 2004 PhD dissertation in theology.

A HEAVEN ON EARTH PERSPECTIVE

MICHAEL ALLEN

Thinking Backward: An Initial Orientation from Last to First

In the end God consummates the heavens in the earth.[1] The beginning finds a fitting end. Or the end is fittingly framed in the language of the beginning. One hallmark of modern theology has been a focused attention to eschatology—even, at times, to apocalyptic—as mother of all Christian theology.[2] Lest we treat eschatology as an afterthought, modern theologians of varying stripes have sought to alert Christians to the systemic and vital place of eschatology in shaping the whole spectrum of Christian faith and practice. Karl Barth interjects, "Christianity that is not entirely and altogether eschatology has entirely and altogether nothing to do with Christ."[3]

Eschatology includes many elements. The creeds speak of the return of Christ, the final judgment, the resurrection of the body, and life eternal. Other lineaments arise in particular ecclesiastical traditions (e.g., purgatory in the Roman Catholic eschatological imagination, the millennium in the dispensational expectation). Still further concerns

---

1. Unless otherwise noted, the following essay employs the ESV translation for biblical citations.
2. Ernst Käsemann, "The Beginnings of Christian Theology," in *New Testament Questions for Today*, trans. W. J. Montague (London: SCM, 1969), 102.
3. Karl Barth, *The Epistle to the Romans*, trans. Edwyn C. Hoskyns (Oxford: Oxford University Press, 1933), 314.

attend theological reflection in all traditions, not least the experience of judgment in hell or the unique significance of the Jews in God's eschatological plan. That these matters have captured the attention of Christians around the globe and through the centuries in no way suggests that they have ceased to challenge.

This essay will focus on the experience of the redeemed as fits the theme of this book, viewing the doctrine of heaven as a central concept not only for thinking about the end but also a clarifying concept for attending to Christian reality today. In this essay the end will be considered first: Where will the redeemed live? What will the redeemed be? What will the redeemed do? And what sort of vision of God will the redeemed enjoy? The essay will address the interim next, asking how the intermediate state relates to the final glory of the heavenly existence. The essay concludes by returning to the present, asking how the end shapes our beginnings and our journey. We long to know where life goes, of course, but we seek such clarity not only for the purpose of planning well but also of investing wisely today.

The End

The heavenly hope of the redeemed warrants reflection. Four questions will demand attention. Before we tackle those specific questions, though, we are wise to reflect on a key distinction in thinking biblically about eschatology. The Bible speaks in two diverse ways about redemption, sometimes using concepts like new creation, at other times using imagery of restoration. In the Old Testament, sometimes the heart needs to be taken out and replaced (that is, transplanted, as in Ezek 36:26); at other times the heart needs to be circumcised (Deut 30:6) or to have the law written upon it (Jer 31:33). In the New Testament, sometimes the scale of redemption is conveyed in terms of new creation (2 Cor 5:17), while other texts use imagery of renovation and restoration (2 Cor 4:16). Some texts use both sorts of concepts; for example, Ephesians 4:23–24 speaks of being "renewed" and also of putting on a new self, "created" according to God's own likeness. In each of these instances, new-creation language evokes the radical and fundamental change needed, whereas restoration or renewal language speaks to the fact that this kind of redemptive change comes to *this* one or *this* world. The key, doctrinally speaking, is to note that the Bible mandates both conceptualities because radically transformative change really does come to these persons, places, and things. The distinction, then, reminds us (as all good systematic-theological distinctions do) of the need to keep alert to both emphases. Salvation ushers in something so radically new that it can be likened to starting from scratch, a completely new creation, as it were. Salvation comes to *this* person or *that* people, however, bringing redeeming grace to them in their unique identities and in ways that involve personal continuity, as in a renovation project. While they may seem disparate, somehow they serve canonically complementary functions in framing our eschatological and soteriological imagination.

That basic prompt in hand, then, we shall consider these four questions: Where is the final destiny of the saved? What will we be there? What will we do there? And how, what, and who will we see of God? Along the way we will address related matters, such as whether we will be able to sin in that state, whether we will still know loved ones, and whether we will remember traumas from this life.

> 1. **Where is the final destiny of the saved?** How do you understand "the new heaven and the new earth"? Will we live forever in heaven or on earth?

It was the genius of Abraham Kuyper and Herman Bavinck and, by extension, of the wider Neo-Calvinist movement to reassert teaching regarding the earthiness of our hope in the late nineteenth and early twentieth centuries. Concerned by dispensationalism, which has regularly been positioned or characterized as a spiritualist foil, Kuyperian theology has reiterated God's concern for spiritual, social, and cultural flourishing. At times analyses from this tradition have fallen foul in identifying modern dispensationalism (with its rapture theology) as somehow representative of the classical Christian hope of centuries past (see, e.g., the appendix to Richard Middleton's *A New Heaven and a New Earth*, where the documentation of a spiritualist hope comes from dispensationalism, but the rhetoric blurs this distinct modern movement with mainstream Christianity as expressed long before and well outside those theological circles).

The gospel promise has always involved not merely a word regarding persons but also a claim concerning place. Abraham was not only pledged descendants as numerous as the stars in heaven but also a land flowing with milk and honey (Gen 12:1–3). The liberating work of the exodus not only brings freedom from Pharaoh's oppression but also a meeting with God at his mountain (Exod 3:12) or in his wilderness (5:1). This spatial specification varies, of course, but it always comes by divine direction. Deuteronomy calls the Israelites to journey in worship to wherever the Lord may summon them (Deut 12:5–7), while later times will see that summons call them again and again to Jerusalem and the temple. The late Jewish theologian Michael Wyschogrod observed, "The God of Israel has an address, 1 Jerusalem Way."[4]

The New Testament does not spirit away that spatial promise, even if it does transform it and extend its reach. Jesus defines happiness as such: "Blessed are the meek, for they shall inherit the earth" (Matt 5:5). It is not that Jerusalem or the promised plot in Canaan ceases to be important; rather, it is that Jerusalem encapsulates the whole earth as a universal city of God's dwelling (Rev 21:22). Jesus does not introduce this universalizing of Jerusalem and of the temple out of nowhere. This has been prepared by earlier revelation. For example, each building of the temple brings expansion of its courts. The temple adds a court of women to the original tabernacle structure, then the second temple adds a court of gentiles to the first temple.[5] So, eventually Revelation 21–22 envisions the whole earth as a temple, fulfilling this trajectory.

The Christian hope takes the form of a civic word: "Here we have no lasting city, but we seek the city that is to come" (Heb 13:14). Herman Bavinck saw a shift here, though it in no way involves a denigration or dismissal of the spatial character of gospel hope:

> Present in the New Testament there is undoubtedly some spiritualization of Old Testament prophecy. . . . But this does not confine this blessedness to heaven. This cannot be the case as is basically evident from the fact that the New Testament teaches the incarnation of the Word and the physical resurrection of Christ; it further expects his physical return at the end of time

---

4. Michael Wyschogrod, "Incarnation," *Pro Ecclesia* 2.2 (1993): 210.
5. Jon D. Levenson, *Sinai and Zion: An Entry into the Jewish Bible* (New York: Harper & Row, 1987), 166.

and immediately thereafter has in view the physical resurrection of all human beings, especially that of believers.[6]

That a place may prove expansive to the meeting of God and creatures warrants astonishment. Solomon exclaimed:

> But will God indeed dwell on the earth? Behold, heaven and the highest heaven cannot contain you; how much less this house that I have built! Yet have regard to the prayer of your servant and to his plea, O LORD my God, listening to the cry and to the prayer that your servant prays before you this day, that your eyes may be open night and day toward this house, the place of which you have said, "My name shall be there," that you may listen to the prayer that your servant offers toward this place. (1 Kgs 8:27–30)

Biblical monotheism trains us to wonder how God might be present in a place: "Heaven and the highest heaven cannot contain you!" But the covenantal promise of God outbids such limits: "You have said, 'My name shall be there.'"

The Bible depicts a promised land, a city, a mountain, a new creation. The images are varied and overlapping, multiform and evocative. The range of portraits surely leans against any crass or literalistic fixation on one to the exclusion of others. The fullest portrait comes in Revelation 21–22. New Jerusalem is depicted here as a city, to be sure, marked by majestic descriptions of both its build and its earthly environment. Its scale is overwhelming, and its beauty almost beyond recounting. And, most notably, it is marked above all by God's presence. The final account is book-ended by his call, "I am coming soon" (22:7, 12, 20). No built temple exists there—its one absence—because "its temple is the Lord God the Almighty and the Lamb" (21:22). Indeed, its very proportions make out a cube like the holy of holies; it has become—all of it, by God's grace—the most intimate sphere of a temple (v. 16). And lest we miss those later features, the account begins with these words: "And I heard

---

6. Herman Bavinck, *Holy Spirit, Church, and New Creation*, vol. 4 of *Reformed Dogmatics*, ed. John Bolt, trans. John Vriend (Grand Rapids: Baker Academic, 2008), 718.

a loud voice from the throne saying, 'Behold, the dwelling place of God is with man. He will dwell with them, and they will be his people, and God himself will be with them as their God'" (v. 3).

2. **What will we *be* there?** Presently we are an integrated combination of body and soul, two distinct parts intertwined in a mysterious whole. What will we be in our final, glorified state? How will we be changed, and how will we remain the same? How do you understand Paul's phrase, "spiritual bodies" (1 Cor 15:42–50)?

We look to the resurrection of the body and the life everlasting. Jesus communicates or makes common those blessings he receives from his heavenly Father to those who are united to him by faith. That is the gospel message (e.g., Luke 24:47; Acts 5:31). The Bible points to many such blessings, with communion with God being the highest and most fundamental. The creeds remind us, however, that there are other crucial facets to the many-splendored beneficence of Christ's work. The same glorified body enjoyed now by our incarnate and risen Lord shall be ours, for he is the firstfruits of that resurrection (e.g., Rom 6:5; 1 Cor 15:49).

In prompting our attention to the bodily benefit of Christ's redemptive work, the creeds signal a wider reality, namely, the universality or totality of the reconciling and restorative work of Jesus Christ. While the Bible does not present a universalism by which all persons are reunited with their God (against which see the words of Jesus in John 5:29 and elsewhere), the Bible does portray a universalism whereby all things are reconciled to God and every facet of the redeemed is restored and renewed in him (see esp. Col 1:15–20 with its repetition of the language of "all"). In other words, the people of God are not saved by being siphoned through a strainer with only some ultimate or most spiritual portion being kept as an apportioned remainder, whether that might be an intellect or a soul. Quite the contrary, the biblical portrait involves the remarkable claim that Christ Jesus has come to reconcile all things and to renew every facet of human existence. "Behold, I am making all things new" (Rev 21:5).

This confession looks not only to new life but to risen and thus embodied life in Jesus. In considering what that fleshly life and existence shall be, then, we look nowhere more significantly than to Jesus's own resurrected and glorified being. Humility is demanded of us, for the portrayals of bodily glory involve not only mundane or common realities but also incomprehensible or strange incandescence. Sure, the glorified Jesus does bear his earlier wounds (such that he can invite Thomas to touch them; see John 20:27; cf. Luke 24:38–40), and he does even partake of the fish of the sea (Luke 24:41–43). Yet the glorified Christ suddenly appears in rooms, seemingly without walking through any doorway; his disappearing acts (as evident earlier in Luke 24:36–37 and John 20:19) are equally quick and mysterious. And while his wounds are recognizable, two of his disciples do not identify him during a lengthy stroll, only finally catching a sense of his identity when he breaks bread with them (Luke 24:13–31). This mixture of bodily realism and yet glorious mystery was prefigured, to some extent, in the account of the transfiguration (Matt 17:1–8). There Jesus was identifiable in bodily form, differentiated, for example, from Moses and Elijah. And yet the way in which he and his clothes radiated the light of God surely exceeds the bounds of verbal expression, to the extent that its viewers wound up on their knees and in need of the word, "Have no fear" (Matt 17:7). This pairing of the mundane and ordinary with the strange and glorious must prompt a reticence to speculate too far and a humility to admit that eschatological bodily glory exceeds our explanatory grasp now.

Relatedly, it has been asked, *Will we be able to sin in our final condition?* If not, in what sense do we possess free will?

The kingdom will be marked by holiness, precisely because this God fellowships with and rules over holy places and holy people. The Gospel of Matthew notes that "the righteous will shine like the sun in the kingdom of their Father" only after "the Son of Man will send his angels, and they will gather out of his kingdom all causes of sin and all law-breakers" (Matt 13:41, 43). Indeed, "just as the weeds are collected and burned up with fire, so will it be at the end of the age" (Matt 13:40). These promises portrayed in the Gospels are rooted in prophetic words of old. "They shall not defile themselves anymore with their idols and their detestable things, or with any of their transgressions. But I will save them from all the backslidings in which they have sinned, and will cleanse them; and they shall be my people, and I will be their God" (Ezek 37:23).

Part of that great new-covenant promise of Jeremiah 31:31–34 involves covenantal fidelity, where God's faithfulness to his people is finally matched by their fealty to him. Though that failed in the old-covenant era (according to Jeremiah), and whereas that comes in fits and starts in our current era of grace, that promise will finally be delivered in its totality when glory comes. We will see him and be changed (1 John 3:2); his presence transforms us so that we are changed from graced to truly glorious. Indeed, in that place there shall be no sorrow or sickness, no sadness or death (Rev 21:4).

What kind of impossibility is sin in that case? It is not for lack of agency. We remain moral agents, human creatures bestowed with responsibility and volition. It is not for lack of judgment, as if we no longer make decisions or exercise intuitive and conscious judgment. No, the sort of sinlessness that is described here comes as an alien gift that has an internal and transformative effect. It changes us from without by immersing us in the transformative presence of the triune God of glory. It may well be described as an infused and thus internal gift, but it is one whose source is from without. Believing in the glorious God and receiving his strengthening, we are no more capable of sinning (not for lack of its theoretical or logical possibility so much as for its covenantal absurdity).

3. **What will we *do* there?** Can you describe our worship of God in our final condition? Will we do anything else? If so, what? Can you describe these activities?

What shall we do? Our agency must be defined secondarily, which is not new. In creation itself, human action is subordinate to that of God alone. As *imago Dei*, humans are defined first and foremost by something outside themselves, namely, by God. In this regard we could speak of a vocational rule implied by the creator-creature distinction. Similarly, in the new creation human agency must be characterized with a pause whereby we ask first what God will do and will be doing.

"Then the seventh angel blew his trumpet, and there were loud voices in heaven, saying, 'The kingdom of the world has become the kingdom of our Lord and of his Christ, and he shall reign forever and ever'" (Rev 11:15). Whatever else must be said of human action, we must say that God will reign, and we will be the kingdom of God. Texts like Romans 14:17 identify such kingdom living with "righteousness and peace and joy in the Holy Spirit," but we do well to remember that such peace and joy come not at a charismatic remove from fellow humans but amid the life of the body; the apostle immediately turns to commend "mutual upbuilding" (Rom 14:18–19).

In many respects we do not know what all we shall do. That does not necessarily mean that we will do only a narrow slice of things, only that there is rather little said of what we shall do in Holy Scripture. We certainly must beware lest our concern to avoid reductionism leads us to the absurd (which is sadly somewhat common in recent preaching), namely, to apologize for or even mock the notion of us simply singing God's praises forevermore. In fact, just about the only concrete reality that is actually affirmed of our future heavenly life is that we shall be with God and we shall therefore praise God. Playing harps and praising God may sound like drudgery to some, but it cannot be anything less than life-giving for those whose imaginations have been formed by the book of Revelation:

> And when he had taken the scroll, the four living creatures and the twenty-four elders fell down before the Lamb, each holding a harp, and golden bowls full of incense, which are the prayers of the saints. (Rev 5:8)

> And I heard a voice from heaven like the roar of many waters and like the sound of loud thunder. The voice I heard was like the sound of harpists playing on their harps. (Rev 14:2)

> And I saw what appeared to be a sea of glass mingled with fire—and also those who had conquered the beast and its image and the number of its name, standing beside the sea of glass with harps of God in their hands. (Rev 15:2)

Worship constitutes the emphatic center of biblically depicted agency in the new heavens and new earth. Again, that is not to say that liturgical behavior will be the exclusive activity of that time and place, but other behaviors are not depicted at length.

Relatedly, it has been asked: *How will we relate to our spouses and other family members?* Will there be marriage, sex, or family units in our final state? Will we remain gendered, and if so, will we wear clothes?

It may be helpful to begin reflection elsewhere, to use this question as a teaching moment for a wider principle. Likely no text has so generated eschatological speculation as has Isaiah 60:5, 9 with its reference to the ships of Tarshish bringing treasures into the storehouse of Zion. Many argue that here is warrant for confidence that the aesthetic or productive triumphs of society will persist into the eschaton. Labor invested in earthly affairs has value not only for today but bright hope for tomorrow too.

Perhaps so. Yet confidence that we have some concrete sense of what it means for life and its blessings today to persist into the eschaton ought to be chastened. The most basic element of human life that will persist is the interpersonal set of relations that make up our human existence (as brother and sister, as father and mother, etc.). But it is just here that the Bible punctures any sense of clear transference from this life to the next.

The most fundamental relational building block of our earthly life is surely human marriage, wherein companionship and the propagation of children find their appropriate place. Yet marriage will not occur in the eschaton (Matt 22:30). While the first clause might be read as merely limiting any new marriages ("they neither marry nor are given in marriage"), the adversative presses further to speak of a non-erotic life that no longer expresses itself sexually ("like angels in heaven"). Marriage is not abrogated so much as fulfilled in that the great marriage supper of the Lamb will have occurred and the eschatological union of Christ and his bride will have taken place.

How shall we understand that line from Matthew 22 and its implications for marriage? Interpreting this biting statement (part of Jesus's polemic against the Sadducees [Matt 22:23–33]) canonically, we see that marriage does not end in eternity. Rather, marriage is perfected, in as much as the great marriage of the Lamb and his bride is celebrated there and then (Rev 21:9). The fellowship and oneness symbolized so powerfully in the earthly marriage of a man and woman (see Eph 5:25–33, esp. v. 32) need no longer occur because its typological fulfillment has been fully and finally brought to pass in the definitive identification, union, communion, and covenant fellowship of Christ with his church.

The perfection of marriage serves as an intellectual prompt for thinking about the social facets of our eschatological hope more broadly. On the one hand, we see the deepest purpose of human marriage being transposed into the ultimate divine-human covenantal fellowship and intimate presence. Thus, our current commitment to marriage has integrity and deserves our concern and commitment (whether directly or indirectly), precisely because it prepares for and is perfected in eternity to come. On the other hand, marriage will no longer exist in its current social form. It will no longer be marked by sexual activity, by procreation as a related end, and so forth. If marriage's perfection involves such radical changes to its reality, ought we not be humble in our presumptions, much less pontifications, about what other social realities might be like in that new-creational hereafter?

In light of these examples—the bodily nature of human glory (as seen in Jesus) or the social nature of human glory (as foretold with regard to marriage by Jesus)—we do well to keep our eyes on broader theological principles. Our concern to keep first things first need not and should not undermine our simultaneous commitment to be alert to other facets of canonical teaching. Emphases and priorities cannot foreclose awareness of the breadth of scriptural teaching. In this case, understanding the center of our hope as communion with God in Christ (so powerfully typified by that doctrine of the beatific vision) ought not lead to dismissing or denigrating the earthy aspect of our hope as one involving a bodily resurrection and a new creation in its holistic totality. That said, that other aspects of this broad eschatological vision are not at the center but on its edges should prompt a greater appreciation for the epistemological limits of our understanding of their nature. Without undermining the integrity of bodies, of societies, of place, and of other nonhuman creatures, we must remember that there are limits to our grasp of their final form. Eschatology, like other doctrines but in a particularly poignant way, must be pursued by faith and by faith alone.

4. **How, what, and who will we see of God?** Will we only see Jesus, or will we also see the Spirit and the Father? If we see the Spirit and the Father, will our vision require mediation of some sort or will we see them directly?

"Blessed are the pure in heart, for they shall see God" (Matt 5:8). In describing the blessed life, Jesus hearkens to an ancient yearning: "When shall I come and behold the face of God?" (Ps 42:2 NRSV). Central to the biblical and classical description of Christian hope is that promise described by the doctrine of the beatific vision. But what is this vision? Debates have swirled for centuries.

Consider the final words of Matthew's account of the transfiguration: "And when they lifted up their eyes, they saw no one but Jesus only" (Matt 17:8). Paul will later speak of God who "has shone in our hearts to give the light of the knowledge of the glory of God in the face of Jesus Christ" (2 Cor 4:6) and then he names the Son "the image of the invisible God" (Col 1:15). It is for this reason that the Reformed tradition has regularly included not only an emphasis upon the singular mediation of Christ in making the beatific vision possible for sinners but also, as John Owen and G. C. Berkouwer have both suggested in various ways, that Christ singularly defines the very vision itself.[7] Jesus is not just the salvific context of the vision; the good news is also that Jesus is the content of the vision.

Berkouwer went so far as to suggest that the beatific vision somehow requires the denial of divine invisibility.[8] His motivation is noble, of course, in seeking to rigorously commend the promises of the gospel offered in Holy Scripture. But in so doing he has extracted the gospel promise from its wider canonical matrix, wherein we are told that "God is spirit" (John 4:24) or that the "invisible attributes, namely, his eternal power and divine nature" are perceived in nature (Rom 1:20). Indeed, Berkouwer's critique of divine invisibility not only forecloses the breadth of biblical teaching (honoring the promise of divine sight at the cost of losing the repeated witness of divine invisibility) but also renders unsteady the christological character of that sight. If God per se were not invisible, why then would Christ's work as "image of the invisible

---

7. For those who found Owen's "Meditations and Discourses on the Glory of Christ in his Person, Office and Grace" to be overly difficult reading (which is understandable), they can engage his rich argument by reading Suzanne McDonald, "Beholding the Glory of God in the Face of Jesus Christ: John Owen and the 'Reforming' of the Beatific Vision," in *The Ashgate Research Companion to John Owen's Theology*, ed. Kelly Kapic and Mark Jones (Burlington, VT: Ashgate, 2012), 141–58.

8. G. C. Berkouwer, "Visio Dei," in *The Return of Christ*, trans. James Van Oosterom, Studies in Dogmatics (Grand Rapids: Eerdmans, 1972), 359–86.

God" be definitive and noteworthy and not merely the latest episode of a temporary theophanic appearance?

In thinking about eschatological hope, one fundamental rule is that this doctrine and its various subtopics not be allowed to function separately from the wider teaching of the prophets and apostles. The beatific vision, for example, points to a unique and necessary facet of biblical teaching, and it will serve a needful role in supplementing, augmenting, and qualifying other teachings. That said, understanding its character also requires a contextual reception of it that does not forget the basic metaphysical, covenantal, and ethical parameters of Christian existence as sketched by the Holy Scriptures. Issues of coherence and interrelationship, then, are necessary exercises in faithful Christian reflection upon eschatology. In the Reformed tradition, one recurring emphasis has been the retethering of eschatology and Christology. Whereas certain versions of late medieval piety severed the links between Christ and the specific character of the heavenly happiness enjoyed by God's people, the early Reformers sought to think clearly and consistently about ways in which Christ singularly provides the pathway to participatory bliss for those united to him by faith, and even how he might definitively and singularly define that blessedness itself.

Might it be that vision of the Christ opens up a wider vista wherein we somehow see God in the form of the persons of the Father and the Spirit? Perhaps. We can certainly say that there is an ocular focus upon the Christ as the one in whom such vision occurs. We can furthermore say that there are scriptural principles regarding divine invisibility that seem to suggest that seeing the divine persons as such would be impossible: "No one has ever seen God" (John 1:18). And, of course, the incarnational availability of the divine Son for sight owes to his enfleshment or tabernacling presence: "And the Word became flesh and dwelt among us, and we have seen his glory, glory as of the only Son from the Father, full of grace and truth" (John 1:14). Dogmatic restraint will suggest avoiding speculation beyond scriptural promptings. Here the Reformed tradition—especially as typified in the analyses of Owen—has shown a restrained focus on Christ as the image or vision of God. But restraint is not merely prompted by scriptural silence (regarding other visions) alone; restraint from speculation flows also from a concern to think this doctrine together with other adjoining truths (e.g., divine invisibility). With Turretin, then, we must say, "Because the Scripture does not disclose it to us, so neither should we rashly define anything concerning it."[9]

We can surely say that we will see Christ more fully than has been the case in any prior situation (1 John 3:2). And we can attest that our knowledge of the whole Godhead will be greater in glory than in this present time of grace (1 Cor 13:12). To what extent the idiom of sight is helpful in attesting not just the first escalation of intimacy with the God of the gospel but also that second sort of escalation—that intellectual and volitional perfection unto glory in knowing and loving the triune God in his entire blessedness as Father, Son, and Spirit—that is a matter for fine judgment and well beyond this sketch.[10] It is worth noting that the tradition has made use of the language of beatific vision for this spiritual perception of the mind's eye as well. Such growth in theological and personal knowledge and love will surely be a part of our great hope. If we deem the language of vision less than apt, we will need to make use of some other biblical idiom to attest to that gospel promise. Again, the need to think in interconnected ways is crucial here as ever.

Relatedly, it is asked: *Will we remember traumatic events of this life or loved ones who are not with us?* If so, how will that not steal our joy? If not, then have we lost a vital part of our identity?

Again, a christological prompt may help guide reflection. Our one entryway to eschatological existence is the risen Christ, who exists in glory and immortality, to be sure, but also bearing the wounds of his suffering. He is not bleeding out. In fact, no mention is made of any illness or weariness. Death having been defeated, Christ has received "indestructible life" (Heb 7:16). Even so, the wounds are there, and Thomas can be invited to reach out and touch them, while all the disciples can be shown them (Luke 24:39–40).

In what way should we characterize such remembrance? It is more than merely notional remembrance; his wounds are there and can be seen, even touched, by others. Signs of trauma are known as trauma; in this case, these are his wounds and not mere scratches or punctures. But they are not known traumatically; there is no sign of Jesus being

---

9. *Institutes of Elenctic Theology*, ed. James T. Dennison Jr., trans. G. M. Giger, 3 vols. (Phillipsburg, NJ: Presbyterian & Reformed, 1997), 3:611 (20.8.14).

10. Though see Turretin for a keen example (*Institutes* 20.8).

triggered by their mention. Rather, he mentions them with smooth regulation of any emotive reaction.

What about those who will not be in heaven on earth? Revelation 19 raises the most pointed and pertinent voice in this regard, as it depicts the redeemed cognizant of and celebrating over the demise of the judged. The saints—"the loud voice of a great multitude in heaven"— rejoice at the judgment of and vengeance regarding the great prostitute (Rev 19:1–2). Immediately the text will transition to acclaim "the marriage of the Lamb" (v. 7, see vv. 6–10 more fully). While there is danger of overreading based on proximity, there is no cue that suggests the circumference of praise in the latter passage is larger than that of the former passage. In other words, it seems to suggest that all the redeemed rejoice in divine judgment even as they celebrate divine union. Admittedly, the judgment is specifically denoted as that of the great whore and corruptor of the earth, not each individual sinner in opposition to God (at least not necessarily). That said, it is still hard not to observe that clearly delight is taken in final divine judgment; hence, it is not quite clear why that sort of delight would not also take place regarding lesser divine judgments (say, pertaining to those known by the redeemed personally). While we dare not speculate into such detail, we also do well not to lay up objections that fall foul of this explicitly stated vision.

Attending to these questions has suggested ways in which they not only contribute to the full scope of eschatological teaching but also suggest a potential sequence for consideration. We move on, or better, a bit backward, to the interim hope of the redeemed: the so-called intermediate state.

Interim

Our heavenly hope marks the high point or finale of the biblical plotline. It serves not only as a barometer of our desire but also as a canon for marking our progress thus far. In that regard, it brings into relief the character of the happiness experienced by those departed saints who have died in Christ though not yet risen and living in heaven on earth. Such is an interim or intermediate state.

Some have pushed back against the notion of an intermediate state. To expound our own affirmation of its importance, we will consider the most significant recent objection.

5. How does your view of our end relate to the intermediate state? How is it similar and how is it different?

Many push against the idea of an intermediate state. It is hard to grasp the motivating impulses for such a shift apart from a judgment that the material is essential. Note that this is not a simple claim that the material is optimal or original or even normative but that the material is essential and—even more pointedly—essential in every moment. Therefore, a human being whose body has expired and who has not yet been physically raised from the dead cannot exist in any intervening state. Exponents may speak of this as a nonreductive physicalism, but it is surely a variant of physicalism. The argument is premised on the idea that human existence is physical and therefore cannot be anything but physical. At the same time, there is a claim that the Bible in no way speaks of a disembodied human existence.[11]

Nonreductive physicalism goes further and denies not only a soul-ish intermediate state but the very concept of a distinct soul in human constitution, period.[12] Nonreductive physicalists read the diverse terms body, soul, and spirit to refer *aspectively*, rather than partitively, to a human being. James D. G. Dunn describes the difference:

> In simplified terms, while Greek thought tended to regard the human being as made up of distinct parts, Hebraic thought saw the human being more as a whole person existing on different dimensions. As we might say, it was more characteristically Greek to conceive of the human person "partitively," whereas it was more characteristically "Hebrew" to conceive of the human person "aspectively." That is to say, we speak of a school *having* a gym (the gym is part of the school); but we say I *am* a Scot (my Scottishness is an aspect of my whole being).[13]

---

11. Joel B. Green, "Eschatology and the Nature of Humans: A Reconsideration of Pertinent Biblical Evidence," *Science and Christian Belief* 14.1 (2002): 33–50; and especially Nancey Murphy, *Bodies and Souls, or Spirited Bodies?*, Current Issues in Theology (Cambridge: Cambridge University Press, 2006).

12. There is a parallel between nonreductive physicalism, then, and philosophical approaches that reduce mind to brain. While I will not explore the latter issue here, it is worth consulting Marilynne Robinson, *Absence of Mind* (New Haven: Yale University Press, 2011).

13. James D. G. Dunn, *The Theology of the Apostle Paul* (Grand Rapids: Eerdmans, 1998), 54.

Nonreductive physicalism asserts the human being on earth is wholly physical, and there is nothing that can then transverse the experience of death and enjoy a future phase of divine paradise apart from bodily life. The biblical evidence gestures otherwise, however. I leave to the side here the broader question of body-soul dualism and focus more specifically on the question of an intermediate state.[14] While the New Testament does not riff widely or in detail on the nature of an intermediate state, it does pressure us to affirm that such a state exists in some fashion and with at least some definition. See how Christ responded to one of the thieves executed with him on Golgotha (as described in Luke 23:39–43). One criminal mockingly pressed Jesus to save them. The other criminal rebuked the first and affirmed the innocence of Jesus. Turning to Jesus, he implored: "Jesus, remember me when you come into your kingdom." Jesus replied, "Truly I say to you, today you will be with me in paradise" (Luke 23:42–43).

The intermediate state is not the final state. It is a good gift and can be called "paradise," yet it is not perfection. Why say it is imperfect? It is sinless and good, but it is not yet the complete or total culmination of all things; perfection here would mean wholistic completion or final attainment of the world's full and fitting end. The intermediate state is immaculate, yet it has not attained that final intended reality. The conclusion to Hebrews 11 addresses the fate of Old Testament believers, all of whom had died prior to the writing of that epistle. "These were all commended for their faith, yet none of them received what had been promised, since God had planned something better for us so that only together with us would they be made perfect" (Heb 11:39–40). These saints were commended, but they had not yet received the promise or been "made perfect" (a term that connotes not sinlessness but maturity or completion; see also Heb 5:14). Perfection or wholeness only comes when all the redeemed experience it together; the words "together with us" are crucial in this regard. So, the intermediate state is good and even paradise, but it is not the best and final state.[15]

---

14. The two questions are enmeshed together. The existence of an intermediate, disembodied state does demand some notion of soul or spirit, while denial of soul or spirit does demand denial of a disembodied, intermediate state. Though distinct, they do stand or fall together.

15. We ought not use the high bar of perfect eschatological glory as the only measure

The Bible commends some notion of an intermediate state, which involves discontinuity and continuity with respect to our final destiny. There is an elemental continuity in that the spiritual presence of Almighty God, as well as the communion of the saints, may be enjoyed. And yet that interpersonal fellowship exists in a wholly spiritual state that is not yet resurrected or environmentally situated in a new heaven and new earth. We can define the intermediate state only in very broad strokes. It involves the enjoyment of God's presence, occurs in a temporarily disembodied state, is paradisal in character (as opposed to purgatorial in mood), and is not yet the climactic finale of redemptive history.

We should return to the challenge of nonreductive physicalism and its psychosomatic approach to human identity. The apostolic portrayal of the intermediate state in no way limits us from affirming that psychosomatic wholeness marks the perfection or completeness of human identity. Hebrews 11 suggests that no saint receives the promise or perfection until they do so with all the redeemed (in their resurrection state upon the return of Christ). The resurrected and glorified body in the new heavens and new earth remains the consummation of our Christian hope, though neither embodiment nor environmental location is the most significant marker of that glory. God's presence is the prime and central thread in human happiness, and it will be most fully experienced when framed by bodily, indestructible life and by a restored, earthly context.

Beginnings from the End

6. **How does your view of the end relate to our present life?** How is it similar and how is it different? How should our end influence how we live now?

---

for one's hope. It is appropriate for Christian women and men to hope to be with the Lord, even in this immediate and intermediate phase. While that is not the final and full hope of resurrection life with the Lord and all his saints here in heaven on earth, it is still a greater good and an appropriate aspiration. That N. T. Wright and Richard Middleton malign such hopes as Platonic or escapist is unfortunate. Creedal affirmation of biblical eschatology ought not to be forced to choose between anticipating the presence of the Lord in the interim with the greater glory of resurrection life in the longer term. For further examination of the projects of Wright and Middleton, respectively, see Matthew Levering, *Jesus and the Demise of Death: Resurrection, Afterlife, and the Fate of the Christian* (Waco, TX: Baylor University Press, 2012), 7–10 and passim; and Michael Allen, *Grounded in Heaven: Recentering Hope and Life in God* (Grand Rapids: Eerdmans, 2018), 1–58.

"Blessed be the God and Father of our Lord Jesus Christ! According to his great mercy, he has caused us to be born again to a living hope through the resurrection of Jesus Christ from the dead" (1 Pet 1:3). Christian anticipation of heavenly glory serves as "living hope," which spurs our vital and active service and love. In fact, Peter goes on to speak of how that "inheritance that is imperishable, undefiled, and unfading, kept in heaven for you" sustains the "genuineness of your faith" even if "now for a little while, if necessary, you have been grieved by various trials" (1 Pet 1:4–7). Grit finds its foundations in expected glory.

The breadth of our heavenly hope prompts us to commit all of life as loving devotion to God. God is making all things new. Our concern ought not be any less expansive than his divine commitment. We are called to love God with all we are—heart, soul, mind, and strength (Deut 6:5; see also Matt 22:37–38; Mark 12:28–31; Luke 10:25–28). We do not merely foster intellectual or rational growth, but we also tend to environmental and ecological concerns. Spiritual vitality is pursued alongside relational reconciliation and peace. These varied and diverse yet interconnected or overlapping facets of creaturely existence become occasions for faithfulness in as much as they all come from God's good provision and return to God's eventual plan for the glory of bringing heaven to this renewed earth.

The surety of our heavenly hope reminds us that we need not venture forth in fear nor falter in anxiety. Love and devotion always come at a cost. We cannot love our neighbor without giving and, more specifically, without giving ourselves. That price functions as the signal of our level of selflessness, yet it also tempts us to pause, reassess, and hold back from giving ourselves away to love and serve others. Investment in the things of this kingdom invariably dries up when future expectations are less than certain. In the business world, investment dries up when the future remains murky and unclear; similarly, Christian or religious sacrifice will invariably flag to the extent that eschatological expectations are ambiguous or unsettled. So the gospel word that with Jesus Christ the end of all things is at hand is no small matter. The presence of the kingdom, the reign of Christ from heaven's throne on high, and his promised return; each of these realities offers a settled or sure hope. Eschatology has always prompted an ethic; hope always generates a distinctive way of walking the path of life.

Biblical eschatology involves not merely the promise that all our wildest dreams will come true but includes the pledge that God will give us every good and perfect gift (though they may often be that which we didn't know we needed). Our best life later involves the persistent, sometimes painful process of having our desires recalibrated now. As Ecclesiastes reminds us of the futility and vanity (i.e., the temporary happiness and yet ephemeral reality) of every earthly good, so the Song of Songs calls us forward to see that ultimately joy is found in the Lord's presence alone. At the end of the day our cry shall be that of the bride: "Come away, my beloved" (Song 8:14 NIV). Origen of Alexandria viewed this canonical sequence as drawing us away from false paths of happiness found in earthly good and toward the discipleship process of learning to love nothing less than God's own presence.[16] In the New Testament, Paul speaks of learning to "set your hearts on things above" (Col 3:1 NIV) and "we fix our eyes not on what is seen, but on what is unseen, since what is seen is temporary, but what is unseen is eternal" (2 Cor 4:18 NIV). Heavenly mindedness must be learned by those of us who so naturally love the pleasures of this age and the principles of life under the sun.

The transformation of our heavenly hope calls us to ongoing repentance, lest we assume that our desires have fully matured. As we pray that God's kingdom would come and his will be done on earth as in heaven, we invite God to transmute our own longings. We not only need his solution to our problems but also are aware that our deepest problem is our lack of awareness of our ultimate problem. We need him, much more than we understand or appreciate.

The center of our heavenly hope calls us again and again to remember that we are made first and foremost for God.[17] The Bible instructs not merely in what content it teaches, answering particular questions, but also in the way it constrains and guides our curiosity, pointing to some questions at the expense of others. That the Bible focuses on the

---

16. Origen, "The Prologue to the Commentary on the Song of Songs," in *Origen: An Exhortation to Martyrdom, Prayer, and Selected Works*, trans. Rowan Greer (New York: Paulist, 1979), 232.

17. See Allen, *Grounded in Heaven*, especially the introduction and chs. 3–4; and Hans Boersma, *Seeing God: The Beatific Vision in Christian Tradition* (Grand Rapids: Eerdmans, 2018).

presence of God in the new heavens and new earth does not in and of itself disprove the presence of buffets or golf or other entertainments, but it does inevitably challenge us to care more about the things that we ought to care about. Many of our eschatological questions are unresolvable now, to be sure, but more importantly they are rather beside the point and remarkably uninteresting in the grand scheme of things. They persist, and we all ask them (myself included), but Scripture's reorientation of the very questions worth addressing suggests that we all need to undergo the process of theological discipleship or intellectual ascesis whereby our speculations are challenged, our questions are redirected, and our desires are sanctified to more closely relate to the ordered loves presented by God in Holy Scripture's eschatological teaching. We are on a need-to-know basis; more importantly, we are on an evangelical regimen of being formed to know by faith what needs knowing.

JOHN S. FEINBERG

Professor Michael Allen has written a stimulating essay that sees heaven as occurring predominantly, if not exclusively, on earth. He and I see many things quite differently, but there are some things on which we agree. In what follows, I shall first address some of the lesser issues and then turn to more substantial matters.

First, Allen explains what happens when we die. I can agree with his basic points, except that we do not get resurrected and glorified bodies immediately upon death. Allen doesn't say we do, but he also doesn't say when these events will occur and whether there are events or stages of events that will lead to them. One wishes he would fill in more details about when these things happen.

Next, as to whether we will be able to sin and will sin when we are glorified, I basically agree with his answers. However, I believe we will not be able to sin for reasons other than those Allen offers. Moreover, he does not answer whether as sinless saints our actions will be free. The key, here, of course, is how one defines free will, and there are two main definitions theologians and philosophers use. On the one hand, there is *libertarian free will*. This view says an action is free only if it is not causally determined. This does not mean the act is random and disconnected from causes altogether. Rather it means that regardless of how many causes (and the nature of those causes) play upon a person's will when he chooses, and regardless of what he does choose, he always could have chosen and done otherwise than he did. If Allen holds libertarian free will, then he cannot consistently believe that a glorified person is free in the libertarian sense, for a glorified nature makes it impossible to sin.

In contrast, there is *compatibilistic free will*. Compatibilism says that an act is free, even though it is causally determined, so long as the causes do not constrain the person to do something he does not want to do. Hence, if causes succeed in getting an agent to do what he wants to do, his act is causally determined but free (compatibilistically), because he did what he wanted to do. If instead causes push the agent to do what he does not wish to do, then he acts unfreely (in the compatibilistic sense). If causes succeed in changing the agent's mind about what he wants to do, and he does what he then wants to do, his choice is compatibilistically free, even though it is also causally determined.

How does compatibilistic freedom relate to the freedom of a glorified person? The glorified person's new nature will persuade him to do good and not evil. Since he has decided that he wants to do good and not evil, he will do good and do it freely (in the compatibilistic sense of freedom).

Hopefully, readers can see that libertarian and compatibilistic free will contradict each other. Therefore, both cannot be true. Given libertarian free will, a glorified believer is not free, for causal conditions (including his own glorified nature) will prevent him from sinning, and yet the hallmark of libertarian freedom is that regardless of what a person does, he always could have done otherwise. A glorified nature cannot sin and will not sin, but since with libertarian freedom the person can do other than he does, that means a glorified person cannot be free in the libertarian sense.

I hold compatibilism. Allen does not tell us what he holds. Failure to discuss his notion of freedom is hardly fatal to his position, but it does leave things unclear as to whether he thinks glorified believers are free.

Allen also addresses what Scripture means when it says that the righteous will see God. I think he is probably right in thinking that the physical thing or being we will see is Christ. Surely, Christ is the *main* physical thing we will see when we see God. But Allen does not seem to consider that the passage might include something further. Though God the Father and God the Holy Spirit are pure spirit and hence invisible, they can make their presence known in a physical way. At Jesus's baptism, those present heard a real voice say that Jesus is God's beloved Son in whom God is well pleased. Though the Father does not have a physical voice box—or anything else physical as part of his divine essence—those present at the baptism heard physical sound waves.

I could say something similar about the pillar of fire at night and the cloud by day that led Israel through the wilderness after their departure from Egypt. But what is my point? Allen limits whom glorified believers will see to Christ alone. Perhaps that is correct, but it may also be correct that the pure in heart will see God the Father and Holy Spirit. How? By means of some *physical* manifestation of their presence that will allow glorified believers to "see" God, though of course they won't "see" his immaterial divine nature.

Again, my point does not destroy Allen's essay, but it suggests that on the question of how we will see God, his answer could stand nuancing beyond what he offers.

In turning to more significant issues, one of my major concerns is Allen's basis for seeing heaven as only occurring on earth. Though he does not reference many Scriptures, it is clear that most of what he writes relies on Revelation 21–22. I grant that much of those chapters does focus on what will happen on earth once God makes the new heavens and earth. However, I believe it is a mistake to think that heaven will only occur on earth just because Revelation 21–22 speaks in terms that seem to be about the new earth. Let me explain why.

First, while it is true that Revelation 21–22 tell us little about the new heavens and the new earth, John does say that the old heavens and earth have passed away and that God will create both a new heaven and a new earth (v. 1). Moreover, the new Jerusalem comes "out of heaven from God" (v. 2). In verse 3 John says he heard a loud voice from the throne of God saying that "the tabernacle of God is among men, and he will dwell among them." That voice may be coming from the new earth and the new Jerusalem, or it may instead be coming from God as he sits on the throne in heaven; there is not enough evidence to say for sure whether the voice comes from the new heaven or from the new earth, but nothing precludes the voice coming from the new heaven.

Granting what I have just said about Revelation 21–22, what is my point? While these chapters speak predominantly about what happens on the new earth and about the new Jerusalem, the first few verses of Revelation 21 do talk about the existence of a new heaven. While these chapters tell us little more about what happens in the new heavens while life continues on the new earth, nothing in either chapter precludes believers having access to the new heaven. Thus, from Revelation 21 and 22 it is an argument from silence to say that the final estate of the godly will not include the new heavens, and it is also an argument from silence to say just from these two chapters that the final state of the godly will include access to the new heaven.

This would indeed be a problem for anyone thinking that he could support the notion that believers will have access in eternity to the new heavens *based solely on Revelation 21–22*. But I am not saying that Revelation 21–22 is the only support for seeing the godly in heaven (including the new heaven). Those chapters do mention God creating a new heaven and earth. Why would that even be relevant for John to say if believers will have no access to the new heavens? Who will, after all, inhabit the new heavens? If not the saints of all ages, and not angels (nothing is said about where angels will be once the new heaven and earth are made), and if God is to dwell *only* on the new earth (Rev 21–22 is clear that God will dwell on the new earth, but nothing says he will have no access to the new heavens), then who will live in or even have access to the new heavens? If no one, why the need to create them, and why mention them (Rev 21:1–3), even if ever so briefly? Surely, we could all wish that Revelation 21 and 22 said more about the new heavens, but as shown in my essay, these two chapters in Revelation are not the only support for believers having access to and dwelling in heaven, even as they also have access to and dwell on the new earth.

So, from Revelation 21–22, I do not see how we can say with certainty (as Allen seems to do) that heaven for the godly will be to live on the new earth. But there is another problem with this view. Revelation 21–22 reveals what will happen after the events of Revelation 20. Revelation 20:11–15 shows us the great white-throne judgment. Revelation 20:1–10 reveals several things. Verses 1–3 teach that Satan will be bound for a thousand years. Verse 4 shows the kingdom rule of the godly of all ages with Christ. But verse 4 clearly says that all the godly dead enumerated in this verse "came to life and reigned with Christ for a thousand years." The rest of the dead (the ungodly dead) did not come to life until after the thousand years were completed (v. 5). When they did come to life, verses 11–15 teach that they were raised to stand at the great white-throne judgment.

Why do I mention Revelation 20:1–4? Because Allen proposes that the godly dead of all ages live on the new earth (Revelation 21–22). And Revelation 21:1–3 clearly shows that God does not create the new heaven and earth until *after* the thousand-year kingdom. How then, if heaven is to be understood *as only on the new earth*, can believers be resurrected to reign on the *old* earth with Christ for a thousand years (Rev 20:4) before God even destroys the old heaven and earth and makes the new ones? And where are the godly dead of all ages prior to the millennial kingdom when they will reign with Christ, if Allen is right in seeing heaven *only* as a reference to the new earth after the millennium and the destruction of the old heaven and earth?

Thus, even if Allen were right that the ultimate destiny of believers is the new earth alone, that would still be inadequate as an explanation of what happens to dead believers of all ages prior to the eternal state. In my essay I cited various verses that show that during the intermediate state, dead believers' immaterial parts are in the current heavens, and that after the rapture but before the millennium they must be in the current heaven with God in glorified bodies, awaiting their reign with Christ for a thousand years on the current earth. Now if what I am saying about dead believers prior to the millennium and during it is true, then throughout much of human history believers (i.e., their immaterial parts) must have access to the current heaven and live there with the Lord.

Now if prior to the eternal state dead believers can live with the Lord in the current heaven, why can't they live with him and have access to the new heaven once God creates it? Though Revelation 21–22 says little about this, as already said, it does not say believers won't and can't have access to the new heaven, any more than do these chapters say that the godly of all ages will have access to and live *only* on the new earth. Hence, I find that Allen's portrayal of the final estate of believers contains some truth, but it does not tell the full story as Scripture portrays it.

Next, I should say something about Allen's handling of marriage in the eternal state. He writes that marriage will not be abrogated but fulfilled in the church's marriage to the Lamb, and the eschatological union of Christ and his bride will have taken place. Though this may sound cogent, it tends to spiritualize marriage altogether. When speaking of marriage on earth in our natural bodies, we certainly do not understand it in this spiritualized way (such an understanding would not make sense of marriages of nonbelievers).

So why must marriage be given a spiritual meaning (and not taken literally at all) when Allen talks about marriage in eternity? Why not simply say that a glorified body cannot reproduce and forget all the invoking of typology to explain what will happen to marriage? It is not typology that will keep anyone from marriage in the afterlife. Rather, it is the altered ontological state of our glorified being that makes marriage as we know it impossible.

Then Allen makes some claims that just don't square with Scripture. For example, he writes that "the Bible in no way speaks of a disembodied human existence" (130).

Is that actually so? What, then, of Paul's desire to depart this life and be present with Christ? Of all people, Paul most assuredly teaches the resurrection of the body on a future day (e.g., 1 Thess 4:13–18). What also of Christ's promise to the repentant thief that he would be with Christ in paradise? Their bodies would be in a tomb, not in paradise! If upon physical death the body stays with the immaterial part, such language makes little sense. For further evidence of disembodied human existence prior to the resurrection of our bodies, consult my essay.

Surely professor Allen is aware of many of these biblical details I have raised, so why does he reject them? It seems necessary to do so if there is to be any hope of finding biblical support for his views on the afterlife. But when there are biblical details that do not square with the theologian or exegete's position, at some point the anomalies will be so many and so significant that the right course of action is to jettison the theory, not reinterpret the biblical details so that they square with the thinker's views.

J. RICHARD MIDDLETON

I am grateful to Mike Allen for his beautifully written, lucid, and evocative chapter on Christian eschatology. There is much that is valuable
in Allen's articulation of his eschatological vision, including his emphasis
on the glory of God, our fellowship with God as the essential goal of the
Christian life, and the bodily and earthly nature of our final destiny. I also
applaud his articulation of our need to live out the future in the present,
so that our eschatology becomes a prod to faithful discipleship. And I am
impressed with how many times he reminds us of the need for epistemological humility and reticence in claiming to know too much about our
final redemptive state. These are all emphases that I fully affirm.

Therefore, I take Mike Allen to be a faithful fellow traveler on the
theological journey to understand Scripture aright and as a full-fledged
brother in Christ, whose point of view I respect, even though we part
company on some issues.

I see two primary disagreements between my essay and Allen's that
I want to explore. The purpose of my exploration of these issues is not
to "set him right" but to clarify further my own point of view (which he
has critiqued both in this volume and in an earlier book) and to press
him to query his own articulations.[1]

The two main disagreements, as I see it, have to do with the importance of, and biblical evidence for, the intermediate state (as a Christian

---

1. Allen has critiqued my position (along with that of N. T. Wright) at some length in his
book *Grounded in Heaven*. In my response here, I will focus on his contribution to the present
work and leave aside the critique articulated in the earlier book. Suffice to say about that book
that I simply do not recognize myself in some of his characterizations of my position (N. T.
Wright has communicated the same thing to me). Perhaps we can take up that discussion
another time.

hope between death and resurrection) and the primacy of the "beatific vision," conceived as an alternative to ordinary cultural pursuits in the eschaton (I use the words "importance" and "primacy" because of the significant length of his sections on these topics). Underlying both disagreements is the question of the degree of continuity and discontinuity between our present life (which, when lived faithfully to God, is an anticipation of the eschaton) and our future hope (which is the culmination and *telos* of our present life).[2]

The Intermediate State

Let's take the intermediate state first. Allen prefaces his defense of the intermediate state by stating his discomfort with those who have recently pushed back against such a state (I am included in this group). "It is hard," he notes, "to grasp the motivating impulses for such a shift apart from a judgment that the material [that is, the body] is essential" (130). There is a certain truth to his point. Yet this a rather crass, even reductionistic, way of stating matters, since it is the holistic, fully orbed nature of human life (rather than just the "material") that many of us think is important. Although I am not a substance dualist, I affirm that a human being is much more than merely material or physical. However, I also believe that dividing a person into material and immaterial parts is far too artificial. Humans are complex, multidimensional creatures whose dimensions are grounded in, though not reducible to, the body. I simply do not think that a disembodied "soul" or "mind," even if it could exist in such a state, is a full person.[3]

---

2. One further point, which bears mentioning here, is Allen's misunderstanding of my position in the historical appendix to my book, *New Heaven and a New Earth*. According to Allen, I incorrectly treat "modern dispensationalism (with its rapture theology) as somehow representative of the classical Christian hope of centuries past," and he mentions this appendix as my "documentation of a spiritualist hope [that] comes from dispensationalism." Here I agree with Allen that it is illegitimate to view dispensationalism as typical of the eschatology of the historic church or as the cause of the emphasis on heaven in the church's eschatology. I never made either claim. Indeed, only three pages out of thirty in my appendix were devoted to dispensationalism, and this was preceded by seventeen pages of analysis of eschatology throughout prior church history (the remainder of the chapter focused on new developments). Here I will simply note that if it is that easy to misread a contemporary author writing in English just a few years ago, how much more difficult it is to interpret ancient texts written in Hebrew and Greek that come from a different cultural milieu, with premodern theological assumptions. This suggests that even when biblical interpreters need to challenge alternative interpretations, we should do so charitably.

3. I gather that Allen is himself ambivalent about this. In advance of his discussion of the

Allen goes on to quote Jimmy Dunn about Greek versus Hebrew ways of seeing the person. But I do not believe Dunn's formulation of the soul as an aspect of the person is specific enough to Scripture. I do not view the "soul" either as a separable part of the person (which Allen implies is the case, without explicitly saying so) or as an "aspect" or "dimension" of the person (as Dunn seems to say). As I explained in my chapter in this volume, the "soul" in the Old Testament and in Paul is the entire embodied organism.[4] There really is not any significant disagreement among exegetes on this point. Of course, someone might object that we need the concept of a separable part of the person and then call this a "soul" (as is traditional in Christian thought), but this is an argument about metaphysical necessity rather than biblical interpretation.

At one point Allen says that he will leave to the side the question of body-soul dualism and focus on the intermediate state itself. He admits that "the New Testament does not riff widely or in detail on the nature of an intermediate state" (131), which is evidently true. But when he goes on to say that the New Testament "does pressure us to affirm that such a state exists in some fashion" (131), I must demur. Indeed, my primary reason for agnosticism about the intermediate state is precisely the lack of exegetical support in Scripture.[5]

In my book *A New Heaven and a New Earth*, I analyzed the half-dozen biblical texts usually cited for the intermediate state and show that none clearly teach this.[6] I addressed a few of these texts in my response to John Feinberg (those he himself mentioned in his chapter). In the interest of brevity, I will not repeat that exegesis here. While I respect belief in the intermediate state (and do not go out of my way to disabuse

---

intermediate state, he affirms that salvation does not involve a person being "siphoned through a strainer" in order to extract the intellect or "soul" as the essential person (120). Yet it seems this is precisely what he thinks the intermediate state consists of.

4. This may be somewhat different for other New Testament authors; I don't assume that they all utilize a Pauline meaning for *psyche* ("soul").

5. Beyond the lack of exegetical support is the notable absence of the intermediate state in the ecumenical creeds of the church. It is thus strange that in one of his footnotes Allen says: "Creedal affirmation of biblical eschatology ought not to be forced to choose between anticipating the presence of the Lord in the interim with the greater glory of resurrection life in the longer term" (132). But there is simply no reference to the intermediate state in the Apostles' Creed, the Nicene Creed, or the Athanasian Creed.

6. Middleton, *New Heaven and a New Earth*, 227–37.

people of such belief), I counsel the reader to check out what I wrote in response to Feinberg (and my fuller analysis in my book). But since Allen mentions Jesus's conversation with the criminal on the cross in Luke 23, I'll just note here a point I made in response to Feinberg: "paradise" in the New Testament is not equivalent to an immaterial "heaven."

The Beatific Vision

The second main disagreement between Allen and myself is the prominence—and especially the theological significance—of the "beatific vision" as it applies to the eschaton.

While I admit that the vision of God's glory is a prominent theme in the Bible (especially in the Old Testament), I resist the reification of this theme into a doctrine of *the* "beatific vision," as if this is a central and clearly defined idea. As an Old Testament scholar, I am aware of the complexity of this theme. There are texts that say that God has not and cannot be seen and that no one can see God and live. And there are other texts where people see God and then comment that they are amazed that the vision did not kill them. It is inappropriate, then, to simply jump to later Second Temple and New Testament claims about God's invisibility and allow them to trump all the prior revelation of Scripture. I am interested in a whole-canon view of biblical truth.

More importantly, I have problems with thinking that the beatific vision, interpreted as worship of and fellowship with God, excludes our ordinary human life, including our sociocultural activities. So while I affirm Jesus's statement, "Blessed are the pure in heart / for they will see God" (Matt 5:8), I can't ignore his earlier words, "Blessed are the meek / for they will inherit the earth" (Matt 5:5).[7] Although Allen quotes the first beatitude, he omits the second. Of course, he affirms the earthly reality of the eschaton, thus implicitly endorsing the second beatitude. But to take this as a bare affirmation of an earthly future while ignoring the depth of meaning in the phrase "inherit the earth" (which builds on the cultural mandate in Genesis 1 and accumulates throughout the Old Testament and Second Temple Judaism) is to impoverish what Jesus intends.

---

7. On the necessary connection between these two beatitudes, see David A. Miller, "A Holistic Eschatology? Negotiating the Beatific Vision and the New Earth in Recent Theology," *Canadian-American Theological Review* 8.1 (2019): 35–54.

Yes, of course, the eschatological future will be different in significant ways from our present life. And since we do not have a clear picture of the differences, we should be reticent in claiming too much certainty about the future. Yet this cuts both ways. If it applies to my idea that our cultural life will continue (suitably changed for a resurrection context), it applies also to Allen's idea that our cultural life will not be prominent (perhaps even transcended).

One of the primary reasons Allen gives for his understanding of the eschaton is the prominence of worship in the book of Revelation. I agree that the redeemed saints are portrayed as singing praises to God and that there is mention of harps as part of worship (Allen cites Rev 5:8; 14:2; 15:2 for the latter point). However, it is important to note that most of the worship portrayed in Revelation is offered by various nonhuman beings, not specifically by humans. If I were to give a brief catalog of the worship portrayed in Revelation, I would note that the worshipers include four living creatures (4:8), twenty-four elders (11:16–19), the four living creatures together with the elders (4:9–11; 5:8–10, 14; 19:4), angels (5:11–12), living creatures, elders, and angels (7:11–12), every creature in heaven and earth (5:13), and redeemed humans (7:9; 15:2–4). Sometimes the identity of the worshipers is not specified (19:1–3, 6–8).

Further, the references to the four living creatures (who are not human) and the twenty-four elders (who might be human, depending on one's interpretation) praising God and the Lamb in Revelation 5 has them affirming the cultural mandate, using language from Exodus 19:6 to claim that Christ has redeemed believers for the priestly service of reigning on earth (Rev 5:10). And these redeemed humans are described in terms of their cultural and linguistic diversity—"from every tribe and language and people and nation" (Rev 5:9).

Beyond the problem of overreading human worship in the book of Revelation, it is inappropriate to allow the teaching of one particular book of the Bible (especially one dominated by figurative and symbolic language) to determine our eschatological vision so precisely. I fully agree with Allen's "one fundamental rule" for eschatology, namely, that it "not be allowed to function separately from the wider teaching of the prophets and apostles" (127). So suppose we did not have access to the book of Revelation; would our vision of the end be different? I myself have tried to show the relationship of worship (narrowly conceived) to an obedient holistic life in the entire arc and sweep of the biblical story. That is, while Allen's understanding of Revelation leads him to be reticent about the role of "culture" in the eschaton, I prefer to extrapolate from the rest of Scripture, with its focus on earthly activities and its affirmation of our ordinary creatureliness.

Undoubtedly, neither of us is dependent solely on biblical interpretation. Our exegesis is informed by our theological assumptions: his by a theological valuation of fellowship with God (understood in a somewhat decontextualized way) and mine by an understanding of the presence of God mediated by ordinary earthly life (which is therefore intrinsically spiritual).

God's Glorious Rule and Human Agency

Perhaps a word might be said here about some of the theological assumptions that I perceive in Allen's chapter, especially where they embody unnecessary binary oppositions. I certainly do not think that all binaries are invalid. It is perfectly legitimate to distinguish between the creator and the created, good and evil, heaven and earth, etc. But we need to be careful not to read unbiblical valences into such distinctions.

So when Allen hesitates about affirming human cultural activity in the eschaton, claiming that human "vocational rule" should be subordinate to God's (and Christ's) rule, I discern not simply an exegetical decision but a conceptual commitment to the sovereignty of God. Well and good; I also affirm God's sovereignty. But being a Wesleyan (though informed by the Reformed camp), I see no intrinsic competition between God's agency and (righteous, obedient) human agency. So when Allen quotes Revelation 11:15, which states that *Christ* "will reign for ever and ever," I note that the author of Revelation did not think this invalidates his later statement that *the redeemed* "will reign for ever and ever" (Rev 22:5). Redemption restores the *imago Dei*.[8]

Likewise, I simply do not see why we need to diminish human cultural accomplishments in order to emphasize our giving glory to God. Of course, God is glorified in our verbal praise. But in a more fundamental sense, God is glorified by our living out God's normative

---

8. The image of God amounts to more than merely worshiping Jesus as Lord. It has implications for our ruling and representing our Lord on earth.

purposes in the fullness of our embodied lives. Affirming the latter does not contradict or diminish the former, unless we begin with an a priori assumption to that end.

Of course, I may be mistaken in thinking that this assumption (or something like it) underlies Allen's eschatological vision. So I raise this point simply as a suggestion, for pondering and reflection, as we both try to reach toward a faithful, biblical vision of the eschaton that will empower God's people to live out the future kingdom even now.

RESPONSE TO MICHAEL ALLEN

PETER KREEFT

I was impressed not only with Dr. Allen's essay overall, and the fact that he gave the most complete answer to each of the questions we were asked to address, but also with many details. For example, I thought Dr. Allen handled with admirable diffidence the various Scripture passages that depict the rejoicing of God and the blessed over the divine justice of damnation. He reminded us of what is most easy to forget when we deal with such questions, namely, that the thing that must be questioned first of all is our own questions (a lesson Job learned when God spoke to him)—and our natural but false assumption that we are the ones asking the questions and God is the one who must answer them (as Job also learned from God when he answered Job with questions rather than with answers).

So I was grateful for Dr. Allen's reminder that we must first "invite God to transmute our own longings" and follow Scripture's "reorientation of the very questions worth addressing" (135). The very first thing Jesus says in John's Gospel is to ask a question, in fact the most important and fateful of all questions: "What do you seek?" (John 1:38). It is the primary Augustinian question: What do you love? The two "cities" that we live in now and that are consummated in heaven and hell are created by the two loves, and therefore the thing in us that needs most to be "transmuted" is our loves, and therefore our hearts.

I appreciated Dr. Allen's penchant for a "both-and" hermeneutic that I found very Augustinian (I think Augustine is the strongest bridge between Catholics and Protestants). For instance, both the hope of *seeing* God and the divine *invisibility*; both the "mixture of bodily realism and yet glorious mystery" (121); and both "new creation" language and "restoration or renewal" language (116, which, like Matthew 13:52, shows why the church needs both progressives and conservatives). Like Augustine, Dr. Allen revels in exploring both halves of paradoxes (e.g., the sovereignty of divine grace and the reality of human free will). I think this is because, like the author of the book of Revelation, Dr. Allen has an artist's mind, and he sees that Scripture's "range of portraits surely leans against any crass or literalistic fixation on one to the exclusion of others" (119; thus God reveals himself both as the particular and specific "God of Abraham, Isaac, and Jacob" and the universal and unlimited "I AM").

A key feature of Dr. Allen's paradoxical "both-and" hermeneutic is revealed in his title, "heaven on earth": the "already and not yet" tension between present and future, presence and absence, immanence and transcendence. Too often traditionalists, in reaction against modernists, have ignored or downplayed what Dr. Allen, in his very first sentence, calls "the heavens *in* the earth" (115). I was struck by the philosophical consonance between my former Calvinist (Kuyper and Bavinck) tradition and my present Catholic "incarnational" and "sacramental" tradition on the importance of the earth. Though our theological traditions disagree, our philosophical foundations are very similar, especially the ubiquitous and consequential premise that grace perfects nature (and culture, reason, desire, time, place, matter, and freedom) rather than replacing it, thus departing equally from the naturalism of Arianism and Pelagianism and the spiritualism of Docetism and Gnosticism.

Dr. Allen performs a rehabilitation of the sacredness and importance of *place* that struck me as similar to the rehabilitation of the sacredness and importance of *time* that was given by Rabbi Abraham Joshua Heschel's classic, *The Sabbath*. The apparently simple, concrete questions about what seem to be only dimensions of physics turn out to be more complex, more spiritual, and more profound than we think.

I was a bit disappointed that none of the four respondents, including myself, mentioned the fascinating traditional answer to the question about what we will be when we get our resurrection bodies, namely, the three conditions of all resurrected bodies: (1) "quality" (including gender identity and perfect, mature age), (2) "identity" (including redeemed memory), and (3) "integrity" (including martyrs' wounds but not bodily handicaps); and the four conditions of the redeemed: (1) "impassibility" (no pain, sickness, aging, death, or harm), (2) "subtlety" (lightness and levity rather than gravity, and unimpeded communication), (3) "agility" (obedience to the sanctified will in all desires and commands) and (4) "clarity" (brilliance and beauty like Christ in the transfiguration). I am shamefaced to have omitted this because it comes mainly, though not exclusively, from my own Catholic tradition. Dr. Allen comes closest to filling in some of that gap.

Conclusions

I think these four essays show that all four of us are much more deeply united than we are divided, both positively, by our absolute dedication and fidelity to the word of God, and negatively, by our frequent return to 1 Corinthians 2:9. As God had the first word, God must have the last. And this will turn out to be not just the end but the beginning, as in the last chapter of C. S. Lewis's *The Last Battle*, the last of the Chronicles of Narnia. If you have never read it, please do. It does not directly answer the theological questions we have set ourselves to in this book, but it will restore your love of eschatology and put a "maranatha" on your lips.

Lewis's writings, especially his ecumenical masterpiece, *Mere Christianity*, were quoted more often than anything else except Scripture by all the presenters at the most productive week of intellectual discussion that I have ever experienced. This happened a few decades ago, at a conference on ecumenism at the now defunct Eastern Orthodox Rose Hill College in Aiken, South Carolina. The conference included theological luminaries from various Christian traditions, who presented and defended papers to one another all day for five days. At the concluding session, it was proposed that we issue a manifesto declaring that although we come from traditionally warring and mutually exclusive traditions, we found that we are far more united than divided because we all believed and loved and defended the whole canon of Scripture, the ecumenical councils and creeds, and the collected works of C. S. Lewis. All applauded.

REJOINDER

MICHAEL ALLEN

I want to express my thanks to Drs. Feinberg, Middleton, and Kreeft. They each identify areas of commonality as well as varying degrees of concern. I appreciate both facets. Such conversations won't be much help if we aren't willing to express disagreements with candor, and yet I can't help but also agree with Dr. Kreeft that so many times we forget the massive, catholic commonality that varying traditions herald together regarding our final hope, confessing against the voices of other religions and the silence of secularism and materialism.

I will resist the urge to respond point by point to my interlocutors. By and large, they expressed areas of disagreement that are simply legitimate areas of Christian debate, and I hope that readers give them a patient, careful hearing. Interestingly, Dr. Middleton disagrees with my affirmation of the intermediate state, whereas Dr. Feinberg seems to think that I deny its existence. Perhaps, therefore, specific rebuttal on either point is rather less promising. On occasion, I find Drs. Feinberg and Middleton to hypothesize about what I must or might mean and to spend time rebutting it. That I may not identify myself with those critiqued positions is beside the point, and I do not think getting into a round of defending myself is the most productive use of my last moment on the soapbox.

Instead, I wish to step back and reflect briefly, ever so briefly, upon the task of Christian eschatology and the kinds of methodological commitments that need to mark its faithful and wise execution. I conclude with seven aspects of pursuing a Christian eschatology and how they are meant to shape my essay (exemplified even in its very title: "Heaven on Earth"). These seven thoughts do not say everything about how to pursue such a topic, but hopefully they do provide a balanced manner of proceeding.

First, eschatology involves wholes, so we want to avoid splicing or dichotomizing unhelpfully. My title is meant to allude to this concept, "heaven on earth" signaling the marriage of that which is above with the renewal of things below. God's home and this natural world shall be joined by God's grace. "Heaven on earth" is remarkable news for those of us who so often experience earth as a valley, reminding us that the great mountain of the Lord holds eschatological, final promise.

Second, eschatology also involves priorities, so we should affirm a range of things in the right way. Again, my title was intended to gesture in this direction, with "heaven" being the leading term. The presence of God's home precedes and shapes any adequately Christian depiction of "earth." To our perpetual tendency to treat eschatology as that looming payback for all that we might suffer or give up now, "heaven on earth" reminds us that we are made for more than mere earthly goods. Dr. Kreeft does me the honor of identifying this Augustinian emphasis (which Lewis certainly highlighted).

Third, eschatology demands a reshuffled set of connections, as we are duty bound to explore the integration and coherence of varying theological claims so far as we might. My title insists on placing this connection before us through the presence of that single preposition "on." Heaven is not restricted to earth, for God is not dependent on creation or on us, yet nonetheless heaven comes to rest and remain "on earth." "Heaven on earth" is especially *good* news (*euangelion*) in that it is not necessary, but it is nonetheless the will and gracious good pleasure of the God of the gospel.

Fourth, eschatology depends on our willingness to return again and again to the bruising word of the Lord, so that our vocabulary—and the longings that those weighty words signify—might be judged. We are duty bound to ask ever anew how we might be hearing Christian terms in non-Christian ways and must therefore perform an act of intellectual repentance. We dare not assume that we know what "heaven" or even "earth" involves. They can be taken up and described in various settings. But to employ those terms Christianly—that is, with theological integrity—will involve asking how the complex literary context of Holy Scripture disciplines their usage.

Fifth, above all, we will need the "fear of the Lord," which is "the beginning of wisdom" (Ps 111:10; Prov 1:7). Therefore, we must walk with a hopeful yet reverentially humbled pace. Fear requires us to focus attention and foreground priorities, refusing distraction as we flee idols. In attending first and foremost always to God—as much in our end as in our beginning—we are actually better able to tend then to bodies and culture, to earth and to production. "Seek first the kingdom of God and his righteousness, and all these things will be added to you" (Matt 6:33).

Sixth, perhaps not surprisingly, I find that Holy Scripture fixes far more on that primary concern and rather less on other details (whether in the mechanics of Christ's return or of human cultural accomplishment in the hereafter). We are on something of a need-to-know basis, and we do well not only to conform our thoughts to God's but also to increasingly line up our questions with his revelation.

Seventh, if the event of Jesus's return and the daily affairs of the hereafter seem rather murky and underdetermined in Scripture, perhaps that mysterious minimalism is meant to direct our attention more fully to the majesty of his presence itself (revealed in far more vivid and recurring form). That brilliant majesty matches the last scriptural promise vested to us by our incarnate Lord: "Surely I am coming soon" (Rev 22:20). Not, happy days are here again, or world peace is coming, or psychological reprieve shall soon arrive, or clean consciences will soon be delivered, or cultural production will be fully flourishing, or even bodily resurrection is just around the corner. No, he says, "Surely I am coming soon." May our eyes ever be watchful for him and that glorious return.

A CATHOLIC PERSPECTIVE

PETER KREEFT

The four of us who are writing this book were each asked to answer the same ten questions about heaven.[1] I am grateful to this assignment, because I am lazy and love it when other people do half of my work for me by asking the questions. Getting the questions out is harder than we usually think. It is at least half the work; finding the answers is only the other half. Getting the questions out is like getting a baby born. Like childbirth, it takes more effort than we think—we *men*, anyway—all we do is leave a deposit in the bank, and both our money and our baby grow without our further effort. On the other hand, getting the answers is easier than we think, because truth exists and is as available as raindrops—but only in droplets that are too small to quench our thirst.

Questions about heaven are at least ten times better than questions about anything else, because heaven is more than ten times better than anything else. And it is twice as much fun for a philosopher to play with questions as it is for anyone else. That is one of the subconscious motives for becoming a philosopher. So do the math: this assignment is $2 \times 10 \times 2 = 40$ times more fun for me than any other. Thank you, Michael Wittmer, who is responsible for this project, at least forty times for every time you thank me for contributing to it.

---

1. Unless otherwise noted, the following essay employs the RSV translation for biblical citations.

* * *

A Christian philosopher should always be true to both Christianity and philosophy, to both Christ and Socrates. Therefore, my database will be mainly the Word of God on paper, which is all about the Word of God in the flesh, and my method will be mainly to seek true definitions, which is what Socrates always began with.

So, to define our subject we need to begin by distinguishing two meanings of *heaven* in our database, in Scripture. (1) When used in the plural ("the heavens," as in "the heavens and the earth"), the word *heavens* refers to a *place*: the rest of this (present) universe as distinct from the (present) earth. In other words, "what's up there and out there." Thus, when God says that he will create "new heavens and a new earth" (Isa 65:17), this means a whole new universe.

(2) When used in the singular, *heaven* can mean either of two things. The first (2a) is God's eternal "dwelling place." This, of course, is not a literal, physical, and spatial place anywhere in this universe (you can't get there in a rocket ship), since God is not relative to the universe but the universe is relative to him. That is why Christians typically did not refer to the universe by the term *cosmos*, because for the Greeks the cosmos was their absolute, such that even the gods were relative to it. Instead, Christians used the Jewish term *creation* for the universe. Heaven is not literally in "the heavens," although the heavens can symbolize it. It refers instead to God's own life or mode of existence.

Heaven can also mean (2b) our future participation in that "dwelling place," or more properly, that supernatural life of God. This amazing destiny, our sharing in a finite way in the very life and nature of the infinite God, is promised in 2 Peter 1:4. These promises are indeed so "precious and very great" that many Protestants protest against *theosis* (divinization), the word that the Orthodox love to use for that destiny.

Since we must very clearly distinguish the creator and the creature, when we speak of heaven we must ask whether we are intending the meaning of 2a or 2b. And when we do, we ask Hamlet's question: 2b or not 2b.

This (2b) in turn has two meanings. It can mean (2b1) this "eternal life," or supernatural life, as it *begins in this life* by faith and baptism (there are many words for this: being *born again*, *supernatural life*, *regeneration*, *salvation, sanctifying grace, sanctification, justification,* and *glorification*). Different Christian traditions use different vocabularies and different distinctions, which often seem to contradict each other, especially if you look *at* them instead of looking *along* them. It can also mean (2b2), this eternal life *as it is perfected in the next life.* The questions this essay means to answer are about this future eternal life (2b2).

Hardly any question could be more important, for (as commonsensical old Aristotle says) the "final cause," that is, the end, good, purpose, and perfection of anything, is the single most important question about it. Our question is about our own *summum bonum,* "greatest good," or "meaning of life."

My answers will come from four sources. First of all, Scripture. Second, Scripture as interpreted by the two-thousand-year-old history of catholic ("universal") dogma, which is the other part of sacred tradition, indispensable for Protestants as well as for Catholics, particularly when the meanings of Scripture are open to importantly different interpretations. Third, Scripture as interpreted, in less confident form, by the wise yet merely human traditions of mainline theological opinions ("theologoumena"), especially when questions are unresolved by both Scripture and catholic dogma. Finally, I will add a very few of my own personal opinions. So the content of this essay is like a four-level pyramid. Or, to reverse the verticality of the image, I am a flea on the back of a dog on the back of a lion on the back of an elephant.

The four of us who were given these ten questions about heaven were selected to explore the likenesses and differences among different Christian communities, and mine is the only Roman Catholic response. However, I do not think there will be many sharp differences between my responses and those from traditional evangelical Protestants, except for the question about Purgatory and the intermediate state, since I take most of my answers from the central consensus of orthodox Christians for the last two thousand years. Most of my answers are not original but come from Augustine, Aquinas, orthodox mystics, saints, and C. S. Lewis.

(Some decades ago I was at a wonderfully irenic weeklong ecumenical conference sponsored by a now-defunct Eastern Orthodox college [Rose Hill] in Aiken, South Carolina. Papers were read and argued about by ten theologians, philosophers, and apologists from Catholic,

Orthodox, Anglican, evangelical, and mainline Protestant traditions. In our papers we were all repeatedly quoting Lewis. At the concluding meeting, Fr. Joseph Fessio, SJ, proposed that we issue a report saying that we had discovered great substantial agreement among all of us based on our common acceptance of the New Testament, the first six ecumenical councils, and the collected works of C. S. Lewis.)

My interest in this question, and I hope yours as well, is not only scholarly but personal; not merely to define and compare opinions but to try to see some truth, some reality. I will not make the mistake of the theologian who, upon dying and meeting God, was asked to choose between going to heaven and going to a theological lecture on heaven, and chose the lecture.

Here are my answers to the ten questions.

1. Where Is the Final Destiny of the Saved?

Life is a game, a bowl of cherries, a work of art, a war, a dance, a mystery, and many other things, but above all it is a story. That is why the Bible is essentially a story, interrupted and interpreted by theology, morality, spirituality, and liturgy. A story has five dimensions: characters, plot, setting, style, and theme. This first question asks about the setting of the postmortem part of our story. I will try to answer not only that question but also the other four: If our story culminates in heaven, what difference does that make to all five dimensions of the story? What does heaven say about our story?

It says that the characters (us) are heavenly characters, that is, that we are designed by heaven and for heaven. It says that the plot is a (heavenward) journey and that this earth is not our destination but our road. (The journey and the road are the single most common set of elements of all plots.) It says that the setting of our story in this life is only preliminary, like a womb, that little womb that we call the universe. It says that the style of the story, as of its telling, is a beautiful and intriguing mystery. And it says that the theme of the story is the theme summarized by ET in his most memorable and heartbreakingly beautiful word, "Home." We denizens of this third rock from the sun are all homeless aliens, refugees, strangers in a strange land, orphaned, bereaved, and exiled. Just like Christ. That is one of the reasons why we must love our fellow aliens: because we love our Lord, and he became a fellow alien. "This world is not my home, I'm just-a-passing through." If we have forgotten that today, we have forgotten an essential theme of our whole story.

Question 1 asks, "Where is the final destiny of the saved?" If the "where" of this question means merely whether our heaven will be on this planet or anywhere else in this universe, Scripture's answer (and reason's too) is clear: it is not on this planet, which is subject to entropy and death, or on any other planet in this entropic universe. There is no reason to believe that God will miraculously heal the senility of the sun or reverse the second law of thermodynamics. Scripture gives us a very different picture. It promises "a new heaven and a new earth" (Rev 21:1), which will be made (either out of the old one or created *ex nihilo* like the old one) by the One who said, "Behold, I make all things new" (v. 5).

Alternatives are all insufficiently open-minded and imaginative. The same failure of imagination that gave rise to the unduly this-worldly idea of a reincarnation into another body in another time but in this same old world is also the source of this-worldly ideas about heaven, such as the happy hunting grounds, harems with forty virgins, or chummy family reunions on the other side of the river. Like God himself, heaven's best definition is "more than that." Scripture describes it this way: "What no eye has seen, nor ear heard, nor the heart of man conceived, what God has prepared for those who love him" (1 Cor 2:9). No philosopher or theologian, no poet or mystic, no fantasist or moviemaker has even imagined it, nor can they. If you say it is this or that, you can only have said what it is not. Anything positive that we can say about heaven can only be an analogy, not what it is but what it is like. It is more like a garden than a desert, more like a city than a prison cell, more like a family than a fire pit.

2. What Will We *Be* There?

We won't be everything. Neither will we be nothing. We won't be God, angels, or apes with bigger brains. (I love the bumper sticker that has the popular picture of apes gradually evolving into men, and the caption, "My ancestors were humans; sorry to hear about yours.") We will be human, perfectly human. Nietzsche would hate it: he called even mankind on earth "human, all too human." No supermen there.

But "we shall all be changed" (1 Cor 15:51), not into something semi-human or superhuman or nonhuman but into something completely human. Something semi-human or nonhuman is what we all are too often now, alas! And something superhuman is what we all too often try to be.

That means we will have perfected human bodies, like Christ's resurrection body, as well as perfected human souls, like his soul. After all, Christ reveals to us not just who God is but also who we are. These are the two things we most need to know, for we and God are the only two beings we will never be able to escape from for one second, either in time or in eternity.

And body and soul will be not two things that often move in opposite directions but two dimensions of one thing, in perfect union. They will be like the meaning and the words of a perfect poem, not like a ghost and a haunted house, or like a captain and a ship, or even like an interspecies marriage, as Mr. Spock on *Star Trek*, half Vulcan and half earthling.

The glorified body will be totally obedient to the glorified soul, because that soul will be perfectly obedient to God. Therefore, it will be entrusted with powers that we can now only dimly dream of and that would be far more dangerous for us now than nuclear powers.

We will have "spiritual bodies" in the double sense that they will be perfectly obedient to the Holy Spirit and to our own spirit (1 Cor 15:44). No conflict will be possible. That is why there will be no death, disease, pain, or frustration. One of the meanings of *sin* is "separation" (Sünde in German). Once the initial separation of sin between our souls and God is wholly overcome, there will be no cause for any of the other separations that derived from it: between soul and body (disease and death), between reason and passions (un-wisdom and un-freedom), or even between body and world (pain and harm).

We can know what we will *not* have in heaven (death, disease, pain, concupiscence, and sin) because we already know what these things are and that they are not good for us. But we cannot know what we *will* have in detail. We have only analogies of proportion: the relationship between what we will be then and what we are now is like the relationship between a mystic and a blind man, between a clean man and a leper, between a sage and a fool, and above all between a saint and a sinner. What we can know is the direction, so to speak, of the changes: we will be more like Christ in every way.

This change will be a greater work of God than the creation of the entire universe. Unlike us sinners, the nothingness out of which God created the universe did not protest and run away from his word when he commanded, "Let there be light."

3. What Will We *Do* There?

This question reminds me of a crisis of faith I had as a teenager. I thought that in heaven I would be eternally chained to a pew in an unending church service, with a very good, and therefore very boring, preacher. I was saved by Revelation 21:22. There will be no temple there because the God who is symbolized and suggested by sacred things, places, and times (like church services) will be there—and he can't possibly be boring! The thing signified is more, not less, than all the signs. Like the champagne glass at a Jewish wedding, the whole earth, even its holy things, will be shattered because its function will be achieved, and it cannot contain the new wine. This whole world is a placenta.

The question about what we will do in heaven probably means whether we will do "secular" things like gardening, science, poetry, and surfing there, as well as "sacred" things like worshiping God. My answer is yes, but I quarrel with the "as well as." The question is like whether I live in Boston "as well as" in the capital of Massachusetts, or whether four is twice two or half of eight. The two will be totally one, not distinct. The separation between "secular" and "sacred" will end. For instance, I think there will be surfing in heaven, and I will be like Laird Hamilton, and my body will be my longboard, and I will soul surf as well as bodysurf on a forty-foot wave, *which will also be the will of God*. The question with the "as well as" in it is like the question, "When you make love with your spouse, is it your body as well as your soul that is doing it?" Or "When you sing a hymn, are you singing as well as praying?"

Everything human will be there, perfected and glorified. Therefore, this will also apply to our sexuality, which is certainly a very important dimension of our being. We will not be castrated. Sexual identity and beauty will be perfected, glorified, and rightly gloried in. Women will be more womanly, and men more manly. But biological reproduction will no longer be needed, and therefore "they neither marry nor are given in marriage" (Matt 22:30). To ask whether our resurrected bodies will have physical sexual intercourse in heaven is probably like a five-year-old boy asking his father, during a talk about sex, whether he can play video games while he's "doing it." He will not understand his father's laughing answer, "Yes, but I guarantee you won't want to."

I think the best answer to the question "What will we do in heaven?" is that we will do perfectly and joyfully the six things that we were put on earth to do, things that we did here only very imperfectly and incompletely and therefore did with a mixture of joy and pain. There are six things because there are two distinctively human powers that come from being made in the image of God and that raise us above all other animals: to know and to love. And there are only three objects that are knowable and lovable for their own sakes: ourselves, each other, and God. Therefore, the six things we will do in heaven are know and love God, know and love our neighbors, and know and love ourselves.

In his devotional classic *On Loving God*, St. Bernard of Clairvaux says that the progress of love begins with loving ourselves for our own sakes. Then we learn to love God for our own sakes (after all, he is our joy and salvation). We next grow to love God for his own sake (for he is infinitely lovable for his own sake, and self-forgetful love is higher than self-conscious love). Finally, we realize that we must even love ourselves, not for our own benefit but for God's sake. Add the love of neighbor to the mix and you have the agenda of heaven. The journey begins here on earth. If it does not begin here, it cannot flourish there. If the seed is not planted in earthly pots, it cannot flower in heavenly fields.

The three traditional ideas of Purgatory (more on that later), the Communion of Saints, and the Beatific Vision correspond to these three objects of love and knowledge, namely, ourselves, our neighbors, and God (all three activities deserve capital letters, in defense of hierarchy and in defiance of contemporary conventions of punctuation that insist on egalitarian leveling. Decapitalization is a kind of decapitation). In Purgatory we will come to know ourselves completely in all our sinful ugliness and, after all our sinful desires are removed, to know ourselves in all our supernatural beauty and to love ourselves accordingly, as God loves us. In the Communion of Saints, with Purgatorially purified eyes and hearts we will come to know and love more and more people more and more completely. And in the Beatific Vision, we ("we" not just individually but also communally, in the Communion of Saints) will come to know and love the infinite God in a finite but ever-ascending and never-ending spiral of newness and wonder, ever progressing, never finishing, and always rejoicing.

The Communion of Saints includes the idea that there is and ought to be communication and love and aid, not just among the living, or among the dead, but also between the living and the dead. This feels so intuitively right. C. S. Lewis writes: "Of course I pray for the dead. The action is so spontaneous, so all but inevitable, that only the most compulsive theological case against it would deter me."[2]

The Communion of Saints has three dimensions: earthly-horizontal, heavenly-horizontal, and vertical between earth and heaven. The heavenly one remains forever. Lewis explains, "For doubtless the continually successful, yet never complete, attempt by each soul to communicate its unique vision (of God) to all others, and that by means whereof earthly art and philosophy are but clumsy imitations, is also among the ends for which the individual was created."[3]

4. What Will We See of God?

We will see aspects, dimensions, and perspectives of God. We will not see parts, because God has no parts. We will see the Infinite One, but in finite ways. C. S. Lewis says, "Each soul will forever know and praise some one aspect of the divine beauty better than any other can. Why else were we created but that God, loving each infinitely, can love each differently?" So in heaven we will forever tell each other of that unique aspect of God that we were created to appreciate, "and that by means whereof earthly art and philosophy are but clumsy imitations."[4]

How will we see God? Since our natural powers are radically inadequate (and if you don't know that, you don't know God!), it will be by a supernatural power that we do not now have, which St. Thomas calls "the light of glory." We will receive this from God as we now receive the gift of faith from him when we are ready and freely consent. "For now we see in a mirror dimly, but then face to face. Now I know in part; then I shall understand fully, even as I have been fully understood" (1 Cor 13:12).

---

2. C. S. Lewis, *Letters to Malcolm: Chiefly on Prayer* (London: Collins, 1969), ch. 20, para. 3.

3. C. S. Lewis, *The Problem of Pain*, in *The Complete C. S. Lewis Signature Classics* (San Francisco: HarperOne, 2002), 642.

4. Lewis, *Problem of Pain*, as quoted in Peter Kreeft, *Practical Theology: Spiritual Direction from Saint Thomas Aquinas* (San Francisco: Ignatius, 2014), 343.

We will know all three divine persons, of course; and we will know them together and not separately because they exist and act always together and not separately. The divine nature, essence, substance, and being is one, not three, even though the persons are three. It is only in our present fallen consciousness that we cannot help thinking of the one God as either a single person or as triplets with different personalities. Perhaps in heaven, as we teach Jews and Muslims about the Trinity, they will remind us about the unity. Perhaps that can begin even here.

Of course, in order for us to know God, mediation will be necessary. If you don't know that, you don't know the transcendence of God. Christ will be our mediator then as he is now, because only Christ became man, and he remains man in heaven (the ascension was not the undoing of the incarnation). The mediator must be God himself, because only the infinite God can bridge the infinite gap between creator and creature. Christ will do that for us in a glorious way in heaven because he did that for us in a bloody and terrible way on earth. Only he is both the infinite creator, independent of all things, and a finite creature, dependent on one of his creatures (his mother) for his temporal beginning. He is a bit like a moviemaker who puts himself into his own movie as one of the characters (as both Alfred Hitchcock and M. Night Shyamalan have done). That single person is simultaneously the transcendent creator of the whole movie and one of its immanent creatures and characters.

5. What of the Intermediate State?

Perhaps there is none. That is, perhaps there is no such thing as a stretch of temporal extension between this life and the next. Perhaps the transition from death to "deep heaven" is instantaneous. As soon as we are "away from the body" we are "at home with the Lord" (2 Cor 5:8). But "at home with the Lord" may involve within itself at least three temporal changes. First, there is (at least from our temporal perspective here) a gap between the particular judgment of the individual at death and the general judgment at the end of the world. Second, there is a gap between being "unclothed" of our old body and "clothed" with our new, resurrection body (2 Cor 5:4). Third, even though God's work of our justification is complete and "finished" on the cross (John 19:30), the work of our sanctification is not yet finished, so that between death and "deep heaven" most of us need further cleansing, which Catholics call Purgatory. If you don't like the term, drop it; a sanctification by any other name would smell as sweet. You can call the place where you wash your hands before dinner the *bathroom*, the *lav*, or the *loo*, or not name it at all. But all at the banquet have completely clean hands.

The Catholic dogma of Purgatory does not insist on a literal reading of its time language. The language of "three hundred days in Purgatory" or "ten years in Purgatory" cannot possibly mean time measured by earthly clocks, since Purgatory is no part of this universe. The time must be *kairos*, not *kronos*—spiritual time, not physical time. The numbers actually came from the penances imposed in the early church for serious and public sins, and as applied to Purgatory they were used as a relative and analogical comparison: the more sinful you are, the more Purgatory you need, just as the dirtier you are, the more you need to wash. How much spiritual time one's Purgatory takes, if any, is quite a different question, and the answer is uncertain.

That there must be something like Purgatory should be clear to Protestants, as it was to C. S. Lewis, from three clear teachings of Scripture:

1. that our old, sinful nature and habits remain with us, like a dead but bothersome albatross around our necks, till the end ("If we say we have no sin, we deceive ourselves and the truth is not in us," 1 John 1:8);
2. that "nothing unclean shall enter" heaven (Rev 21:27);
3. that the difference between sin and holiness, the unclean and the clean, light and darkness, is enormous.

If you think it takes anything less than Purgatory, anything easier, to make a man into a saint, then either you do not know what a man is or do not know what a saint is. You must have a horribly shallow view either of human sinfulness, or of heavenly holiness, or of the difference between the two if you think that we sinners, as we are when we die, without any further Purgatorial cleansing or sanctification, can just casually sashay into heaven and rub elbows with God.

Perhaps some of us "cheap-grace Christians" need to listen to pious

Muslims about God's unutterably transcendent holiness almost as much as they need to listen to us (and to their own Sufis) about his unutterable love and amazing desire for intimacy with us.

The Protestant C. S. Lewis wrote, after his wife's death, "How do I know that all her anguish is past? I never believed before—I thought it immensely improbable—that the faithfulest soul could leap straight into perfection and peace the moment death has rattled in the throat. It would be wishful thinking with a vengeance to take up that belief now. H. was a splendid thing: a soul straight, bright, and tempered like a sword. But not a perfected saint."[5]

Lewis says, "Our souls *demand* Purgatory, don't they? Would it not break the heart if God said to us, 'It is true, my son, that your breath smells and your rags drip with mud and slime, but we are charitable here and no one will upbraid you with these things, nor draw away from you. Enter into the joy.' Should we not reply, 'With submission, sir, and if there is no objection, I'd rather be cleansed first.' 'It may hurt, you know'—'Even so, sir.'"[6]

Scripture itself speaks of purifying gold by fire (1 Cor 3:12–13). St. Catherine of Genoa, who was given mystic visions of Purgatory, explains this analogy: "Look at gold: the more you melt it, the better it becomes; you could melt it until you had destroyed in it every imperfection. . . . When the soul has been purified . . . it can suffer no more, for nothing is left in it to be burnt away. Were it held in the fire when it has thus been cleansed, it would feel no pain. Rather the fire of divine love would be to it like eternal life and in no way contrary to it."[7]

What will we experience in Purgatory? St. Catherine says that its joys as well as its pains are far greater than anything in this life, for "the love for God, which fills the soul to overflowing, as I see it, gives it a happiness beyond what can be told. And yet this happiness takes not one pang from the pain of the souls in Purgatory. Rather, the love of these souls, finding itself hindered (from full union with God), causes their pain; and the more perfect the love of which God has made them

---

5. C. S. Lewis, *A Grief Observed* (San Francisco: HarperSanFrancisco, 1961), 59.

6. Lewis, *Letters to Malcolm*, 108–9.

7. Catherine of Genoa, "Treatise on Purgatory," in *Late Medieval Mysticism*, ed. Ray C. Petry, Library of Christian Classics (Philadelphia: Westminster, 1957), 407.

capable, the greater is their pain. So the souls in Purgatory enjoy the greatest happiness and endure the greatest pain."[8]

In light of those formidable horizons, it is shameful how Catholics so blithely and cavalierly run through their fleeting five-word mention of "the holy souls in Purgatory" in their Morning Offering, ignoring the enormity of their pain and their passion. Protestants ignore its very existence, but they at least have an excuse: they were told it is a myth.

The title of C. S. Lewis's greatest book, *Till We Have Faces*, is the essential reason for Purgatory, for how can we meet God face-to-face till we have faces? Lewis meant this "myth retold" for all of us, for the name of its heroine "Psyche" means simply "soul."

Ultimately the very question of pleasure and pain drops away, as St. Catherine explains, "For every glimpse that can be had of God exceeds any pain or joy a man can feel."[9] Lewis says the same thing: "As we draw nearer to it (the Beatific Vision, the Great Dance) . . . pain and pleasure sink almost out of sight."[10]

Purgatory is not a third final destination, an alternative to heaven or hell; it is the beginning of heaven. It is heaven's bathroom and hot shower before the banquet room and the dining room and the bedroom. (Yes, the bedroom. That's from Scripture too—"Your Maker is your husband" [Isa 54:5]—as well as from the mystics).

The strongest argument for Purgatory is Christ's own demand: "You, therefore, must be perfect, as your heavenly Father is perfect" (Matt 5:48). This is no exaggeration. Christ never exaggerated. As George MacDonald taught, our heavenly Father is "easy to please but hard to satisfy."[11] We need Purgatory because God is not a wading pool but an ocean, not a warm fuzzy but "a consuming fire" (Heb 12:29).

So now which of you already-perfected saints would like to volunteer to throw the first stone at this doctrine?

It is the formidable biblical doctrine of heaven that demands this formidable doctrine of Purgatory. Heaven is higher than Everest, and

---

8. Catherine of Genoa, "Treatise on Purgatory," 408.
9. Catherine of Genoa, *Fire of Love!: Understanding Purgatory* (Manchester, NH: Sophia Institute, 1996), 84.
10. Lewis, *Problem of Pain*, 141.
11. C. S. Lewis, ed., *George MacDonald: An Anthology of 365 Readings* (New York: HarperCollins, 2001), 30.

our flea-like leaps upward a few inches are, in relation to its full reality, like a toddler's first two staggering steps in relation to her becoming a prima ballerina.

Anything less formidable than that is not even Protestantism but paganism, or secular humanism, or pop psychology.

6. How Does This View of the End Relate to the Present Life?

In the same way as this view of life in the world relates to this view of life in the womb. As marriage relates to courtship. As eating relates to cooking. As the destination relates to the journey. As victory relates to war. As home relates to homecoming. Life in heaven is not an alternative to life on earth, or an escape from life on earth, or a compensation for life on earth, or a payment for performance in life on earth, or even a new and improved version of our life on earth (although that comes the closest to it). It is the transformed fullness of our life on earth, of the life we now have, if we are Christians. It is the thing we were made for, the totally human thing.

Therefore, there is nothing more relevant to this world and this life than heaven. Heaven is exactly the opposite of "pie in the sky by and by." It is the point of the story we are writing, the fullness of the picture we are drawing. We are like *Harold and the Purple Crayon*.[12] It is "home" for the exiled ET. That's why, when we watch that movie and "turn on our heartlight," we identify with the homeless extraterrestrial ET more than with the at-home earth child Elliot.

In heaven nothing earthly will be lost, nothing good will be simply subtracted and replaced. Yet nothing will be unchanged either. When "we shall be changed" (1 Cor 15:52), everything that is ours will be changed too. It will all be transformed and perfected. Just as when bad vision is healed in two little eyes, every single thing in the world suddenly looks different. "Transformed and perfected"—that is the universal principle that answers all questions (though of course not in any concrete detail) about whether this or that earthly thing will be in heaven. There will be transformed and perfected baseball, brown bears, butterflies, and whatever we love rightly. St. Bridget says that

---

12. Crockett Johnson, *Harold and the Purple Crayon* (New York: Harper & Row, 1955). In this children's book, Harold is a four-year-old boy who creates his own adventure with his imagination and his crayon.

heaven will contain a great lake of beer in which we swim. (I suspect that everybody is at least partly Irish. Evidence that that's part of the image of God is the fact that when we talk to God rather than just about him, we always use his Irish name, "O'God"). The only earthly thing that certainly and absolutely and unqualifiedly won't be in heaven is sin.

All the aspects of a complete human life, especially the ones that were tragically lost in this world to some of us, will be found in heaven. Tom Howard puts this eloquently in *Christ the Tiger*:

> Behold I make all things new. Behold I do what cannot be done. I restore the years that the locusts and worms have eaten. I restore the years which you have drooped away upon your crutches and in your wheelchair. I restore the symphonies and operas which your deaf ears have never heard, and the snowy massif your blind eyes have never seen, and the freedom lost to you through plunder, and the identity lost to you because of calumny and the failure of justice; and I restore the good which your own foolish mistakes have cheated you of. And I bring you to the love of which all other loves speak, the Love which is joy and beauty, and which you have sought in a thousand streets and for which you have wept and clawed your pillow.[13]

When in heaven grieving parents meet their children who died at a tragically young age on earth, I think it is very likely that God will arrange for the parents not only to love them as children but also to love them into human maturity and adulthood through all the stages of growth. For just as nothing more effectively matures children than parents, so nothing more effectively matures parents than children. This would fulfill the straightening out and perfecting of the lives of both the children and the parents. For surely the parent-child relationship is just as beautifully codependent as the husband-wife relationship.

7. Will We Possess Special Powers?

Of course we will. Just as physical adults possess special powers that physical babies lack, so heaven's spiritual adults will possess special

---

13. Thomas Howard, *Christ the Tiger* (San Francisco: Ignatius, 1990), 147.

powers that we spiritual babies lack. St. Thomas, summarizing the traditional opinion, lists five of these powers (there are almost certainly many more):[14]

1. *Impassibility* means that no external violence will touch us to crush, kill, or harm us. Elephant guns can kill elephants, and so can a tiny virus, but neither can kill a spiritual body. Garlic may slay vampires, and silver bullets may stop werewolves, but neither can kill a spirit. One of the things meant by "a spiritual body" is clearly immortality. What is true even now of the soul will also be true of the body then, because body and soul will be one, not two.

   This is not hard to see. If an axe could separate the head from the torso of the resurrection body, it would be a pretty poor improvement on the present body. And it would not be a "spiritual body." Of course we will be indestructible. Both reason and faith assure us of that. Reason argues that if we will not be indestructible, then we will be destructible, and therefore eventually destroyed. For if it is not possible that a certain potentiality will ever be actualized, then it is not a potentiality at all. Likewise, faith tells us that "Christ being raised from the dead will never die again" (Rom 6:9) and that "we shall be like him" (1 John 3:2). Therefore, we also, having risen from the dead, will die no more. (Notice, by the way, that faith, like reason, has its syllogisms: major premises, minor premises, and conclusions!)

2. *Levity* is also mentioned in Scripture: we shall be "like sparks among the reeds" (Wis 3:7 Douay-Rheims). This is best understood not with the intellect but with the eyes. You have to actually see this, or at least imagine this movement of sparks among reeds, not just think about it, in order to intuitively understand the point of the analogy. At least part of the message here is that we will fly, like the angels. Chesterton tells us why: "Angels can fly because they can take themselves lightly."[15] There is a deliberate double meaning here: humility and humor. The two are necessarily connected, as are their respective lacks. The point also implies that

---

14. St. Thomas Aquinas, *Summa Theologiae*, Supplement, Questions 82–85.
15. G. K. Chesterton, *Orthodoxy* (John Lane Company, 1908; repr., San Francisco: Ignatius, 1995), 127.

humor will exist, and be perfected, in heaven. The question "Is heaven humorous or serious?" is too humorous to be serious. As C. S. Lewis says, "Joy is the serious business of heaven."[16]

3. *Agility* will enable us to walk through walls, bilocate, and be instantly at another place, just as Christ and the angels can do, because as St. Thomas explains, "The human body and all [the powers] that it contains will be perfectly subject to the rational soul, even as the soul will be perfectly subject to God."[17] We "shall run to and fro like sparks among the reeds," like electrons changing orbits in quantum theory. As St. Thomas says, "A glorified body passes from one place to another without passing through the interval."[18]

4. *Clarity* means that we will be "lightsome"—either made of light or at least full of light and generating light like Christ in the transfiguration. This "will result from the overflow of the soul's glory into the body," says St. Thomas.[19] Like Christ, we shall become "children of light" (Eph 5:8) in a more than symbolic sense. Light is the first material thing God created, and it has always been the favorite material image for the mystics. As gravity is love in material form, light is truth in material form. As love is spiritual gravity, truth is spiritual light.

5. *Subtlety* means that we will be like angels in that no material thing will block us and be impenetrable to us. The fall will be reversed. Before we sinned, our bodies were in our souls; after we fell into sin, our souls fell into our bodies. To use another analogy for the same point, when our souls rebelled against God, our bodies rebelled against our souls and became mortal. Likewise, the material world also rebelled against our souls in becoming painful and full of obstacles: "the garden" became "thorns and thistles" to Adam's work, and childbirth became painful to Eve's (Gen 3:16–19). When our souls become perfectly subject to God,

---

16. Lewis, *Letters to Malcolm*, 93.
17. Peter Kreeft, *Practical Theology: Spiritual Direction from Saint Thomas Aquinas* (San Francisco: Ignatius, 2014), 331, citing Supplement, Question 82.1 of *Summa Theologiae* (New York: Benziger, 1947).
18. Kreeft, *Practical Theology*, 331 (citing Supplement, Question 84.3).
19. Aquinas, *Summa Theologiae*, Supplement 85.2.

172 •   FOUR VIEWS ON HEAVEN

our bodies will be perfectly subject to our souls, and the matter of the "new earth" will be perfectly subject to our bodies (this is their "subtlety").

8. Will We Remember Tragic Events of This Life? And Will We Remember and Regret the Absence of the Loved Ones Who Are Not with Us in Heaven because They Are in Hell?

These are two quite different questions. Let's answer the last and hardest one first.

The question is a trilemma. If we will not regret their absence because we will not remember them, then our happiness would depend on our ignorance of the truth that they are in hell. If we will remember them but not regret their absence, then our happiness would depend on our lovelessness. But truth and love are the two divine and heavenly absolutes. And if we will remember them and regret their absence, then a third heavenly absolute would be sacrificed, namely, joy.

C. S. Lewis answers this trilemma—a truly difficult and worrisome one—in *The Great Divorce*, first by proving that the answer must be that we will have no loss of joy or love or truth. However God does that, we will do it too. The facts are certain and clear, even though the explanation of *how* that can work is not. For heaven cannot meet "the demand of the loveless and the self-imprisoned (in hell) that they should be allowed to blackmail the universe; that till they consent to be happy (on their own terms) no one else shall taste joy: that theirs should be the final power; that hell should be able to *veto* heaven. . . . Either the day must come when joy prevails and all the makers of misery are no longer allowed to infect it, or else forever and ever the makers of misery can destroy in others the happiness they reject for themselves."[20]

Lewis then explains how this can happen, applying St. Thomas's distinction between activity and passivity, or act and potency, to the affection of pity or compassion:

The action of Pity will live forever, but the passion of Pity will not. The passion of Pity, the Pity we merely suffer, the ache that draws men to concede what should not be conceded and to

---

20. C. S. Lewis, *The Great Divorce* (San Francisco: HarperSanFrancisco, 2001), 135–36.

flatter when they should speak truth, the Pity that has cheated many a woman out of her virginity and many a statesman out of his honesty—that will die. It was used as a weapon by bad men against good ones: their weapon will be broken.

[But the action of Pity is] a weapon on the other side. It leaps quicker than light from the highest place to the lowest to bring healing and joy. . . . Every disease that submits to a cure shall be cured, but we will not call blue yellow to please those who insist on still having jaundice.[21]

Even in this life we can distinguish these two aspects of pity or compassion, even though they are always mingled together. When someone we love does something self-destructive, we say, "How could you do that to yourself?" This is active compassion, pure and unselfish charity. But there is always also an undertone of, "How could you do that to me?" And that is passive and self-centered pity. We cannot and should not try to separate these two aspects in this life, but God will separate them in the next. The activity of love, charity, pity, and compassion will persist, but the passivity or passion will not.

As to the other question: We *will* remember the tragic events in our life on earth (heaven is not a happy dementia!), but here again action will trump passion. We will remember them not simply passively, like photographs, our minds simply conforming to the events and adding nothing more. Rather, we will remember them actively and creatively, like an artist making a painting from a photograph or like an author writing a beautiful commentary on his own less-than-beautiful book. Even poor books can have great commentaries. We will see these tragic events as God sees them, not as we saw them at the time. This correction and reinterpretation will bring out their deeper meaning. We will see how even these evils were worked out for good by God's perfect providence (Rom 8:28). We can *believe* that now (and that is an action, not a passion, for it is a free choice), but we will *see* it and *rejoice* in it then, as God does, because we will see our imperfect stories as part of his perfect story. We will see history as His-story.

Thus, in a sense we will make causality work backward in time: our

---

21. Lewis, *Great Divorce*, 136–37.

corrected heavenly vision will act on these past earthly events to change their significance, but not their facticity. It will subtract nothing, but it will add the divine interpretation to them. The heavenly commentary we will write on our earthly lives will add no *data* but will add *light* to the dark data of our lives on earth. We will see even these dark parts in the light of God's perfect plan.

I think this must apply not only to tragedies or physical evils suffered but even to sins or spiritual evils done. St. Peter will probably even glory in confessing his greatest sin, his threefold denial of Christ, because it furnished the material and the occasion for his repentance and for God's amazing grace of forgiveness and because God used this evil for the great good of the edification of millions of Christians. "Where sin increased, grace abounded all the more" (Rom 5:20). Evil cannot become good, but God can work even evils together for good (Rom 8:28), as he did two thousand years ago on Calvary. His revealed will and law is like the published score of a symphony, which we members of the orchestra badly misplay; but his secret will and grace is like a greater score, in which he uses our clunkers for his higher harmonies. We do not usually see this, but we can believe it. Why can we believe it? Simply because he has told us. There are no exceptions to this: "Behold, I make all things new" (Rev 21:5).

This is true even concerning the fall—the primal sin and the source of all the evils in the world. Augustine says of it, "O felicitous fault [*felix culpa*] that brought about so great a redemption!" Furthermore, we remember the greatest sin ever committed on a holy day that we call "Good Friday."

Everything, not only tragedies (physical evils) but even sins (moral evils), can be elements in heaven's glory and joy. But the tragedies enter only through the gate of divine providence and the sins only through the gate of human repentance. Not all things are good, but all things work together for good. Not all things are virtuous, but all things, even sin, can be occasions for virtue. St. Thomas says that this is the reason why God deliberately withholds the grace to cure some of our most obvious and embarrassing sins. God foresees that if he gave such grace, the result would be a worse sin (pride), while if he does not, the result will be a great good (humility, self-knowledge, and repentance). God is a utilitarian. We dare not be because we are not God.

Scripture tells us that in heaven God "will *wipe away* every tear from their eyes" (Rev 21:4). It does not tell us that there will *be* no tears. If there were no tears, how could we understand Shakespeare, Dostoyevsky, or Tolkien? If tears were not there to be wiped away, what would happen to that unique joy that Tolkien calls the "eucatastrophe" ("the sudden happy turn in a story which pierces you with a joy that brings tears, produced by a sudden glimpse of Truth")?[22] If heaven does not simply remove or destroy anything that is part of our fulfillment and flourishing and identity but rather transforms it, then this must also be somehow true of tears and tragedy.

9. How Will We Relate to Our Spouses and Other Family Members?

We will certainly relate to them with recognition, understanding, and love, for we will not be greater fools then than we are now. Everything positive in these relationships, including the irreplaceable uniqueness of them, will remain. But the negative factor, the exclusiveness of some of these relationships (most notably, marriage), though necessary on earth, will no longer be needed in heaven. There may well be a kind of virtuous promiscuity of the spirit that will enable us, without lust or betrayal, to enter the spirit of anyone and everyone in pure and perfect personal and spiritual intimacy—an intimacy of which we can taste only the remotest appetizers in our friendships in this life.

And since we are neither pure spirits nor ghosts inhabiting machines, either in this world or in the next, and since gender is an important aspect of our spiritual as well as physical identity—in fact something that colors even the most spiritual parts—we therefore will not lose our gender in heaven. We will not be castrated but perfected, not diminished but enhanced, in everything that is good (but not, of course, in anything that is not good, such as gender confusion). And gender is a great good, since God not only invented but declared it to be an essential part of the very image of God. Genesis 1:26–27 is the first mention in the Bible of the image of God, and one of the very first things it says about that image is that it is "male and female." Our gender will not be for reproduction but for glory and beauty. It will be then as it is now, a dimension

---

22. Tolkien Gateway contributors, "Letter 89," Tolkien Gateway, http://tolkiengateway.net/w/index.php?title=Letter_89&oldid=268504.

of our total identity, and not just in a spatially isolated physical organ. As to the details, the only thing we know is that we cannot know.

What about clothing? Those who have glimpses of the blessed in heaven (saints, mystics, and out-of-body experiencers, whose numbers have radically increased because of modern CPR), when asked whether the people they saw in heaven were naked or clothed, always say the same thing: they are clothed, but the clothes there do not hide but reveal their bodies' beauty, as if they grew out of their bodies as flowers grow from their stalks.

This is a good illustration of how heaven's answers always transcend our categories and our either-or questions. The same is true of age: the blessed seem, to us who see them, to be young and old at the same time. (It is especially child visionaries who say this.)

I strongly suspect that this kind of category transcendence will also be the pattern of heaven's answer to the question of comparative religions. Will Hindus and Muslims either not get to heaven, or at least attain an inferior position there because they were not Christians (the "exclusivist" or "conservative" option), or will there be total equality among religions (the "inclusivist" or "liberal" option)? Somehow when we give God a multiple-choice question, the answer is always "none of the above." Because "the above" options are really from below.

10. Will We Be Able to Sin in Our Final Condition? If Not, in What Sense Do We Possess Free Will?

The factual answer is clear: we will not sin (because that would infect heaven with actual evil), nor even, in a practical sense, will we be able to sin (because that would infect heaven with at least the real possibility of evil). It is certain, not merely probable, that no one will ever sin in heaven.

Yet it is also certain that we will not become robots and lose our free will (because free will is a good thing), but we will have it perfected. But how? That is not as clear.

Augustine helps answer the question by distinguishing three conditions of our free will:[23]

---

23. Augustine, *Admonition and Grace* 33.

1. In the garden of Eden we were able not to sin (*posse non peccare*) and also able to sin (*posse peccare*).
2. In our present fallen condition, we are not able not to sin (*non posse non peccare*) unless God supernaturally intervenes. But this inability not to sin refers to our life as a whole; for every individual moral choice, we are able both not to sin and to sin. If this were not so, we would not have free will and thus not be morally responsible. However, in our present fallen condition, our depraved appetites, weak will, and darkened mind create concupiscence, a positive force toward evil that makes sin very easy and virtue very hard, so much so that in our life as a whole we are not able not to sin.
3. In heaven we will be not just able not to sin (*posse non peccare*). We will be confirmed in righteousness, so we will also be not able to sin (*non posse peccare*). This is not because we will lose our freedom but because God will have perfected it. True freedom, or liberty (*libertas*), is freedom from all that impedes our perfection, fulfillment, and joy; and that impediment is, above all, sin. The lower freedom, *liberum arbitrium*, or free choice, is our means to the end of this higher freedom. (Unlike Calvin and Luther on the one hand and Pelagius and Arminius on the other, Augustine was strong on both predestination and free will.)

We will not be able to sin in heaven because we will see God face-to-face, and this vision of divine beauty will be so attractive and so full of light as to make it impossible for us to be tempted. Darkness and deception are necessary for the devil to do his work. In order to be tempted by evil, we must see it as somehow desirable, and this is ignorance, so that ignorance is a necessary, partial cause or condition for sin. This ignorance will be removed in heaven. Plato was wrong in thinking that the lack of this vision of the Absolute Good (which is what he meant by ignorance) was the sufficient and only cause of our evil, but he was right to believe that was a necessary part of it.

We will have the power to choose evil (free choice) but not the *motive*—as a math whiz has the power but not the motive to write "twenty-two" as the answer to the question, "How much is two plus two?" Or, better, it is as a man whose blindness has been healed. He has the power not to see the beautiful colors and shapes of the world around him—he could deliberately gouge his eyes out, like Oedipus, if he wanted to. But he will never want to. And once we see God, we will never not want to love and obey him.

All will get what they want, in the end. That is why Christ's very first words in John's Gospel were, "What do you seek?" (John 1:38). For "he who seeks finds" (Matt 7:8). The point of life is to purify our seeking.

This whole essay has been a mental seeking. Its findings have been mixed because its motives have been mixed: partly holy (God's will), partly innocent (truth for its own sake), partly low (idle, selfish, animal curiosity), and partly dark (look how wise I am!). Mea culpa.

RESPONSE TO PETER KREEFT

JOHN S. FEINBERG

Early in his essay Professor Kreeft states that he believes his answers to most of the questions we were given will coincide with the answers of the three of us who are Protestants. However, his views on purgatory and the intermediate state are decidedly different from the rest of us. In what follows, I want to focus on two major issues. The first is the issue of authority, and the second has to do with purgatory.

As to authority, the key issue is what he uses as the sources of his theologizing on our topic, and how he ranks each in importance. Fairly early in his essay, Professor Kreeft clearly articulates the sources of his theologizing on heaven and related themes. He writes:

> My answers will come from four sources. First of all, Scripture. Second, Scripture as interpreted by the two-thousand-year-old history of catholic ("universal") dogma, which is the other part of sacred tradition, indispensable for Protestants as well as for Catholics, particularly when the meanings of Scripture are open to importantly different interpretations. Third, Scripture as interpreted, in less confident form, by the wise yet merely human traditions of mainline theological opinions ("theologoumena"), especially when questions are unresolved by both Scripture and catholic dogma. Finally, I will add a very few of my own personal opinions. . . .
>
> The four of us who were given these ten questions about heaven were selected to explore the likenesses and differences among different Christian communities, and mine is the only Roman Catholic response. However, I do not think there will be many sharp differences between my responses and those from

traditional evangelical Protestants, except for the question about Purgatory and the intermediate state, since I take most of my answers from the central consensus of orthodox Christians for the last two thousand years. Most of my answers are not original but come from Augustine, Aquinas, orthodox mystics, saints, and C. S. Lewis (p. 157).

I have quoted Professor Kreeft at length because what he says and where he places the emphases are key to his essay. The first paragraph cited above might seem quite consistent with the strategy of Protestant, evangelical theologians. As for Kreeft's four sources, no evangelical should have a problem with the first. As to the third, I suspect that it means what Protestant theologians refer to as historical theology or the history of doctrine; it is also relevant to Protestant theologizing. The second could be seen as relevant to historical theology, though Protestants would not likely give it an elevated status over many of the thinkers included in his third source. And, of course, there should be little objection to the fourth, as it is impossible to exclude completely one's worldview, prior training, etc. as one theologizes. A theology may be faithful to Scripture, but it will still bear the marks of being composed by a human writer with his or her particular style of writing, worldview, and specific theological beliefs.

For someone to say, "We only use Scripture as our source of theology," is naive, if he thinks that use of Scripture alone results in a pristine, thoroughly precise statement of theology that all Christians hold.[1] Of course, as a Protestant, I am dubious about elevating items in (2) beyond the importance of things in (3). I surely would not refer to items in (2) as the other part of sacred tradition (with Scripture as the first part of sacred tradition).

Many readers may think what I am saying is roughly equivalent to Kreeft's claims about sources and their importance in his theologizing.

---

1. Here I am not suggesting that humans, using their own conceptual grid, must get it wrong when articulating any point of view. Elsewhere I have argued at length that it is possible to do theology that accurately reflects, for example, what Scripture teaches. My point is that one is wrong if he or she thinks any mere statement of a doctrine can escape entirely the mindset of the one making the statement. See my *Can You Believe It's True: Christian Apologetics in a Modern and Postmodern Era* (Wheaton, IL: Crossway, 2013), section 1.

But I give Scripture an even higher status than Kreeft appears to give it. For me, Scripture is the inspired, inerrant word of God. It is the final authority on every topic it covers. Thus, if anything in the other sources contradicts Scripture, it must be rejected in favor of scriptural teaching. But that said, readers may not see a lot of difference in Kreeft's methodology and mine.

This is a large part of why I included a quote of Kreeft's second paragraph. By his own admission, Kreeft says, "I take most of my answers from the central consensus of orthodox Christians for the last two thousand years. Most of my answers are not original but come from Augustine, Aquinas, orthodox mystics, saints, and C. S. Lewis" (157).

Here we must be fair to Kreeft. He is not eschewing using Scripture altogether in favor of these Christian luminaries through the centuries of church history. In fact, in his answers to the first five questions especially, there is an appeal to Scripture. Though I think at times he goes beyond what the Scriptures he cites demand, his answers are not devoid of scriptural backing. The problem, as I see it, is that when he discusses purgatory, there is very little, if any, scriptural support for his views. He cites passages that say God requires holiness (as God is holy), but those passages say nothing about purgatory or any kind of probation time after death in which to acquire that holiness.

In contrast, Scripture teaches that in this life on earth, we must first repent of our sins and accept Christ as Savior. Once that happens, the Holy Spirit works powerfully in our life to sanctify us (i.e., to help us resist temptation and put sin out of our life). In this life, sanctification will not be complete (see 1 John 1), but those genuinely saved do make progress in their growth in holiness. According to Scripture, sanctification of a believer comes, so to speak, in stages. During our current life on earth, both our soul and body grow closer to the Lord as we follow and obey him. At death our body goes to the grave, as it has not completely escaped the effects of sin, but our soul is immediately in God's presence (2 Cor 5:8—absent from body but present with Christ). There is no biblical evidence that a believer's soul can sin or that it needs more purification once the believer dies.

There is, however, one last step in the sanctification process, but it has nothing to do with time in purgatory. Rather, at the end of the current age, believers in Christ will be raised bodily. Their bodies will be rejoined to their immaterial parts (see 1 Cor 15; 1 Thess 4:13–18), and as Paul puts it, "We will all be changed" (1 Cor 15:51). Protestant theologians refer to the reunion of body and soul and the removal of sin and any of its effects on us as *glorification*. As John says, "We will be like Him [Jesus]" (1 John 3:2). Clearly John does not refer to Jesus during his earthly pilgrimage, nor is he suggesting that we shall become "mini-gods." Rather, he means that we will have a resurrection body and be fully glorified, even as Jesus was after his resurrection.

So, what is my concern here with Kreeft? It is that on key theological issues, his answers, by his own admission, come more from Aquinas, Augustine, and Lewis than from Scripture. Now I have great respect for these thinkers, but they cannot be allowed to trump what Scripture teaches. My complaint, then, is ultimately with the issue of authority. What, when you see a piece of Kreeft's theology (as we have it here), is the ultimate authority for Kreeft? Though he might protest that Scripture is his ultimate authority (even though I haven't seen that), I simply ask the reader to read his essay again. There is some Scripture, but far more seems to rest on the thinking of various historical figures and historical dogma (see his espousal of the two-thousand-year-dogma of the church). I have great appreciation for the great theologians of the church down through the centuries. They can be especially helpful in explaining doctrines that come from Scripture but have little explanation in Scripture. But for me, Scripture is both the starting point and the touchstone for biblical exegesis and theology. If a point of view is not taught or even generally supported by Scripture, then it must be rejected. Scripture is the supreme authority for doctrine for me, whether it be about heaven or any other topic. On that matter, Kreeft and I disagree, both in what we say about the sources of our theology and in what we use when doing theology (as evidenced in our essays in this volume).

In the space that remains, I want to address problems I have with the idea of purgatory. According to the notion of purgatory, it seems that regardless of what sort of life one has lived on earth, after death sins can be purified in purgatory. Depending on the sins you committed on earth and how far the sanctification process advanced, the amount of time you must spend in purgatory will be determined. Once that period of purification ends, a person enters into the beatific vision. My problem with all of this is that I don't find anything about purgatory taught in Scripture. Let me explain some key problems I have with this idea.

First, as Kreeft presents it, it seems that the answer to the question, "What must I do to be saved?" or "to inherit eternal life?" includes "spend the required time in purgatory." But where does Scripture ever say that, and where does it even mention purgatory? In contrast, Scripture does answer the questions just raised, and the answer has nothing to do with purgatory. According to Luke 10:25–28, an expert in the Mosaic law asked Jesus what he must do to inherit eternal life. Jesus asked him what the law says. The expert replied, citing Deuteronomy 6:5 and Leviticus 19:18, that one must love the Lord with all one's heart, soul, and strength and love one's neighbor as oneself. None of these are things that can be postponed until after death. Moreover, when the young man tried to justify himself in the eyes of the law by asking who one's neighbor is, Jesus answered with the parable of the good Samaritan (Luke 10:29–37). What does that parable have to do with anything one could do after death?

In John 3 we have another case of someone wanting to know how to be saved (Nicodemus). Jesus replied that one must be born again if one wants to see the kingdom of God (John 3:3; also 3:5). A bit later in the conversation, Jesus said that God's love moved him to give his Son so that whoever believes in him should not perish but have eternal life. The phrase "believe in" (*pisteuein eis*) means more than an intellectual acknowledgment that Jesus existed and said and did various things. It means that one must repent of one's sin and commit oneself to accepting Jesus as one's Savior. There is no evidence in this passage or any other that this transaction can happen after one has died.

Acts 3 records the event of Peter and other disciples healing a sick man. The day after the healing, the rulers, elders, scribes, and high priests of the Jews were in Jerusalem (4:5). They brought Peter and his companions before them and asked by whose name and by what power they had healed this man (v. 7). They answered that it was by the name and power of Jesus Christ (v. 10). Moreover, they added, "And there is salvation in no one else; for there is no other name under heaven that has been given among men by which we must be saved" (v. 12).

In Acts 16 we read about the Philippian jailor. Paul and Silas were in prison, but there was a great earthquake so that the foundations of the prison were shaken, the doors were opened, and everyone's chains were loosed (v. 26). The jailor was roused from his sleep, and seeing Paul and Silas freed from their chains, he asked, "Sirs, what must I do to be saved?" (v. 30). They answered, "Believe in the Lord Jesus, and you shall be saved, you and your household" (v. 31).

Note as well 1 John 5:11–12. John says that the one who believes in Jesus has a witness within himself that he is saved. "And the testimony is this, that God has given us eternal life, and this life is in His Son. He who has the Son has the life; he who does not have the Son of God does not have the life." How does one get the Son? As the verses cited above teach, one gets the Son by accepting him as one's personal Savior.

What is the point of these verses? The point is that one inherits eternal life by believing in Christ as personal Savior. This involves understanding that he has died for your sin and wants to save you and accepting the salvation he offers. Where do any of these verses say anything about spending time in purgatory?

Let me close with a final question. How does the notion of purgatory relate to Scripture's teaching on how to gain eternal life? Does this doctrine require anyone to accept Christ as Savior? If so, when does that happen? Before one dies, after death while one is in purgatory, or some other time? Kreeft says nothing about trusting Christ as Savior and how that relates to purgatory. I doubt that there are many, if any, discussions of purgatory that say that to be saved one must trust Christ and then stay in purgatory.

We seem, then, to have two different answers to how one gets saved. According to the first, regardless of the shape of one's life on earth, if one spends enough time in purgatory, he or she will be purified enough, eventually, to get into heaven. Or, one accepts Christ's death on Calvary as payment for one's sins, making Christ one's Savior by faith, and so one receives eternal life. These two methods of attaining salvation seem mutually exclusive. If you can get into heaven via purgatory, why must you trust in Christ as Savior? And if you trust in Christ as Savior, your sins are forgiven, and you stand clothed in the perfect righteousness of Christ. Why, then, would you need to spend any time in purgatory?

These two ways to get to heaven contradict each other, so they can't both be true. Which should we believe? We should believe the one taught by Scripture and reject the one Scripture does not teach!

But what if Scripture teaches both? It doesn't! Scripture teaches that salvation comes through faith in Christ alone (see the passages above). What biblical passages teach that there is such a place as purgatory or that after death believers must undergo what Kreeft and other Roman Catholics say happens in purgatory?

With the way Kreeft describes purgatory and what is supposed to happen there, it sounds as though everyone (or almost everyone) goes there upon physical death. Even more, it sounds as though, given enough time, everyone there will be purified to the point where they are ready to enter heaven. Readers should realize that this amounts to universalism. Kreeft never uses that term or mentions that concept, but in light of what he does say it seems hard to escape the view that his position leads to universalism. And yet, as Jesus said in speaking about the course of one's life and one's ultimate destiny, "Enter through the narrow gate; for the gate is wide and the way is broad that leads to destruction, and there are many who enter through it. For the gate is small and the way is narrow that leads to life, and there are few who find it" (Matt 7:13–14). This does not sound like universalism (or anything close to it) to me.

J. RICHARD MIDDLETON

I first read Peter Kreeft's *Between Heaven and Hell* and *The Unaborted Socrates* when I was a graduate student and campus minister in the 1980s.[1] Even back then I was in awe of his sharp philosophical mind. So it is a distinct privilege to respond to his chapter in this volume. I only hope that in his rejoinder to my response I won't be pricked too sharply for my disagreements!

Kreeft is an engaging writer whose prose is full of wit and vivid analogies. If he had fun writing his chapter (as he admits), I found his (serious) levity infectious, and I often laughed along with him at his imaginative turns of phrase amid incisive analysis. I suspect that, like God, he might also be Irish, as many times I wanted to exclaim, "O Kreeft!"

Having now read my chapter on the new earth, Kreeft will realize that there is something of a gulf between our positions on eschatology. Here I want to record, at the outset, that none of my dissent from Kreeft's classical theological viewpoint is meant to demean either him personally or the venerable tradition that he articulates so eloquently.

However, I am compelled to dissent on certain points. I will raise questions both about terminology and about the underlying concepts or categories.

Heaven

First of all, I wonder why Kreeft continues to use the term *heaven* to describe the eschaton. He himself refers to the eschatological future as

---

1. The first book is now in a revised edition: Peter Kreeft, *Between Heaven and Hell: A Dialog Somewhere beyond Death with John F. Kennedy, C. S. Lewis, and Aldous Huxley*, rev. ed. (Downers Grove, IL: InterVarsity Press, 2008); idem, *The Unaborted Socrates: A Dramatic Debate on the Issues Surrounding Abortion* (Downers Grove, IL: InterVarsity Press, 1983).

a "new earth" and as "new heavens and a new earth," noting that the latter phrase "means a whole new universe" (156). *Heaven* is, of course, the traditional term used in the history of theology for the eschatological future, but this term is never used in the Bible for the final destiny of the righteous.[2] In my opinion, the use of the term *heaven* for this destiny contributes to a confusion of meaning.

Even Kreeft's opening definitions of the various meanings of *heaven* do not clear up the confusion. Kreeft distinguishes between the plural "heavens" and the singular "heaven." He takes the plural to refer to "what's up there and out there" (that is, part of the created order, p. 156). He uses the singular for "God's eternal 'dwelling place'" (understood not as being literally in the sky; this is a symbolic use of the term to refer to "God's own life or mode of existence," p. 156) and also for "our future participation in that 'dwelling place,' or more properly, that supernatural life of God" (156). To these three meanings, he adds a variant of the third: our *present* participation in that "supernatural life" (156–57).

So, let us do some linguistic and conceptual clarification.

First, while there may be a distinction in English between the singular "heaven" and the plural "heavens," this is not relevant to the Hebrew word *shamayim* (or the Aramaic *shemayin*) found in the Old Testament. This word is technically a dual (a form of plural); there is no singular form. It is translated in English Bibles variously as "sky," "heaven," or "the heavens." Over the years some have suggested that the dual originated as a reference to the visible sky and the invisible realm where God dwells or to the upper heavens/sky (where the stars are found) and the lower heavens/sky (where atmospheric phenomena occur). However, neither hypothesis is borne out by the usage of the term in the Old Testament. Whether translated into English as singular or plural, *shamayim* in the Old Testament is understood as that transcendent realm (beyond earth) whose residents include God and the angels, together with celestial and meteorological phenomena such as sun, moon, stars, clouds, wind, and lightning (these are portrayed as inhabiting the same realm in texts like Pss 104:1–4 and 148:1–4).[3]

---

2. I began my study of eschatology years ago by verifying this exegetical point, and I have explained this in my published writings on the subject.

3. It is more likely that the dual (like the plural term *'elohim* used for God) is meant to communicate majesty or excellence, or (in this case) is used to signify a complex whole with

188 • FOUR VIEWS ON HEAVEN

Whereas Hebrew *shamayim* is dual, the Septuagint (LXX) translators almost always used the Greek singular *ouranos* (though they do use the plural *ouranoi* a few times).[4] The singular is also dominant in the New Testament, though the plural predominates in a few books. One of those is Matthew's Gospel, which uses the plural and the singular with precisely the *opposite* meanings that Kreeft proposes. For Matthew, the singular refers to the visible heaven (the sky above), and the plural is used for the (invisible) abode of God (as in his distinctive phrase, "kingdom of heaven"—literally, "kingdom of the heavens").[5]

But Matthew is not thinking there are literally two heavens. Rather, Matthew is dependent on the logic of the Old Testament's symbolic use of heaven/sky to refer to "where" God is. Since heaven/sky is transcendent to us earth dwellers (it is literally *beyond* us), heaven/sky can be used metaphorically to emphasize God's transcendence (thus, God is "in heaven"). I believe that Kreeft is on the right track when he explains that "'Heaven' is not literally in 'the heavens,' although the heavens can symbolize it. It refers instead to God's own life or mode of existence" (156). Although Kreeft here flips Matthew's use of the singular and plural, his point resonates with Matthew's distinction.

Leaving aside the flipping of the singular and plural, the real problem is to move from this symbolic or metaphorical use of heaven as the (temporary and partial) abode of God (analogous to God's "location" in the holy of holies) to a fixed metaphysical identification of God with heaven. If, however, we read the Bible not in terms of later metaphysical developments but through a Jewish temple lens, we would be prepared for the eschatological coming of God to earth, which begins in the Old Testament, continues through the incarnation and Pentecost, and culminates in the new Jerusalem. Thus the rending of the veil of the holy of holies in the Jerusalem temple, which signified the missional presence

---

many parts (a plural of extension or amplification).

4. Jonathan Pennington's survey of the Septuagint (both the canonical Hebrew Bible and the Apocrypha) suggests that only about 9 percent of the time is the plural used (the plural is also rare in classical Greek outside the LXX). See Jonathan T. Pennington, *Heaven and Earth in the Gospel of Matthew* (Grand Rapids: Baker Academic, 2007), 100. For Pennington's study of the singular and plural in the LXX and Second Temple Judaism, see *Heaven and Earth in the Gospel of Matthew*, 39–65 (ch. 5).

5. For Pennington's full analysis of Matthew's use of the singular and plural, see *Heaven and Earth in the Gospel of Matthew*, 67–76 (ch. 6).

of God going out into the church and the world, was a precursor to the parousia, when the heavens (the cosmic holy of holies) would open and Christ would return to claim (and fill) all creation (earth included) as his cosmic temple.

To put it starkly, whereas much of the Christian theological tradition views life as a journey of ascent from earth to God/heaven, the Bible depicts exactly the opposite—the coming of God into earthly existence.[6]

Supernatural

There is a similar confusion with the term *supernatural* (with *natural* as its opposite). As Kreeft surely knows (given his familiarity with Aquinas), the natural/supernatural distinction became prominent with the angelic doctor in the thirteenth century. The precedent for Aquinas's use of "supernatural" (*supernaturalis*) is found in the writings of Peter Lombard, who spoke of God's working both in and beyond the ordinary functioning of nature (the latter being "praternatural" (*praeter naturam*).[7] But this distinction is somewhat different from the later theological usage of these terms. Originally, "natural" and "supernatural" did not distinguish between creaturely reality and God's own life but rather referred to two modes of divine causation—"one in which God works with the order he embedded into things; the other when he acts miraculously and independently of created causes."[8]

I submit that if we used the terms *natural* and *supernatural* in this way, they would have some validity. But slippage occurs when the term *supernatural* comes to refer to God himself or to God's own form of life, then is subsequently extended to refer to our salvation (present or eschatological), which is then understood as equivalent to participation in that divine life.

---

6. New Testament scholar George Eldon Ladd has been particularly clear on this point: "Thus the final redemption is not flight from this world to another world; it may be described as the descent of the other world—God's world—resulting in a transformation of this world" (George Eldon Ladd, *The Pattern of New Testament Truth* [Grand Rapids: Eerdmans, 1968], 37).

7. Peter Lombard, *Sententiae in IV libris distinctae*, 2.18.5. For a historical account of this distinction, see Robert Bartlett, *The Natural and Supernatural in the Middle Ages* (Cambridge: Cambridge University Press, 2008), 1–33.

8. Peter Harrison, "Introduction," in *Science without God? Rethinking the History of Scientific Naturalism*, ed. Peter Harrison and Jon H. Roberts, Ian Ramsey Centre Studies in Science and Religion (New York: Oxford University Press, 2019), 8. See also Peter Harrison, "Naturalism and the Success of Science," *Religious Studies* 56 (2020): 279 (entire article 274–91).

The paradoxes then begin to multiply, so that it becomes necessary to say that although we participate in the divine life, we don't become God but remain fully creatures and fully human (indeed, to use Kreeft's terminology, we become, perhaps for the first time, fully human).

But I think we could avoid such paradoxes by reference to a temple-centered sacramental framework that maintains the creator-creature distinction while speaking of the coming of God's presence or Spirit to indwell and thus transform earthly creation into what God intended. Then we can unashamedly say with Paul that at the last day God will be "all in all" (1 Cor 15:28), with no worries of sounding pantheistic.[9]

The Relationship of Scripture to Tradition

As may be discerned from the above discussion, the main underlying issue that I perceive between my position and Kreeft's is the tension between an inner-biblical (or *emic*) framework for understanding Scripture and an external (or *etic*) theological conceptuality that is brought to the text.

I fully recognize that what I am calling an external/*etic* set of concepts has become a venerable theological tradition. And I have no desire to invalidate tradition simply because it is postbiblical. I may not be committed to tradition in the same way that my Roman Catholic brothers and sisters are, but as a Wesleyan theologian I value tradition (including the ecumenical creeds) as important to my faith. So I am not proposing a simple commitment to the Bible alone, as if anyone could read Scripture without a theological framework (and many other assumptions, besides).

However, the fundamental issue for me is whether the church's later theological concepts, developed from Scripture in dialogue with the issues of the times (all theology is contextual), should have a unilateral

---

9. Michael Gorman is a prominent New Testament scholar who fully embraces the notion of our participation in Christ and in God (even using the term *theosis*), but he does so in a way that is grounded in inner-biblical conceptuality, without drawing on an external metaphysical (essentially Neoplatonic) framework to do so. See Michael Gorman, *Becoming the Gospel: Paul, Participation, and Mission*, The Gospel and Our Culture Series (Grand Rapids: Eerdmans, 2015); *Participation: Paul's Vision of Life in Christ*, Grove Biblical Series 88 (Cambridge, UK: Grove, 2018); *Abide and Go: Missional Theosis in the Gospel of John* (Eugene, OR: Cascade, 2018); and *Participating in Christ: Explorations in Paul's Theology and Spirituality* (Grand Rapids: Baker Academic, 2019).

influence on our reading of the Bible, or whether our contemporary reflection on Scripture might generate fresh understandings that can renew (and even correct) our theology. This is a complicated question, which I do not expect can be resolved here. Yet it is this very question that generated my own shift from initial undergraduate and graduate studies in theology and philosophy to a focus on biblical studies (primarily, but not exclusively, the Old Testament) for my doctoral studies and my subsequent teaching and research. I wanted my theological reflections to be as informed as possible by an interpretation of the Bible read in terms of its own historical contexts.[10]

Purgatory

Early in his chapter Kreeft commented on his theological location as a Roman Catholic, noting, "I do not think there will be many sharp differences between my responses [to the ten questions] and those from traditional evangelical Protestants" (157). Kreeft suggests only two points on which his Protestant interlocutors might demur—the doctrine of purgatory and the intermediate state. However, I seem to be the only dissenter on the intermediate state among the Protestants who contributed to this book (perhaps this is because, while I attempt to be biblical and I sometimes accept the label "evangelical," I go against tradition when I deem it necessary).

Surprisingly, it is Kreeft's exposition of purgatory that I find most appealing. This is because I am fully on board with the claim that we need to be radically transformed in order to be fit for the new creation that God has in store for us. However, I don't see the need to posit purgatory as a (presumably disembodied) state between this world and the world to come. Rather, given the open-endedness and progressive nature of the new creation as described in Revelation, I assume that this transformation is itself part of embodied life in the eschaton. Put another way, I don't assume any sort of stasis for the redeemed in the age to come.[11]

---

10. On the importance of the ancient historical context for responsible theological interpretation of Scripture, see Joel Green, "Rethinking 'History' for Theological Interpretation," *Journal of Theological Interpretation* 5.2 (2011): 159–74.

11. Here I might draw on Kreeft's own dependence on Aristotle, via Aquinas, in order to characterize our future perfection as continuous *energeia* or activity. However, many

I close with thanks and appreciation to Peter Kreeft for his playful, lucid, and thoughtful answers to the ten assigned questions. My critical response to his answers is offered in a spirit of iron sharpening iron, in order to stimulate conversation about these important issues. May the conversations continue!

theological conceptions of *energeia*, conceived as "pure actuality," end up being equivalent to a kind of stasis (which I resist).

MICHAEL ALLEN

I begin with thanks to Professor Kreeft. Some contrasts between a Roman Catholic philosopher and a Reformed dogmatic theologian are perhaps unsurprising. I don't believe in purgatory and find his framing of the issue to jump past the rather obvious excluded middle, namely, how to reconcile the arduous journey toward glory of the departed faithful with the divine promise to transform us immediately at Jesus's return (not in some long-lumbering process of moral machination). But I also believe that to engage there polemically at any length would be to miss the thrust of what Professor Kreeft has done and, frankly, to compel readers into what may feel like a purgatorial polemic. I leave that disagreement to the side and am happy to turn elsewhere.

His essay traverses so many topics prompted by the ten questions we all have been given. I could salute a range of his arguments. I especially appreciate the way he addresses relationships now and in the hereafter, the move from signs to a still deeper, even if mysterious, substance, and his turning to the risen Christ as the perfected human. He also identifies Christ as mediator in the heavenly life, the one we can see in that beatific or blessed vision. In these and other areas, I'm thankful to have had opportunity to think along with him and to be challenged and strengthened by his capable intellectual work.

I am especially struck by where he begins, commenting that getting the right questions—productive and important questions—is actually half the work of the life of the mind. We don't merely seek answers, in other words, but need first to settle on the right questions. In that spirit, then, I want to pull out a couple strands in what he does say and frame a new question as a means of trying to think with Professor Kreeft. I will be eager to see what he might say, then, by way of response. That kind of dialectical give and take is crucial to theological growth and the work of what we might call intellectual discipleship.

I want to wrestle with one question then, and it can be framed more broadly and more bluntly. Broadly, in what ways do we live with individuality and distinctness in our heavenly, eternal state, and in what ways are we conformed along with our brothers and sisters to a particular model of humanity found in Jesus Christ? More bluntly, how do we think both individuality and conformity together?

Why might this even be a question? Two strands of eschatological doctrine are affirmed capably by Professor Kreeft. First, individual women and men are redeemed and glorified by God; every time we hear the gospel promise "Christ died and rose for you," that *you* names a specific and discrete person. The professor goes further in his essay to tease out some of the particularities enmeshed in that specificity. In his discussion of the beatific vision, he turns to C. S. Lewis's pondering: "Each soul will forever know and praise some one aspect of the divine beauty better than any other can. Why else were we created but that God, loving each infinitely, can love each differently?"[1] Professor Kreeft then adds: "So in heaven we will forever tell each other of that unique aspect of God that we were created to appreciate" (163).

Others may see more of the whole, while still others may strive for synthesis, looking across the interstices of divine self-revelation's seemingly discrete moments. The project of intellectual and theological growth described by Professors Lewis and Kreeft seems to leave much room for unique powers and capacities, each of which serves in a steward-like fashion to share with others.

Another reflection from Lewis proves helpful at this point:

In each of my friends there is something that only some other friend can fully bring out. By myself I am not large enough to call the whole man into activity; I want other lights than my own to show all his facets. Now that Charles is dead, I shall never again see Ronald's [Tolkien's] reaction to a specifically Charles joke. Far from having more of Ronald, having him "to

---

1. C. S. Lewis, *The Problem of Pain*, in *The Complete C. S. Lewis Signature Classics* (San Francisco: HarperOne, 2002), 642.

myself" now that Charles is away, I have less of Ronald. . . . In this, Friendship exhibits a glorious "nearness by resemblance" to heaven itself where the very multitude of the blessed (which no man can number) increases the fruition which each of us has of God. For every soul, seeing Him in her own way, doubtless communicates that unique vision to all the rest. That, says an old author, is why the Seraphim in Isaiah's vision are crying "Holy, Holy, Holy" to one another (Isaiah 6:3). The more we thus share the Heavenly Bread between us, the more we shall have.[2]

This notion of individual giftedness that sees more, draws out more, shares more of the holy not only for one's own good but for all one's company helps gesture toward the specificity and particularity of each redeemed, glorified saint.

It is often overlooked, but I take the Song of Songs to attest this truth in that it not only speaks of the song of the bride for her lover but also of the lover's song over his beloved.[3] "Behold, you are beautiful, my love, behold, you are beautiful" (4:1). The Song does not remain abstract or ambiguous. It moves to more specific acclamation: "Your eyes . . . your hair . . . your teeth . . . your lips . . . your cheeks . . . your neck . . . your two breasts" (4:1–5). God takes delight in the specific shape of his own people, and this will be evident when they will have been not only redeemed by grace but also transfigured in glorious resurrection at the return of Christ. So we see here that the divine acclamation of each saint lingers over their particular gifts and graces and glories, like the song of a lover praises the contours of their beloved's body. God does not tolerate us or love us in some merely generic way—God delights, ultimately, in the glorified particularity of each member of his body. That is the first strand of biblical teaching about our glorious end that we dare not lose.

---

2. C. S. Lewis, *The Four Loves* (New York: Harcourt, Brace, and Jovanovich, 1960), 92.

3. This paragraph depends on a distinctly Christian reading of the Song as being ultimately a song to be sung about divine love (God and Israel, and then Christ and church) rather than ultimately about human sexual love (though this is the penultimate figure for that deeper theological truth). One does wonder how an erotic song could ever be called the "Song of Songs" in Scripture, greater than the many other songs of Miriam, or Hannah, or Mary, or Zechariah, or of the Psalms. For analysis of the role that this reading of the Song played in the development of early Christianity, see Karl Shuve, *The Song of Songs and the Fashioning of Identity in Early Latin Christianity*, Oxford Early Christian Studies (New York: Oxford University Press, 2016).

A second element also presses itself upon us. Professor Kreeft calls the risen Christ the image of perfected humanity and goes on to say that the promise of the gospel is that "we will be more like Christ in every way" (160). Underneath that crucial affirmation is biblical teaching that we are to experience a conformity. Romans 8 not only affirms predestination but names its purpose: "Those whom he foreknew he also predestined to be conformed to the image of his Son" (8:29). There is a specific aim for all the elect, namely, conformity to the image of God's own Son, the incarnate Son named Jesus of Nazareth. The text goes one step further in teasing out this promise: "In order that he [God's Son] might be the firstborn among many brothers" (8:29). This conformity fills out family resemblance as well as what it means to bear the name "Christian," that is, to be and become increasingly a "little Christ" or one who in some small way is marked by the character and presence of the Messiah.

We obey the "law of Christ" and bear the "yoke of Christ," but we also "imitate Christ" (Gal 6:2; Matt 11:29–30; 1 John 2:6). These terms not only speak of doing something said by the incarnate Son but also of being shaped or molded to walk as he walked. That conformity involves all sorts of things, from prayer to cross bearing. Terms such as *Christoformity* or even *cruciformity* are used to convey the idea that the good news not only brings forgiveness but also the promise that God will, by his Holy Spirit, eventually transform us into Christ's own glory. "We shall also bear the image of the man of heaven" (1 Cor 15:49). As "we" each bear that common image, surely there is a sense in which Christians drawn "from every tribe and language and people and nation" (Rev 5:9) are increasingly sharing qualities (whether the beatitudes [Matt 5] or the fruit of the Spirit [Gal 5] or the gifts of the Holy Spirit [Isa 11]). In so doing, there is a unifying thread of Christian transformation. In conformity to Christ, we experience greater commonality with one another.

One element suggests that each person has a distinct perspective and gift, while the other element reminds us that we are all being conformed to Christ (and thus presumably becoming more like each other). The trick is how to respect each of these claims, neither collapsing the one into the other nor acting as though they must contradict each other. If they collapse into one another, then we may fall into the dangers of colonialism, where the personal or cultural idiosyncrasies of some person or persons are taken as being themselves part and parcel to the shape of Christoformity. Such is the way of cultural superiority and a font of ills. Or we collapse in the other direction, as if personal qualities of one sort or another are simply viewed as beside the point when one is identified with Christ, for his personal properties—in every respect— are mandated: such would be to proceed as if his maleness or carpentry are as morally significant as his footwashing and prayer. Here, too, we would fail to distinguish between universal and particular.

The way of contradiction is no better, and it has implications for our lives now. It can result in an attitude of secular self-preservation, as if we imitate certain elements of Jesus though the rest of us remains untouched by him or by God. We might parcel matters out in terms of time: Sabbath or Lord's Day conforms to his path, but the workweek or that blessed weekend remains outside his purview. Perhaps we consider parts or aspects of the self, as if some faculties are more or less of consequence: the mind or soul for Christ, yet the body being beyond his concern. Each of these contradictory approaches—viewing conformity and parti- cularity as competing and not overlapping concerns—ultimately leads to a division of loyalties: God reigns in facets of life but not all; devotion to God or love of God marks some aspects of the self though not every one of them. Against these pitfalls, Deuteronomy 6:5 must call us to love God with all we have, every nook and cranny. God makes all things new, in the cosmos and in our selves.

Is there a way to think about the eternal self—resurrected, transfig- ured, and conformed to Christ as a particular self—that can bear both specificity but also this sanctified commonality with other sisters and brothers who share this birthright? Well, the first thing is to say that the paths of confusion and contradiction each serve as warnings to keep our eyes ever on both realities. Personal identity remains (signaled perhaps by the identification of Moses and Elijah in the transfiguration), and that does involve unique and varied appearance, ability, and perspective in certain respects. Professor Kreeft does speak to greater "agility" in the glorified life, but that need not suggest that we all become superhero- like and possess each and every agile capacity in the same degree. And yet personal identity is true there and then of those who are washed in the blood of the Lamb and bear the name of Jesus Christ. Not only do they bear that name, but they bear his image as the man of heaven. They have been transformed to manifest those godly qualities.

I think we are left with what I take to be a significant question, some warnings about false paths, and some reminders about its significance, as well as a need to be cautious lest we speculate in ways undisciplined by and unconstrained by the norming voice of God's own word. The question is: In what exact ways are cultural particularities going to be manifest? Somehow, but these may vary and will surely exceed our current imagination. More personally, the question can be focused: In which manner will various personality traits or unique ability sets (intellectually or physiologically) display themselves? Somehow, but a range of possibilities present themselves, and it is perhaps more important to be committed to the significance of that question than to dare an actual, particular answer at this point. The question reminds us to be alert to both strands of biblical teaching and Christian doctrine: namely, that God saves and glorifies *me* (and a whole host of other Christians, each one an individual person with specificity) and that God simultaneously glorifies *us*, each and every one, by conforming us all by his Spirit's power to the image of the man of heaven, Jesus Christ. I do not think lingering over and hopefully more fully appreciating the challenge of a particular question, even if it cannot be fully answered, is time wasted. The question prompts alertness to Scripture and also frames how we might think about unity and diversity more broadly. It provides one unique angle on how we think about what binds us together (as Christians one day to be resurrected and glorified) and what distinguishes us (as being individuals of unique backgrounds and experiences). I am grateful to Professor Kreeft for his many reflections, as well as for prompting me to wrestle again with this profound topic of human nature and its glorified character in Christ.

PETER KREEFT

First, hearty thanks to my three fellow truth seekers and for Mike Wittmer for setting up this format of "iron sharpening iron." It should be replicated again and again. Three substantive issues arise: Purgatory with Dr. Feinberg, the relation between the eschaton and heaven with Dr. Middleton, and individuality in heaven with Dr. Allen.

Dr. Feinberg cuts to the heart of the issue by focusing on our sources of authority for theologizing. Of course, he disagrees with the level I ascribe to the Roman Church's magisterium; if he didn't, he'd be a Catholic. But this does not downgrade Scripture, because Catholic dogmas are founded upon, interpretations of, and tested by the touchstone of Scripture. Aquinas even *identifies* theology (*sacra doctrina*) with Scripture (*Summa Theologica* 1.1.1), at least in its "material cause" or data.

True, the word *Purgatory* is not in Scripture, but neither is the word *Trinity*. The doctrine of the Trinity is the theological explanation that accounts for all the scriptural data: that God is one, the Father is God, the Son is God, the Holy Spirit is God, and they are different persons. And the same is true of Purgatory, which rests on two clear scriptural teachings: that in this life even saints are sinners (1 John 1:8) and that nothing in any way sinful can enter heaven (Rev 21:27).

There are many popular misunderstandings of Purgatory (as there are of the Trinity); for example, that it means Christ did not finish the job on the cross, that it makes death gloomy rather than joyful, that it defers our meeting with Christ until our time of purgation is over, and that it is a third alternative to "the great divorce" of heaven or hell. Dr. Feinberg's misunderstanding is to call Purgatory a "probation time."

But its purpose is not probation or justice. It is not the completion of justification but of sanctification.

Dr. Feinberg admits that sanctification is "in stages" rather than once for all, as with justification. But it is evident that few reach its final stage in this life; only fools and Pharisees think they are perfected saints. Does any honest Christian actually believe that he has done what Christ says is necessary to enter eternal life (Luke 10:25–28), namely, to love God with one's whole heart, soul, mind, and strength, to be "perfect, as your heavenly Father is perfect" (Matt 5:48)?

Another common misunderstanding about Purgatory concerns *time*. Purgatorial time is not measured by clocks or calendars. In fact, it may even be instantaneous. The language of "days" in Purgatory is symbolic, not literal—an analogy taken from the days of penances assigned in the early church, which were proportioned to the gravity of sins.

Purgatory purges our sinful habits and desires, not sins themselves. After death we can no longer sin. But we can still learn and grow spiritually. Purgatory deals not with what we do but with what we are, not with sins but with sinners.

Most Protestant objections to Purgatory stem from Luther's innovative heresy of a merely "forensic justification," the "legal fiction" that he called "a dunghill covered by snow."[1] Thus Dr. Feinberg speaks of us as "stand[ing] *clothed* in the perfect righteousness of Christ" (italics mine, p. 184). But that simply will not do. A coward wearing a knight's armor is still a coward. Heaven is not a costume party. God requires perfected *hearts*. Few things in Scripture are clearer than that. And our own hearts concur. Surely our holiest desire is not merely to be "reckoned" as perfect but to really become perfect, not merely to receive but also to merit the divine accolade. For our heavenly Father is total truth as well as total love—which is why he is "easy to please and hard to satisfy" (George MacDonald), like our good earthly fathers. Of course, we can satisfy him only by his own grace, but grace does not bypass or replace nature, including human nature, but perfects it.

---

1. Actually, this exact saying cannot be located in Luther's writings, but the sentiment is there and can be pieced together by bringing together a few various statements found in his writings. See Dave Armstrong, "Luther's 'Snow-Covered Dunghill' (Myth?)," Patheos, April 7, 2016, www.patheos.com/blogs/davearmstrong/2016/04/luthers-snow-covered-dunghill-myth.html.

I still remember the thrill of liberation I felt as a student at Calvin College when, having known nothing but Luther's doctrine of forensic justification, I read in C. S. Lewis's *Mere Christianity* the simple truth that what God wants with us is not a certain kind of action but a certain kind of person. He is our lover, not our lawyer; our Father, not our employer.

Finally, Purgatory does not imply universalism, or salvation of all on earth, but only of all in Purgatory. Purgatory is Heaven's bathroom, but some refuse even to enter the front door of the heavenly mansion. No one lives in the bathroom forever. Whether Purgatory is temporal or not, it is temporary. This "bathroom" is where the "snow on dung" is flushed away so we can enjoy the banquet in the dining room.

Protestants rightly protest the common misunderstanding of Purgatory that undermines the scriptural hope of a happy death by anticipating a long prison sentence and work camp before we can enjoy the light of Christ's face. But if we have lived "in Christ" and have died "in Christ," he will be with us in Purgatory too, even more interiorly and intimately then and there than he is now and here, teaching, purifying, and showering us with the total love we find appealing as well as the total truth we find appalling. Purgatory is intensely joyful as well as intensely painful, like a snake shedding its old skin, like Eustace's "de-dragoning" in C. S. Lewis's *The Voyage of the Dawn Treader.*

Dr. Middleton, as a Wesleyan Methodist, is typical of Protestants outside the Lutheran (and usually the Calvinist) traditions, who see sanctification as metaphysical, not just legal, even though they do not embrace what they understand (or misunderstand) to be the Catholic dogma of Purgatory. (Lewis believed in Purgatory but not what he called the "papist" version of it. Yet he praised Newman's view of it in "The Dream of Gerontius," which is in fact the "papist" version!).

Dr. Middleton's main focus is the important question of the relation between Heaven and the earthly eschaton. Do we "go up" to heaven, or does heaven "come down" to us? I think the answer has to be both and neither: both, because both of these images are scriptural and traditional; neither, because heaven is not in this universe, like another planet, whether we "go up" to it or whether it "comes down" to us.

The new heavens and new earth both is and is not another world. It is our world, but it is not just perfected but radically transformed. For example, it can hold a population of all the blessed dead, living, and future saints (and angels too), unlike our small planet. It is also immortal and thus not subject to entropy, as is everything in this universe. The best fictional description I know of this both/and and neither/nor paradox is the end of C. S. Lewis's *The Last Battle*.

Perhaps our problem is that we always think of this issue in terms of space rather than time. (We also tend to think of time itself as a kind of space, like a road or a line, which generates all kinds of philosophical and scientific conundrums.) In heaven and/or the eschaton, our whole past will be resurrected, not just remembered. Eternity is neither time abolished nor time continued but time transformed and made totally present. How that will happen and what it will look or feel like is probably as unimaginable as the world outside the womb is to an unborn baby. The key concept is transformation—neither a utopian perfecting of the old nor a simple substitution of a new thing for it. As with God, we know what it is not more clearly than we know what it is.

Jesus said, in Scripture's next-to-last chapter, "Behold, I make all things new" (Rev 21:5). That probably includes the very nature of space, time, motion, matter, and energy. We know from Scripture that the resurrection body is not a physical body like those in this universe (1 Cor 15:35–50). And we know from modern science that space and time are relative to matter, motion, and energy, not vice versa. There is no Newtonian absolute space and time. Put these two truths together, and you may begin to see something about the new world our new bodies will live in. The most certain thing we can say about it is that it is "what no eye has seen, nor ear heard, nor the heart of man conceived" (1 Cor 2:9). I hope to see all three of you there fairly soon, and to share a good laugh together about our childish speculations.

Dr. Allen's focus is probably the most important one of all, but one we can deal with without much controversy. He wonders, broadly speaking, in what ways do we live with individuality and distinctness in our heavenly, eternal state, and in what ways are we conformed along with our brothers and sisters to a particular model of humanity found in Jesus Christ? More bluntly, how do we think both individuality and conformity go together?

The answer is surely *in all ways*, for in Christ all are supremely individuated *and* supremely one—in fact, individuated *by* being one with

Christ. The paradox is similar to human love. Lovers are never more individuated, unique, irreplaceable, and fulfilled than when they are most totally lost in self-forgetful love of each other. Similarly with the sexes: men find their unique masculinity only by understanding and uniting with women, and women find their unique femininity by understanding and uniting with men.

This is an application of the theological principle that grace perfects nature, as light, by transcending all colors and shapes, perfects and brings out each color and shape, and as intelligence reveals both differences and similarities among its objects. It is precisely the transcendence of light to color, of thought to its objects, of God to man, and of grace to nature that allows light to be more present to each color than any other color is to another and that allows thought to do the same to its objects, divinity to humanity, and grace to nature.

In Thomistic metaphysics, the act of existence is so supremely actual that it transcends all essences, which are only potentialities for existence. Yet it also actualizes all essences, all natures, from within, not from without, as an accident. And in Augustine, God is "more intimately present to me than I am to myself."[2] Supreme transcendence allows supreme immanence.

This same paradoxical dialectic holds between individuality and community, in *both* directions. Each of these two poles of the dialectic is perfected by the other, because each transcends the other. (1) Individuality, the unique "I"-ness that is the image of the God who is "I am," transcends group identity and therefore perfects it. The more distinctive the individuals are in a community, the stronger the community can be. (2) As individuality perfects community, so community perfects individuality. The organs in a body are both more unique *and* more unified than soldiers in a parade or pennies in a pile. The common good perfects the private good because the common good transcends the private good. The more individuals give themselves to their community, the more individuated and fulfilled they are as individuals.

To quote *The Three Musketeers*, "One for all and all for one." Or to quote two *Star Trek* movies, "The good of the many is greater than the

---

2. Augustine, *Confessiones*, ed. James J. O'Donnell, 3 vols. (Oxford: Clarendon, 1992), 1:27.

204 ● FOUR VIEWS ON HEAVEN

good of the one," *and* "The good of the one is greater than the good of the many."

Every sage and saint in every world religion has some glimpse of the profound psychological paradox: the self finds itself only by losing itself. Christians alone know why: it is true of God's creatures because it is true of the creator himself. For God is not only "I" but also "We"; both a single unified nature and a Trinity of persons who totally give themselves away to the others in love. The unified nature *is* the love. Love is a stronger glue, a stronger unity, than mere arithmetical oneness. And that love-unity supremely individuates: the three divine persons are not triplets but the most individuated and unique personalities in all reality. This is why saints are all wonderfully eccentric: they are unique selves because they have died to themselves and been conformed to Christ. Great saints are weird and wonderful; great sinners are boring and predictable.

So how should we imagine this dialectic of individuality and conformity to Christ in heaven? As Christ often did, Dr. Allen questions the question itself: "It is perhaps more important to be committed to the significance of that question than to dare an actual, particular answer at this point" (198). And "at this point" means before our Purgatory and before the transformation of our eschaton.

CONCLUSION

MICHAEL WITTMER

I use several Counterpoints books in my classroom because students get a big bang for their buck. It is always enlightening and sometimes thrilling to hear leaders in their field hash out their differences. Flashes of insight often come in the response essays, as each seeks to clarify his or her position and push back on perceived errors in the others. The quality of the interaction depends on the expertise of the contributors and their eagerness to engage opposing views. In our case, I think we have a winner. John Feinberg, Richard Middleton, Michael Allen, and Peter Kreeft have illumined where Christians agree on heaven, where and why we disagree, and what work may still need to be done. They have moved the conversation forward.

Every contributor agreed on one main point: many of our questions about the final state will not be answered until we get there. It is as if we are standing on the shore of a vast ocean, peering out into a thick fog. Every thirty seconds a rotating lighthouse beam sweeps past, and for a brief moment the spot where we're looking shines bright as day, then it plunges back into the mist. Each of our contributors is looking in a somewhat different spot, and so brings a varied and important piece about what they see. John Feinberg looks straight toward the eschaton through the lens of Scripture. Richard Middleton uses the same lens but widens its angle to start at the beginning with God's plan for creation, his cosmic temple, and humans made in his image. Michael Allen uses the same lens with an additional filter—Scripture as interpreted by the Reformed and catholic tradition—and focuses much of his attention on Christology. Peter Kreeft's gaze is the most diffuse. He collects insights as his eyes dart among philosophy, Scripture, Roman Catholic tradition, and the reflections of C. S. Lewis.

Sometimes the contributors' visions overlap. They all agree that our souls will reunite with our resurrection bodies to live with Jesus in the new heavens and new earth. We will enjoy satisfying, unbreakable communion with God, each other, and the renewed creation. We will be unable to sin, suffer, or die. In a way that we cannot fathom, God will wipe every tear from our eyes.

Sometimes their visions differ. Regarding our journey to the new creation, our contributors disagree about the intermediate state and purgatory. (1) Will our souls exist for a time without our bodies, (2) and will we use this time to grow in holiness until we are ready to meet the Lord? Kreeft says yes to both, Middleton says no to both, and Feinberg and Allen say yes to the first and no to the second.

The contributors also disagree somewhat about the relation between the new creation and our present one. Middleton argues that our present creation will be restored rather than replaced. Humanity's best cultural works will survive the purging fire, so we ought to labor well for the Lord now. Feinberg believes our present creation will be destroyed, then its matter reconstructed into a new heaven and new earth. Kreeft says our final destiny is not on this planet, though the new creation might be fashioned out of this one (or created from scratch). Allen claims our present creation will be redeemed, but its transformation will be so radical that it is called "new."

The contributors also disagree somewhat about the relation between the new heaven and the new earth. Feinberg believes the new heaven and earth will remain distinct, and we will be able to travel between and live in both places. Middleton emphasizes that ultimately heaven comes to earth, and heaven and earth will be one. Allen agrees with Middleton that redeemed humans are meant to live on earth. Kreeft does not explicitly speak to this question. He seems to take the new heaven and earth as a unit, without noting a distinction.

The contributors also disagree somewhat about what we will be and what we will do in the new creation. Kreeft follows Thomas Aquinas in suggesting we will possess indestructible bodies that will be able to walk through walls, tele-transport, and fly like the angels. Allen observes that the resurrected Jesus could do these things, and perhaps so will we. We should humbly refuse to speculate with a firm yes or no. Feinberg agrees that our spiritual bodies will be indestructible, but as humans we will not necessarily be granted superpowers that we do not currently possess.

Middleton does not comment on this question, other than to say our resurrection bodies will be immortal.

All contributors agree that the center of the new creation will be Jesus and that through him we may in some intimate way "see" our invisible and ineffable God. Yet they differ regarding how our worship of God through our Lord Jesus relates to ordinary human life. Middleton fears a sacred-secular divide, and he argues that the "narrow" worship of God will inspire the "broader" worship of our continued task to develop the culture of the new earth. The beatific vision "will be intertwined with our ordinary, earthly activities." Kreeft asserts that in heaven the sacred act of worshiping God will become "totally one" with our "secular" activities of "gardening, science, poetry, and surfing." Conversely, Allen warns against giving too much weight to our future cultural tasks, lest we distract from "the emphatic center" of our redeemed creation, the presence of God in Christ. The new earth may have various cultural entertainments, but we should keep our focus on the worship of Jesus. Feinberg agrees that worship is the primary business of our final state and that Scripture is silent about lawns, gardens, and houses, though we will be able to perform physical and mental tasks.

Their disagreement on the activity of the new creation signals an important point. We must embrace the apparent tension between worshiping Jesus and doing cultural tasks, while pondering the relative weight given to each. If we minimize the development of culture, we will minimize an important aspect of being human. God commanded us to make something of this world. It is what we do. But if we minimize the worship of Jesus, we forfeit the most essential part. As the NBC sitcom *The Good Place* inadvertently showed, getting to heaven is not all it's cracked up to be if Jesus isn't there. We can only drink so many milkshakes, stare at flaming sunsets, and get perfect scores on video games until we get bored with it all. If there is no Lord and Savior to worship, we will eventually tire of existence and decide we are better off dead. In sum, Jesus is the center of the new creation, but there is a circumference. There is a circumference, but Jesus remains the center.

The disagreements among the contributors reveal something else. As they stand at water's edge and peer into the foggy distance, the looping searchlight of divine revelation both illumines the spot where they are looking and throws the surrounding surf into dark relief. The

208 ● FOUR VIEWS ON HEAVEN

light and the darkness indicate that when it comes to salvation's final place, we have both answers and questions. We may seem to have more questions than answers, but both should excite us. What we know about our final home may be merely a few spots in a vast ocean, but they are a sign of more to come. Given the spectacular promise of what we do know, can you imagine the parts we don't? It is enough to make us shout the closing prayer of Scripture, "Come, Lord Jesus!"

SCRIPTURE INDEX

SUBJECT/AUTHOR INDEX

Four Views on Hell
Counterpoints Series

Contributors: Denny Burk, John G. Stackhouse, Robin A. Parry, Jerry L. Walls
General Editor: Preston Sprinkle

Recent years have seen much controversy regarding a unified Christian doctrine of hell. Do we go to heaven or hell when we die? Or do we cease to exist? Are believers and unbelievers ultimately saved by grace in the end?

By focusing on recent theological arguments, *Four Views on Hell: Second Edition* highlights why the church still needs to wrestle with the doctrine of hell.

In the fair-minded and engaging Counterpoints format, four leading scholars introduce us to the current views on eternal judgment, with particular attention given to the new voices that have entered the debate.

Contributors and views include:

- Denny Burk – representing a principle of Eternal Conscious Torment
- John Stackhouse – representing a principle of Annihilationism (Conditional Immortality)
- Robin Parry – representing a principle of Universalism (Ultimate Reconciliation)
- Jerry Walls – representing a principle of Purgatory

Preston Sprinkle concludes the discussion by evaluating each view, noting significant points of exchange between the essayists. The interactive nature of the volume allows the reader to reflect on the strengths and weaknesses of each view and come to an informed conclusion.

Three Views on the Rapture
Counterpoints Series

Contributors: Douglas J. Moo, Alan D. Hultberg, Craig Blaising
General Editor: Alan D. Hultberg

The rapture—or the belief that Jesus's living followers will, at some point, join him forever while
others do not—is an important but contested doctrine among evangelicals.

Scholars generally hold one of three perspectives on the timing and
circumstances of the rapture, all of which are presented in this important
volume of the Counterpoints series, *Three Views on the Rapture*:

- Alan D. Hultberg explains the Pre-Wrath view.
- Craig Blaising defends the Pre-Tribulation view.
- Douglas J. Moo sets forth the Post-Tribulation view.

Each author provides a substantive explanation of his position, which
is critiqued by the other two authors.

A thorough introduction gives a historical overview of the doctrine of
the rapture and its effects on the church. The interactive and fair-minded
format of the Counterpoints series allows readers to consider the strengths
and weaknesses of each view and draw informed, personal conclusions.

Four Views on the Role of Works at the Final Judgment
Counterpoints Series

Contributors: Robert N. Wilkin, Thomas R. Schreiner, James D. G. Dunn, Michael P. Barber
General Editor: Alan P. Stanley

Through a discussion of biblical texts, this book presents four perspectives on the role of works at the final judgment.

The final judgment is the last and final act before God dwells with his people forever. Scripture makes that clear, but what function do our actions play in the final assessment of our souls—especially those of professing Christians?

The contributors each state their case for one of four prominent views on the effect of works at the end of time:

- Robert N. Wilkin: Works will determine rewards but not salvation
- Thomas R. Schreiner: Works will provide evidence that one actually has been saved
- James D. G. Dunn: Works will provide the criterion by which Christ will determine eternal destiny of his people
- Michael P. Barber: Works will merit eternal life

This book allows each contributor to not only present the case for his view but also to critique and respond to the critiques of the other contributors, allowing you to compare their beliefs in an open-forum setting to see where they overlap and where they differ.

Five Views on the Extent of the Atonement

Counterpoints Series

Contributors: Andrew Louth, Matthew Levering, Michael Horton, Fred Sanders, Tom Greggs
General Editor: Adam J. Johnson

Explore the question of the extent of Christ's atonement: To whom will grace be extended in the end? Will only professing Christians be saved? Or does the Bible suggest that the breadth of grace is greater? And, if so, what does that mean for the church?

These are questions of great importance for the Christian faith and to our understanding of Scripture. This volume of the clear and fair-minded Counterpoints series elevates the conversation about atonement to include a range of contributors who represent the breadth of Christian tradition:

- Michael Horton: a Traditional Reformed perspective
- Fred Sanders: a Wesleyan perspective
- Matthew Levering: a Roman Catholic perspective
- Andrew Louth: an Eastern Orthodox perspective
- Tom Greggs: a Barthian Universalist perspective

This book serves not only as a single-volume resource for engaging the views on the extent of the atonement but also as a catalyst for understanding and advancing a balanced approach to this core Christian doctrine.